Good Vibrations:
Crossing Europe on a Bike Called Reggie

Andrew P. Sykes

A <u>CyclingEurope.org</u> book

Good Vibrations:
Crossing Europe on a Bike Called Reggie

"When I see an adult on a bicycle, I do not despair for the future of the human race."

H.G. Wells

To Reggie, of course.

For more information on Andrew P. Sykes and his travels, see his website at CyclingEurope.org

Acknowledgements

Although the cycle itself was a journey of only six weeks, the Eurovelo 5 adventure was two years in the making and has been one year in the telling. Countless people have helped me along the way with their advice and guidance via the website CyclingEurope.org. A full list of people can be found on the website itself, but those of particular note, I shall mention here as well.

First words of thanks must be to Basil & Liz Ford, my friends in the south of Italy who didn't recoil in horror when they first realised that I intended paying them a visit by bike. They offered support and encouragement and never once questioned my abilities to make it all the way to Puglia. If you are interested in finding out about the villa that is mentioned at the end of this book and which they rent out, visit their website at www.euronaissance.com.

Friends, old and new who welcomed me along the way and were willing to not only spend time with me but in many cases provide food and accommodation as I travelled south need also to be thanked most sincerely. Paul who calmed my nerves on the first day of cycling in London, Iain & Carly in Deal who welcomed me and provided me with a bed on my second night on the road and then Alain in Boulogne-sur-mer and his cousin Anaïs in Lille who did the same on the third and fourth nights respectively. Thanks to my fellow teacher & friend Claus who came across from Stuttgart to spend the day with me in Strasbourg. In Italy, I was ably supported by Simone and Elettra who moved out of their flat in order that I would have a comfortable bed for the night, Marcello in Rome and then Massimo in Benevento who both provided a friendly welcome as I passed through their home cities.

For the online support they provided while I was en route with technical suggestions and pointers as to where I could mend my bike, Jim & Sally and the man who followed in my wake, Chris.

And finally, many thanks to the man who has been the inspiration for many 'small-time' cycling adventures such as this particular jaunt across Europe, Mark Beaumont, long-distance cycling guru. May you live long, continue to do lots of cycling and prosper.

Andrew Sykes, August 2011

The Eurovelo 5
(minus Belgium)

Start

Reading • • Abbey Wood
• Deal
Boulogne-sur-mer • • Lille
• Maubeuge
Charleville-Mézières • • Luxembourg
Metz •
Dabo • • Strasbourg
Eguisheim •
Huningue •
Sursee • • Lucerne
Andermatt • • Bellinzona
• Como
Pavia • • Salsomaggiore Terme
• Berceto
Pisa / Lucca •
• Siena
• Bolsena
Rome •
• Sora
Benevento • Finish
Laghi Di Monticchio • • Brindisi
Matera Cisternino

Prologue

There is a t-shirt you can buy that states that there are three reasons to become a teacher; Christmas, Easter and summer and although I don't subscribe to the cynical sentiment, there is a pertinent message for all teachers in the smugness; we are very lucky to have such a long period away from our workplaces every year so we shouldn't waste it. Unfortunately, that's exactly what I was doing in the summer of 2008. No plans, no adventures. In fact, nothing apart from a six-week period of sloathing from one unimportant activity to the next. The far off Beijing Olympics were successfully filling the gaps in between.

The previous academic year must have been a difficult one and for some reason I had resolved to do as little as I possibly could come the summer holidays. As I sat on my sofa watching the rain-drenched cycling events at The Great Wall of China, I was effortlessly working my way to achieving an A* in procrastination.

However enticing a period of six weeks of doing very little may seem as you are tearing your way through the corridors of a school trying to fit in all those tasks that clearly the person who originally designed the working life of a teacher had no idea existed, the novelty can soon wear off. How wonderful it must be to do something exciting. Really exciting. The kind of exciting that makes other people stop and want to know more. My eyes and thoughts returned to cyclists at the Great Wall. That was exciting.

Although never quite at the standard of an Olympic competitor, I had always been a committed cyclist. Through a combination of necessity and desire, I had been cycling almost without interruption since the age of ten and was proud of the fact that by my mid 30s I had disposed of my car and was an enthusiastic cycling commuter. Admittedly it hadn't quite turned me into the svelte, Lycra-clad muscle machine that I had once dreamt might be the knock-on effect, but my morning and evening efforts were keeping me relatively fit and healthy.

So the idea of planning an adventurous trip by bike didn't take a great leap of imagination. Seeing the cyclists pedalling in the rain at the Olympics in China merely flicked the switch that had been waiting to be activated for some time. The more difficult question was where to?

How could I challenge myself? I had never done any long-distance cycling before. The furthest I had been was down the Thames Valley to London and, on a separate occasion in the other direction to Oxford. Hardly the stuff of adventure. John O'Groats to Lands End? Exotic? Perhaps not. Around the World? A bit too adventurous, especially on my budget. Somewhere closer to home but not too close seemed to be the compromise. Europe. OK. But from where to where? Who did I know on the continent? It would be useful to have not just somewhere but someone to aim for. That way I would have a friendly face in situ to help me celebrate upon arrival! Family in Spain? Friends in Germany? A former colleague in southern Italy... Yes, that would work. Cycling from my flat in Berkshire to my friend's villa in Puglia, in the heel of Italy. Not a bad idea. It certainly ticked the box of being a little bit out of the ordinary. I could hear the staffroom conversations already

"Any plans for the summer Andrew?"

"Yes, I'm going to cycle to southern Italy to see a friend".

"Oh!"

A frenzy of planning ensued. I had no great delusions about what I was intending to do. There are countless numbers of people who have made their way from England to Italy over the centuries. Travelling from Canterbury to Rome, two of the great centres of the Christian world has been on the to do list of many a pilgrim for at least the last thousand years. And it was in this direction that my research first went.

The ancient route from Canterbury to Rome has become known as the Via Francigena and it was first formally described by Archbishop Sigeric in AD 990. Much of my time in August 2008 was spent looking into the Via Francigena, its origins & its history.

Archbishop Sigeric's original manuscript – now over a thousand years old – is kept at the British Library so one morning I made my way to London to see it. I had to arrange everything in advance (it wasn't just a case of turning up at the desk and asking for the reference section) and I was ushered through corridors in the hulk of the depository next to St. Pancras station. Unfortunately an upstart like me wasn't allowed to see Sigeric's handiwork which was a little bit of a disappointment but not altogether unsurprising. What I was permitted to look at was a copy on CD-ROM which I perused at my leisure in the corner of a room full of people wearing white gloves who did have the credentials to handle the real things. I contented myself with the (possibly erroneous) thought that I was only a few steps away from the original document.

What I could see on the computer was actually very short and to the point. Not much more detail than a list of places that he stayed on his way back from Rome. It was about as far removed from a modern day guide book as you could possibly get and went as follows;

Canterbury – Calais – Bruay – Arras – Reims – Chalons sur Marne- Bar sur Aube – Besancon – Pontarlier – Losanna – Gran San Bernardo – Aosta – Ivrea – Santhia – Vercelli – Pavia – Piacenza – Fiorenzuola – Fidenza – Parma – Fornovo – Pontremoli – Aulla – Luni – Lucca – S.Genesio – S.Gimignano – Siena – S.Quirico – Bolsena – Viterbo – Sutri – Roma.

When I plotted these places on a map, they traced a more or less straight-line journey from Canterbury to Rome. Why would he want to do otherwise? He wasn't a tourist, he was a pilgrim and pilgrims back in the 10th century weren't on some gap-year jaunt. The purpose was to get to where you were going, do whatever religious thing you had to do and get back, hopefully in one piece. Straight lines made for short distances.

My research continued online. One source described how the first pilgrims were expected to prepare, and made reference to their chances of being successful;

"The person had to pay his debts, prepare a will, receive from his local priest his pilgrim costume, ask forgiveness of anyone whom he might have offended and finally to say goodbye to everyone before leaving. The chances of returning were not all that good."

Quite a sobering thought but one that had resonances with my own situation; I needed to sort out my finances, I needed to get some appropriate equipment and I also needed to carefully consider the problems that I may experience on my own journey to Rome and beyond.

I was only scratching the surface of research about the Via Francigena and Archbishop Sigeric but there was one thing of which I was certain; he didn't cycle to Rome. Since the invention of the bicycle however, many must have attempted to cycle where Sigeric had trodden, certainly more recently as people have rediscovered the bike as a form of mass tourism.

It was then that I found the Eurovelo network and more specifically, Eurovelo route number 5. The word 'vélo' is French for bike and it's not much of a leap of logic to work out that Eurovelo has something to do with cycling in Europe. Put simply, it is a network of long-distance cycle routes in Europe and is a baby of the European Cyclists' Federation or ECF. Now if I tell you that the ECF's mission (according to their own website) is to... "...ensure that bicycle use achieves its fullest potential so as to bring about sustainable mobility and public well-being and economic development via sustainable tourism and to change attitudes, policies and budget allocations at the European level" you will see that we are in serious danger of entering the world of Euro-babble so let's keep things simple. The network, set up and promoted by the ECF consists of twelve routes than criss-cross the continent and they each have a name so, for example number 6 is the "Rivers Route" and runs from Nantes in the west to Constanta on the shores of the Black Sea in Romania in the east. Number 12 is the "North Sea Cycle Route" which runs where you think it runs (linked up by a few ferry journeys) and is the world's longest sign-posted cycle route. Number 5 is the "Via Romea Francigena" from London to Rome and (importantly for me) Brindisi in the south of Italy. It is, officially at least, 3,900 kilometres in length.

This was fantastic news. Not only had I discovered that the Via Francigena had a cycling route equivalent but also that it didn't stop in Rome; it continued all the way to Brindisi in the south of Italy, just 50 kilometres away from my friends in Puglia. Someone, perhaps Sigeric himself, was looking down upon my fledgling plan and giving me a blessing from on high. I immediately ordered the map of the Eurovelo network. A few days later it arrived and I had the first description of a cycle route from London to Brindisi. My work was done!

What had originally started as a slow, boring summer stuck in my flat drinking endless cups of coffee while watching hour after hour of Olympic endeavour had turned out to be a very active few weeks of research and planning. I had decided upon summer 2010 for the trip itself so by the end of August 2008, I was still 700 days away from setting off. That would allow me plenty of time to sort myself out with a detailed route plan, equipment and also to transform myself into the lean Lycra-clad cyclist that I would need to be to ensure success.

Unfortunately, despite my initial hopes, it became apparent that the description given by the ECF in their documentation about the route of the Eurovelo 5 was far from the detailed "turn left, turn right, continue for 800 metres and you'll find the perfect campsite" kind of thing that I had been hoping for. What the ECF had produced was a good overview which highlighted the sections of the route where the Eurovelo 5 piggy-backed upon other national or regional cycle routes but it was lacking in any kind of detail, especially when the route arrived in Italy and gave precious little extra information over and above of that provided originally by Sigeric a thousand years previously.

Over the winter months, things went quiet although I never stopped thinking about what I was intending to do in summer 2010 and my mind was constantly full of thoughts of cycling through the sun-bleached countryside of southern Europe, but I did nothing concrete to make the dream a reality. Even the website that I had set up during the previous summer lay dormant without a single update from the end of August to the start of April.

As spring approached however, my thoughts turned once again to the practicalities of what I was planning to do. I needed to spend less time dreaming and more time doing.

I had never done any kind of long-distance bike ride before. Come to think of it, I had done nothing long-distance before. I had never walked the Pennine Way, never run a marathon and even my relatively infrequent flights had only ever been short-haul. Should I be worried that I wasn't a long-distance person? Would I arrive in Dover and think to myself "the last two days of cycling have been complete hell, this is not for me. I'm off home". Poring over maps, watching inspirational cyclists like Mark Beaumont on television, reading about their adventures in print is one thing, but to actually do it yourself quite another. How would I cope with the day-in, day-out requirements of long-distance cycling? Would I get saddle sore to the extent that I wouldn't be able to even sit on a bike never mind ride the thing? How would I confront the loneliness and solitude that I would inevitably have to experience as I made my way south? Would I be still be a happy camper after several weeks under canvas? I had no answers to my questions as I had no experience to call upon. I realised that in order to avoid that horrid 'Dover moment', I would need to do some kind of practice run.

We may not have the best cycling facilities in Britain, but we are blessed by some very enthusiastic individuals and well-run organisations which promote cycling and are gradually pulling the population out of their cars and onto the roads. And it was beginning to have effect. In 2006, The Independent newspaper reported the following;

"After a decade of stagnation in the number of bicycle journeys, new figures show there has been a dramatic leap in commuters and leisure cyclists focused on Britain's cities and the burgeoning network of cycle routes. In London, trips by bike have increased by 50 per cent in five years to 450,000 per day while figures obtained... show use of the National Cycle Network, covering 10,000 miles of urban and rural pathways, rose last year by 15 per cent to 232 million journeys."

The National Cycle Network has its origins in Bristol in 1977 when the charity Sustrans was set up. The name Sustrans comes from "sustainable transport" and let's face it, apart from going somewhere on foot, there is no form of transport quite as sustainable as cycling. The first route was between Bath and Bristol along a disused railway track; perfect for leisurely cycling as trains are not great at steep climbs either. With generous allocations of cash from the National Lottery, the network has grown gradually but substantially to the point where today, 57% of the population lives within a mile of one of the national cycle routes.

I needed to find myself a route on the National Cycle Network that would be a bit of a shakedown for me as a prospective long-distance cyclist. One that would confirm my dreams that cycling is all about escape and freedom, but at the same time challenge my suspicions that actually, I was just a fat middle-aged bloke who would have trouble making it to Birmingham by bike never mind Brindisi.

Having been born and brought up in Yorkshire, it was an annual summer habit to return to the county where my family still live. Could I use the opportunity of my trip north to also test out my mind and body as a cyclist? I stumbled upon National Cycle Route 68. Starting in Berwick-upon-Tweed on the English-Scottish border, it made its way south alongside the Pennines, through Northumberland, across Yorkshire and finally Derbyshire before finishing at the county town of Derby itself. If I completed the whole thing I would end up cycling about 350 miles but I would have the option of cutting that short by just cycling from Berwick to West Yorkshire where I would be staying with family for a few days.

Maps purchased, bike serviced and mentally prepared for the unknown, I set off, caught the train to Northumberland and made the following notes on arrival at Wooler, my first evening destination after cycling from Berwick;

Arrived bang on time in Berwick and the first thing that surprised me was the weather; it wasn't raining and was actually quite warm... The first 25 miles from Berwick to Wooler were quickly demolished in about three hours. The most beautiful part was as we approached the Cheviot Hills, especially the last 5 miles of the journey from Fenton to Wooler. With the hills as a backdrop, it was hard not to be impressed. Arriving at the youth hostel in Wooler, the first person I chatted with was far from being a 'youth'; an 82-year-old former miner called Jack. He had cycled from South Shields and put my efforts to shame! I will sleep well tonight.

And I think I did. It had all gone to plan and although this was only the first day of nine in the saddle, many of my anxieties concerning life as a long-distance cyclist were already melting away. The greatest relief was that I never once felt lonely; I realised very quickly that most people out there were interested in what I was doing and this was a reason to strike up conversation. They were curious and perhaps even a little bit admiring. I had a small story to tell and in the main, they were willing to listen. My diary was testament to nine days of meeting new people, mile upon mile of stunning scenery and a thoroughly enjoyable holiday. I even began to tell the people I met en route about my plans for the following summer and the cycle to southern Italy.

Back home in Berkshire however I was still keeping quiet about my journey along the Eurovelo 5. On the night of my 40th birthday, a few weeks prior to my trip north, I had dined out with a group of fellow teachers, including my friends from Puglia who were the only ones who knew of my intention to cycle to see them in 2010. They mentioned my plans and another friend just laughed and then immediately changed the topic of conversation. I wasn't annoyed as I knew, subject to the successful trial run along the Pennine Cycleway, I was getting to the point of no return, I had invested too much time and effort in the planning and it was slowly becoming an unstoppable juggernaut.

I wasn't the only person who had plans to cycle the Eurovelo 5 (or at least part of it) and those people had started to contact me via my website. The problem was that I was still as ignorant as they were about the route and many emailers assumed that I was an experienced cyclist. I certainly wasn't that, despite my nine-day trip in the north of England during the summer of 2009. I was spending hours online doing roughly the same thing as all the people who were contacting me; trying to find that definitive, detailed route map that seemed to be the Holy Grail of everyone wanting to cycle from London to Rome and beyond.

It became very much of a jigsaw, piecing together snippets of information that would allow me to successfully navigate a path all the way to southern Italy. The first bit in England, thanks to the National Cycle Network was relatively straightforward and I had already cycled the very first part of the journey from my home in the Thames Valley to London several times. From London to Dover, I had to hook up with route number 1 which starts in Edinburgh and runs all the way to the Kent port. I had quite a detailed map and the Sustrans' website provided me with the kind of detail I needed.

However, once in France, I would have to start following the rudimentary instructions from the European Cyclists' Federation;

Cross the channel by train or ferry to France at Calais. Then you follow Canal de Calais to Saint Omer signed as LF1 and continue through Lille / Roubaix into Belgium. Here you follow the river / canal Escaut, which is the border between Flanders and Wallonia and then through Ronse and into Brussels.

My efforts to find any kind of detail about the LF1 were in vain but I could locate the Escaut Canal. The vague "through Ronse and into Brussels" left me with many possibilities.

I also started to question whether I wanted to make the detour to the Belgian capital or not. I referred to it as the Belgian kink (nothing to do with any salacious activity of Eurocrats I'm afraid) as it appeared from the map that a route straddling the French-Belgian border would allow me to make much more rapid progress in the first week of my trip. That said, I never considered the trip as a race. If I had, I would have taken up the Calais to Brindisi Audax Route.

Audax cycling was, I discovered, cycling as far as you possibly could in the shortest amount of time available. It seemed to be closely related to credit card cycling where, to maximise the speed that a person can cycle, the luggage is kept to an absolute minimum. Everything – hotels, food, replacement clothing, repairs – is paid for with the credit card and the cyclist can therefore cycle 'light' as if they are doing a circular route at home. The audax route from Calais to Brindisi had been written about in an edition of the magazine Arrivée by audax devotee Abraham Cohen who summed up his trip as follows;

I must say that this ride took me through some amazing scenery, beautiful architecture, lovely little roads but the pressure to complete my task stopped me from enjoying the tranquillity of the places.

Quite.

John Davies, another audax cyclist from London who had been reading my website and who had pointed me in the direction of Cohen's article told me about two of his cycling colleagues who had completed the trip from Calais to Brindisi in a remarkable nine days! Even he admitted that they would have chosen the shortest route rather than the most interesting and it was certainly true for Cohen. I plotted the places he mentioned in his article on a map and, with no surprise, found his route to be almost identical to that of Sigeric as far as northern Italy at which point he skipped over to the flat eastern coastline of Italy to continue his journey all the way to Brindisi in the south.

So although I was making my trip for the sake of the journey itself just as much as the arrival (doesn't the name of the audax magazine, Arrivée speak volumes about the philosophy?), I did want to make decent progress in the first week or so to build a bit of momentum and get to the point where I had no choice but to carry on. Even in Brussels, it would have been easy to jump on a train and be back in London within a few hours. So I made the decision to iron out the Belgian kink.

I didn't do this lightly as I had started to become, online at least, the leading light in the fledgling Eurovelo 5 movement and I wanted to be as faithful as I possibly could to the route as set out by the European Cyclists' Federation but I came to the (probably erroneous) conclusion that the only reason Brussels was actually on the route of the Eurovelo 5 was because it was the home to the ECF itself. In one way it was a shame as I had been contacted by a keen Belgian cyclist called Jean-Marie Vion. He supplied me with the very detailed route maps that he and his fellow club members had used when cycling from Brussels to the Italian border and had even suggested that he join me for one of the sections of the route in southern Belgian;

"Lors de ton passage en Belgique on pourrait peut-être organiser avec le club que l'on fasse une partie de la route avec toi..." but the lure of making good time across northern Europe was too strong and I didn't take him up on his offer.

Returning to the official Eurovelo 5 description, the section south from Luxembourg seemed relatively straightforward;

The next stage leads via the Moselle cycle path back to France, this time the eastern part with very nice landscape, towns and wine (Alsace). Strasbourg has many nice cyclist facilities and Colmar invites you in with beautiful old houses and nice cafés. Basel is an international city between 3 counties and also the entrance to the well signed national cycle routes of Switzerland.

The Rhine forms the border between France and Germany all the way from Strasbourg to Basel and this would hopefully be straightforward to follow. No mention, however, of the small matter of the Vosges mountains which separate the Moselle Valley from the Rhine Valley, but there was a clear indication that in Switzerland, life would be very easy following way-marked paths. Indeed the Swiss, true to their reputation of being the masters of organisation had an excellent website that allowed a prospective cyclo-tourist to see every possible detail of all of the numerous routes that create a lattice across the country. I was going to be following route number 3 from the border with France at Basel to the Italian border at Chiasso.

The final part of the route was described as follows;

Continue to... Como in Lombardy. Northern Italy has several initiatives to build cyclists facilities. [For the] last stage to Rome you follow the national cycle route of "Ciclopista del Sole". It is not signed yet, but maps and guidebooks are available.

There we had it! More or less the entire second half of the route of the Eurovelo 5 summed up in fewer than forty words. What's more it didn't seem to be accurate when compared to the scant amount of information available from FIAB, the Federazione Italiana Amici della Bicicletta. Just as the Swiss had ticked the box marked organised, the Italians appeared to be doing the opposite. I make no comment.

On the overview map of La Rete Ciclabile Nazionale, the Italian Cycling Network, the Ciclopista del Sole didn't start in Como. It actually kicked off at the Brenner pass some 200 kilometres further east. It did continue all the way to the south of Italy, via Rome but sticking to the west coast and terminating west of Palermo in Sicily. The route I wanted was, unsurprisingly, the Via dei Pellegrini, The Pilgrims' Way. That did make sense! It started in Como and it too continued all the way to the south but this time heading east towards Brindisi once it had passed through Rome.

Perhaps I was being hard on the poor Italians; it was, after all, the description of the Eurovelo 5 that was erroneous, not their own national cycle network. And the FIAB website did give a little more detail about route number 3, the Via dei Pelligrini, including a useful list of places, Sigeric-style, that the route visited;

Itinerario: Chiasso, Como, Milano, Lodi, Corte S. Andrea, Piacenza, Parma, Passo della Cisa, Lucca, Siena, Roma, Fiuggi, Frosinone, Cassino, Benevento, Melfi, Gravina, Matera, Taranto, Brindisi.

This was more or less the route I was to take but I tried in vain to find any further details. One email correspondent from Italy pointed out that the network was 'aspirational'. What was said about the building of Rome?

I always imaged that I would get to a point, probably sometime in late spring or early summer 2010 when everything was ticked off on a list. It didn't quite happen like that. I kept chipping away in a haphazard manner at the tasks I had to do but the running theme throughout my preparation was one of severe procrastination. Perhaps the Internet is to blame. In the time before the World Wide Web, life must have been fairly simple (although we were never able to recognise the fact at the time). If you wanted to do something 'big', you might have discussed it with a friend or two, perhaps read a book about it and if it involved purchasing something, the chances are you would have bought the relevant Which...? guide to assist you. You then got on and did it.

Following the information and communication revolution that has been taking place since the mid 1990s, things no longer seem so simple and straightforward. If you choose to, you can welcome, literally, the world into your life and I had managed to do this big time. Via the website that I had set up, I was in contact with people around the globe, from Australia, New Zealand, Canada, America, all corners of the European continent and, of course, throughout the British Isles. On most levels this was fantastic; people were contacting me because they were genuinely interested in my plans, wanted to share experiences they themselves had had and were keen to advise me on all aspects of my trip whether it be the route planning, the bike I needed to purchase, the weather prospects en route, the best way to cross the Alps, where I should stay and what I should do. It was amazing and there seemed to be no aspect of what I was planning to do upon which someone, somewhere out there in cyberspace didn't have a view.

However, on the level of getting things done and making some key decisions, all the information I was receiving was, at times, a little overwhelming and simply lead to indecision and delay. Clearly my own lack of experience in cycling long-distance didn't help and I was very grateful for assistance being offered but the issue was that I was all too often torn between different options whose advocates had equally strong arguments.

Slowly, however, I started to distil all the pros and cons of this piece of equipment or that, whether to take one route or another and things did start to coalesce.

In early 2010 I purchased a Ridgeback Panorama bike; it fitted my requirements well as it had pannier racks back and front and was made of steel which, apparently, would be better than aluminium on long journeys as it could be welded back together if it broke. That said, as I was cycling in Europe I suspect that if that had happened I would just have jumped on a train south and called it a day! The Ridgeback also looked good. I am just as vain as the next person and I saw no reason why I shouldn't look the part as I pedalled my way across the continent. There was one aspect of the Ridgeback that I didn't like however; the drop handlebars.

And here we enter a classic area of Internet head banging. You would not believe the number of web pages, discussion forums and blogs that are devoted to the multitude of handlebars that exist. Drop, flat (or riser), upright (or north road), porteur, touring (or trekking or butterfly), triathlon (or aero), pursuit, BMX, cruiser, moustache, ape hangers, recumbent, whatton to name but some. And many of these, inevitably, have many variants due to some slight change of direction of the piece of tubular metal of which they consist.

It was time for a face-to-face consultation back at the bike shop so there I cycled to obtain the view of an impartial observer. I was hoping for too much. The staff at my local bike shop, an establishment which I have frequented for many years were just as fundamental in their views about the drop handlebars as anything I could have find on the Internet. "You'll get used to it...I really wouldn't recommend that you change them...give it time". Now your average employee of a bike shop, certainly this bike shop is usually a male in their early twenties who is a lean and keen cyclist. They are the ones who, when they do wear anything in Lycra, people stare in admiration rather than sorrow or ever horror. They have bodies that bend and I am sure are perfectly comfortable when hunched over a pair of handlebars that seem closer to the road than is feasible or indeed safe. I didn't. My own finely tuned body was stuck in a relatively upright cycling position and I wasn't about to cycle over 3,000 kilometres to Italy trying to prove them right and me wrong. But they were having none of my silly talk of changing the drop handlebars to the touring (or trekking or butterfly!) bars that seemed to be the bars of choice of the world's long-distance cycling community. Well, Mark Beaumont anyway and he didn't seem to complain.

Instinct is a useful quality and in respect of my handlebars, I knew my instinct was telling me that by adopting flatter handlebars and as a result more upright cycling position, my journey along the Eurovelo 5 would be so much more enjoyable. Not only would I benefit from being able to see all the beautiful places I was passing (rather than amass a detailed knowledge of the tarmac used on Europe's roads), I wouldn't have to return home to months of physiotherapy on my back. I purchased some touring handlebars online, went to a different bike shop and got them fitted. I didn't ask the shop assistants' opinion for fear of getting one; I simply walked in and explained that I needed the old bars changing. Within 48 hours they were and I didn't regret it.

So I had a (slightly) customised bike. All I needed now were the panniers, a tent, a sleeping bag, a camping mat, some appropriate pieces of clothing, a complete set of maps, insurance, a medical kit for me and a repair kit for Reggie, a method of updating the website from a distance, some guide books, a ferry ticket, a GPS device for tracking my route, some camping equipment... I refrain from listing a cuddly toy but at times it seemed that it would be the only thing I didn't need to get hold of. Gradually, thanks to (but often in spite of) advice from the Internet and my growing band of online advisors, I was nearing a state of readiness.

Reggie? The Ridgeback Panorama was too much of a mouthful so, as he was to be my only constant companion along the way, he was given a name: Reginald Ridgeback. But to you, me and my band of online followers, he was called Reggie.

Cycling Day 1:

Sunday 18th July: Reading to Abbey Wood

7 hours, 40 mins in the saddle, 130 kilometres

I had a distinct feeling of being out of my depth. I couldn't quite believe or indeed understand how my idea of doing something exciting which had first come to me while sat on the sofa watching the cyclists at the Beijing Olympics had come to fruition. Well, the fruition bit would come in a few weeks time if I managed to make it all the way to Brindisi and that was a big if. I had modified the bike and purchased the equipment, I had bought the maps and had made contact with people I was to meet en route but my plan was lacking in one subtle way; detail. My attempt at planning each day from Reading to Brindisi in any kind of intricacy had failed. Much of what I was about do would be done ad hoc, en route. I had the dots but I still wasn't sure how I would be joining them up.

My two years of preparation had been low key and my departure was equally discrete. Predictably, I didn't sleep well and woke at an unfeasibly early hour. I couldn't just set off however as I had arranged for a send-off breakfast with my friend and ex-colleague Basil. Not only was he the last person I would see as I set off, he would hopefully be one of the first people I would see on arrival in southern Italy as it was Basil and his wife Liz who were the friends I had in Puglia, the friends who would hopefully welcome me as I collapsed into their arms after five weeks of arduous cycling. That seemed so far away.

To fill time, I spent a few moments re-reading what I had written on my website in the summer of 2008 in those initial weeks of excited planning and I added the first entry for the trip itself;

I'm proud to say that, despite the grey sky outside and all the unknown elements of what I am about to do, I am even more motivated now than I was all those days ago during that

Olympic summer. It would be a cliché to say how quickly time has passed but since I have never held back on the odd cliché in the past two years of writing on this blog, today doesn't seem an appropriate place to stop!

My flippant comments were an outward sign of bravado. Inside, it was a mixture of excitement and severe anxiety. Even if I had not been as motivated as I claimed to be, I was not really in a position to change my mind. I had invested too much in what I was about to do; money, time and credibility. The moment of any kind of choice had passed. I had to do it.

So I pushed a heavily-laden Reggie out of the flat, locked the door behind me, squeezed him into the lift, pushed the button for the ground floor, descended, exited the building, activated the satellite sensor which was strapped to the tent above the back wheel and climbed on board. No one saw me leave. If they had, they would never have imagined I was setting off for southern Italy.

It was a cold, grey but dry morning. I comforted myself with the fact that very soon I would pass that line somewhere in northern France after which the sun shines every day in summer. If I was lucky, it may even stretch itself over England for a couple of days as I cycled towards the port in Dover. Little did I know that it was actually pushing itself south, not north and it would be quite a few weeks of cycling before I would experience day after day of guaranteed blue skies

Basil's flat wasn't far from my own so it was only a few minutes before I had to dismount for breakfast. As we chatted over tea and toast I wondered how he rated my chances of seeing him in Puglia towards the end of August. We took the obligatory farewell photograph, shook hands, commented a little nervously upon how we would see each other again at the end of August and then I was gone. I waved towards Basil's video camera as Reggie carried me down the road away from the familiarity of home and friends towards a summer of unknown people, places and experiences.

The first few hours of that first day were, however, very familiar as I had previously cycled to London along the National Cycle Network route 4 on at least three previous occasions. It's nice to complete a familiar journey under your own steam once in a while. The train from Reading to Paddington speeds you to your destination in just over thirty minutes on a good day but to make the same journey by bike never fails to give a sense of satisfaction as you lay back on the stone benches around Trafalgar Square upon arrival in the capital. That said, the cycle route stays well away from the mainline train track and both the M4 and A4 especially once it cuts south towards Windsor which is where I paused for the first time to catch my breath. As I gazed along the Long Walk that runs from the castle down through the expanse of the Great Park, I was a little concerned by the slight pain that I had in my left knee. During the three years that I had been a cycling commuter it was this part of the body which had always given me a nagging worry, especially towards the end of the working week. After a weekend off the saddle, it had more often than not sorted itself out come Monday morning. Although I would be taking the occasional day off over the next few weeks – I had scheduled five of them for when I hit the main cities – my knees would not benefit from a good 48 hours of rest and they would also be expected to do far more work than they had ever done on any previous day, wake up in the morning and do the whole thing over again. And again, and again. How frustrating it would be if I had to stop because of injury. I put the thought to the back of my mind and snapped a picture of Reggie in front of the gates of the castle. I wondered if anyone inside was following my little adventure online but rationalised that this journey would continue without royal approval; for cycling monarchs I would have had to detour via The Netherlands and that wasn't part of the plan.

I had no time to hang around as I had arranged to meet a friend in the centre of London at one o'clock so off I cycled through the mainly pleasant and certainly affluent outer suburbs of south-west London. This being a Sunday in July, the tourists were out en masse as I weaved my way along the cycle path by the Thames, past the Tudor splendour of Hampton Court and into the surprising wilderness of Richmond Park. It's often said that one of the great pleasures of London is its abundance of green space and sprawling parks but none feels quite as countrified as the park at Richmond with its ancient trees and grazing deer. In the distance I could see the skyscrapers of the East End and marvelled a little nervously that my destination at the end of the day lay beyond what already appeared to be very far off buildings.

The cycle route I was following – number 4 – was well signposted but as with most trans-urban bike paths it did take me round the houses as it approached the heart of the city itself. The logic of the cycle path planner, I assume, is to try and keep the cyclist away from heavy streams of traffic. This was something that I was to encounter time and time again over the trip and I learnt to abandon my attempts at following the signs in such areas and cycle according to my own internal sense of direction, often with the help of such fundamental guides as the position of the sun in the sky. I would invariably bump into the appropriate signage on the other side of a town or city which would then lead me onwards and southwards. By the time I arrived in Chelsea, I had resorted to simply following the ordinary traffic signs for 'The West End'.

Arriving in Trafalgar Square to meet my friend Paul I felt good. Even my left knee had decided to play ball and had stopped hurting. The grey, cool morning had developed into a warm sunny afternoon and we chatted about my plans as we slowly made our way on foot towards the city and a pub in the East End. Leaving Reggie chained to an upright in the small garden in front of the watering hole (which made me a little nervous; even more embarrassing than having to give up because of a dodgy knee would be abandoning my trip because some London hoodlum had made off with my faithful steed and all the equipment he was carrying), we tucked into some pub grub and a pint as we speculated upon what lay ahead of me in the weeks to come.

Paul wasn't the only friendly face I was planning on seeing as I cycled south although his face and the face of Claus, a good friend from Stuttgart who I had arranged to meet up with in Strasbourg were the only ones with which I was remotely familiar. The other people I had arranged to meet were all online cycling enthusiasts who had kindly offered to guide me through their part of the route; Iain in Kent, Alain in Boulogne-sur-mer, Simone in Pavia near Milan, Marcello in Rome and Massimo in Benevento half-way between the Italian capital and my final destination of Brindisi.

Fully refuelled with pie and chips, I bid farewell to Paul and continued my journey. I had found, and was heading for a campsite tucked into a corner of east London near Woolwich but for the first time I was in unfamiliar territory. The moment I had left Paul I had developed a knot in my stomach because I knew that this was now the real thing. I wasn't re-visiting well-worn cycle paths and familiar locations, I was pedalling into the unknown.

My first problem was how to cross from north of the river to south of the river. Paul and I had gone our separate ways just north of the Isle of Dogs, the piece of land upon which the skyscrapers I had seen early from Richmond park are built. Although there are no over-the-river crossings further east than Tower Bridge some four kilometres away, there are a couple of tunnels and the one that seemed most appropriate for me was the Greenwich Foot Tunnel which linked the bottom of the Isle of Dogs bulge with the maritime complex south of the river. The entrance – a distinctive circular red brick structure with a glass dome - should have been easy to spot but with all the development that has taken place in the area over recent years it took some time before I actually located it. And when I did, I noticed that they appeared to have the builders in. I dearly hoped that it was still open. This is the kind of detail, I thought, that I should have been checking up upon over those two mis-spent years of planning. As I approached I could see that it was indeed open but my problems were yet to come. The chap sitting inside the ornate entrance took one look and me and Reggie and laughed.

'There's no lift on the south side mate'.

It was not operating due to renovation work. I weighed up my options. It was quite late in the afternoon and I had yet to find the campsite in Woolwich where I was intending pitching the tent, a tent which I had so far only erected once in a friend's garden as a trial run so if at all possible, I wanted to avoid putting it up for the second time in the dimming light of dusk. What's more, I hadn't even booked a place at the campsite. It wasn't impossible that my day could end up in a local B&B. Did I have the time or inclination to cycle all the way back to Tower Bridge?

I decided to risk it and use the tunnel, lift on the north side, stairs on the south side. Cycling in the tunnel itself was banned so as I trudged along its four hundred or so metres I wondered just how steep and foreboding the stairs at the other end might be. It's one thing to carry a bike up a flight of stairs but quite another to do it laden with four panniers full of clothes and equipment. If my personified bike Reggie did have a mind, he was no doubt cursing me at that moment although he had no reason to as it would be me doing all the lifting. One thing kept me walking; the thought of not having to see the smug face of the attendant on the south side again. He wanted to be proved right and was probably just tapping his finger awaiting my return. He would have some time to wait as my determination was strong and when I arrived at the circular flight of stairs wrapping themselves around the redundant lift I seized Reggie by the top bar and hauled him upon each step to the top emerging triumphant but smothered in a fine gloss of sweat from another glass-domed structure on the south of the river. It had been my first climbing challenge of the Eurovelo 5, albeit a little bit different from the climbing challenges I had imagined, and I had done it. If I had had a flag, I would have planted it, Edmund Hillary style in the nearest patch of ground. I looked around for applause but there was none, just lots of tourists looking quizzically at the damp cyclist who had just appeared before them. I mounted Reggie and we cycled on.

The challenges of the day were not, however, finished. Putting aside the not insignificant job of the pitching of the tent for only the second time, I only had a vague idea where the campsite was. I found it difficult to imagine how anyone would consider setting up a campsite in such an urban area. I headed east following the signs for Woolwich, then Eltham, Plumstead and Abbey Wood, the location of the site. I could see a small wood in the distance beyond all the urban clutter. Was that the location of my camp-site? If so, why was the dual carriageway upon which I was cycling not getting anywhere nearer to it? Indeed I was even more disturbed to notice that I was passing the perimeter fence of Belmarsh Prison, a category A establishment housing some of the most notorious offenders in the country. Gulp. Somehow I suddenly seemed to be travelling just a little bit faster as I made my way away from the gaol.

Arriving at a large roundabout I was more than gratified to see a brown sign with a tepee and caravan pointing in the direction of the clump of trees I had noticed earlier. Within a few minutes I was at the gate of an urban oasis. Behind me lay the ugly sprawl of south-east London. In front of me a pocket of countryside at odds with its surroundings. My praise was gushing when I later wrote my first end of day update for the blog;

What an amazing place... you could quite easily be in the Dordogne. And at £11.90, a bargain to boot... British campsites are not supposed to be like this; it breaks the cardinal 'Carry On Camping' rule that campsites in the UK should be on the wrong side of crap! ...This one is up there with the most pristine places you might find in the Swiss Alps. I wandered around a few moments ago to see what I hadn't already seen and am pleased to report that I cannot find fault.

If was a truly amazing find. The washrooms were deluxe, the space plentiful and the welcome outstanding. I was in two minds whether to chuck the whole Eurovelo 5 idea in the bin and spend a tranquil five weeks within a stone's throw of Belmarsh prison. I could have done a lot worse.

The only thing I had to complain about was my own inability to locate a patch of ground that was flat. As I lay in the tent, blood rushing to my head and sun setting between the trees, I wondered if every day would present me with the same range of challenges and variety as I had experienced on day number one. I also turned my thoughts to Kent, the coast and France but before I could put too much flesh upon the bones of my plan, I fell soundly asleep.

Cycling Day 2:

Monday 19th July 2010: Abbey Wood to Deal

6 hours 49 minutes in the saddle, 128 kilometres

My last full day in England started as pleasantly as the previous day had ended although I wasn't able to say that I had experienced one continuous night of sleep. I don't think I ever did in the tent, but when I opened my eyes for the final time, I had to spend a few moments reflecting upon, indeed reminding myself of, my situation; in a tent, on a campsite in the East End of London, with a bike, heading for Dover, a ferry and France. I paused and did for the first time something that would become a habit everyday for the next five weeks; I checked that Reggie was still with me. He was. Phew.

Bike security while travelling is a much discussed issue on Internet cycling forums. The traditional accepted method of keeping a bike as secure as you can is to use a D-Lock through the frame and front wheel with a second cable-type lock to secure the back wheel and saddle (if they have easy release levers). The problem with touring is the weight of the D-Lock. Mine weighed exactly 1kg which was almost as heavy as the tent. Was it worth it? In the May before my trip I had been to see my long-distance cycling guru, Mark Beaumont give a lecture in glamorous Camberley and I was very surprised to hear him say that he never locked his bike when he was cycling. I suppose for much of his time cycling however, he was in very unpopulated places as he made his way around the World. Mary Bryant, author of the book Four Cheeks To The Wind which recounts the story of her decision, quite late in life to head off from her home in Berkshire to Australia by bike, told me when I met her that she always insisted upon the bike staying with her in her hotel rooms. On the occasions when I myself stayed in hotels, I tried (not always successfully) to do the same but as far as Mark Beaumont's advice went (sorry Mark), I ignored it. I was after all travelling through relatively heavily populated Western

Europe and I'm sure that Reggie would have made a nice Christmas present for the off-spring of any passing thief. When camping I would, in addition to the D-lock, wrap the cable lock around the pole of the tent so if anyone did decide to try and move the bike, I would be alerted via a shaking of the canvas although what I would have done if that had happened I'm not quite sure. Shoo?

Relieved that Reggie hadn't disappeared in the night, I crawled out of the greenness of my tent and sat for a few moments on the grass trying to warm up in the fledgling rays of the sun. Another routine I would have to master over the coming days would be the morning ritual of packing up. It had taken me the best part of a week back at the flat in the run-up to the trip to position everything in the panniers in what I thought would not only give me perfect balance on the bike but allow me to access the things I would need to use the most often with ease. I now had to repeat that entire exercise in just a few minutes.

As I deliberated over what should go where, an elderly chap appeared and started to chat. He was from New Zealand and was travelling around Europe in a camper van with his wife. It was a conversation that would be replicated many times over the subsequent few weeks. If you remember, one of my main concerns prior to embarking on my trip to the north of England during the previous summer had been the solitude and potential loneliness I would have to deal with. But it never happened. And here I was on only the second day of my big trip having an in depth conversation about what I was doing with a complete stranger. I seemed to attract the curious attentions of many people as I made my way south; if I had wanted solitude, I wasn't going to get it while completing a solo cycling trip.

Indeed, once the New Zealander had wandered back to his van, I was joined by a pensioner from South Africa. He was not quite as friendly as my first interviewer and seemed quite sceptical about my plan which was fine with me; I wasn't offended if the odd person thought I was completely barking. What did annoy me slightly however were his parting comments,

'Well, at least you'll come back a completely different shape'.

He was of course alluding to the fact that one of the things that I hadn't managed to do in two years of preparation prior to the trip was to transform myself into a lean, mean cycling machine. He left me to pack.

Breakfast was a Ginsters pasty from the Co-op along the street from the campsite. The abrupt change from leafy idyll to suburban sprawl was a jolt to the system and I marvelled once again upon how the owners of the campsite had managed to create what they had, where they had and charge me only ten quid for the privilege.

My route to Canterbury was simple; follow the National Cycle Network Route 1. The A2 road was a direct link between south-east London and Canterbury which I would use if needed to, either because I had lost my way along the cycle route or because I was running late. The plan was to arrive in Canterbury mid to late afternoon and meet up with my online contact Iain. Once in Canterbury, I would decide whether to camp or to take Iain up on his offer of a bed in his spare room in Deal but that was a good twenty-five kilometres further on past Canterbury. Would I have the energy left in me? Reading to London had already been a 130 kilometre haul and potentially, I was looking at the same distance on day two.

I picked my way along the cycle route and it was a relief, after an hour or so to escape into the countryside once again. Blue sky, golden brown fields and oast houses in the distance. It ticked all the boxes of what Kent should be.

I was soon approaching the mini Rochester-Chatham-Gillingham conurbation. Rochester was quite a pleasant place and I was a contented cyclist as I made my way alongside the ever-widening River Medway on my right. Hang on. That wasn't right! I stopped and examined the map only to realise that I was beginning to head north-east onto the Isle of Grain. I tried to fix my bearings and worked out that I was seriously off course. I had two options; I could either cycle all the way back along the river to Rochester Bridge or...

I've never knowingly broken the law while cycling. OK, perhaps the odd left turn at a deserted set of traffic lights or cycling after one too many beers, but apart from the odd minor indiscretion, I am one of those boring cyclists who follow the rules of the road. I wait at traffic lights, use lamps when it's dark and, probably most annoyingly, tut at others who don't. Sanctimonious? Me?

It was either the Rochester Bridge or the 'cycling-is-prohibited' Medway Tunnel. The tunnel option would allow me to do in about five minutes what otherwise might have been thirty via the bridge. I paused at the roundabout where a decision had to be made. Straight ahead and continue to be a cycling saint, turn left to become a cycling sinner.

Putting my hitherto good cycling name to one side, I turned left and passed the signs that repeatedly shouted what I wanted to ignore; that I shouldn't be there. I tried to pick up as much speed as I possibly could; I was able to see in the distance the black hole of the tunnel and had quickly worked out that my best tactic would be to use momentum gathered on the down side of the tunnel on the up side to try and prevent me from being shunted at high speed by an irate lorry driver. As I plunged into the tunnel itself, I glanced at the security cameras and didn't smile. Would this moment come back to haunt me?

The irony of the whole thing, as I later found out, is that despite being banned by Act of Parliament, cycling through the Medway Tunnel was allowed in 2007 for the passage of the Tour de France. Ok, it would have been shut off to normal traffic at the time but principles are principles, certainly if they come packaged in Acts of Parliament. If you can make an exception for a whole bunch of lean Lycra-lads, one slightly podgy one is surely fine, no?

As I emerged from the tunnel, I couldn't hear the siren of a chasing police car so I calmly, if a little guiltily, continued my journey to Canterbury contenting myself with the fact that if I never told anyone, I would be able to maintain the facade of a sanctimonious cyclist. Oops.

My Medway towns incident had put me off continuing to follow the cycle route along the Kent coast so I stuck to the A2 instead. Now, think of the straightest road you have even travelled along and straighten it in your mind just a little bit more, iron it and then put it under your mattress for a week. You'll be somewhere near the straightness of the A2 from Gillingham to Faversham. It must have Roman origins and made for relentless cycling. I finally arrived in Canterbury at around 4 o'clock.

I wasn't cycling the Via Francigena, I was cycling the Eurovelo 5 (or at least my variant of the route). I wasn't starting my journey in Canterbury and didn't intend finishing in Rome. Unless I was to experience some sort of conversion on the road to Brindisi in the few weeks that lay ahead of me, I remained an unbeliever. However the Eurovelo 5 is inspired by the Via Francigena and they are very similar. Indeed, as I had decided to chop Brussels from my route, my journey was, in the first stages at least a hybrid between the two. So it seemed churlish to miss the opportunity of visiting the little plaque that sits in the precincts of Canterbury Cathedral and which marks the official starting point of the Via Francigena. Mind you, it cost me £8 for the privilege! Bah, humbug...

I'm being a little disingenuous if truth be known. In March I had attended the annual meeting of The Confraternity of Pilgrims to Rome in, appropriately, St. James' (he of the Camino de Santiago fame) Church in Piccadilly, London. Before I decided to go, I did question whether it would be an appropriate event for an atheist such as myself. Shouldn't I feel at least a little bit guilty about elbowing myself into a clearly Christian-based society? Fellow blogger Silvia Nilson, as keen on atheism as she is on pilgrimage routes reassured me;

'The church has always welcomed all – as is evidenced by the 12th century Latin hymn, La Pretiosa used as a part of the blessing on the Camino at Roncesvalles:

Its doors are open to the sick and well

to Catholics as well as to pagans,

Jews, Heretics, beggars and the indigent,

and it embraces all like brothers'

I was absolved of my guilt and it was no surprise that when I attended the meeting of the Confraternity, I received a warm welcome and picked up quite a few useful bits of information, both cultural as well as practical. This included the itinerary of a cycling journey that a chap called William, the chair of the association had made with his wife some years previously although he had split the journey into three as he didn't have one long six-week period available to him as I did. Another member called Ann spoke to the twenty or so people who were present about her experiences walking to Rome and camping every night along the way. She had a salutary tale to tell about travelling companions having originally set off with two other walkers that she hadn't known prior to meeting them in Canterbury. All had not gone to plan and the three split up at a relatively early stage in what sounded like slightly acrimonious circumstances, which she clearly regretted. Her advice on how to avoid this included suggestions such as deciding upon how far different people are willing to walk in a day, how much to spend on accommodation and in what kind of restaurants to eat. I had once toyed with the idea of trying to find a cycling companion for my own trip but her words helped me focus my mind and I decided to stick with just Reggie. He wasn't very good in rebutting my arguments so I was able to dictate what we did very successfully indeed.

Back in Canterbury, my day was far from over. I exchanged a couple of texts with Iain from Deal as I was resting in the precincts of the cathedral, making the most of the £8 investment and we arranged to meet for coffee just opposite a cycle shop next to the ancient walls of the city.

This was a new experience; I was meeting someone who had, for some reason, fallen upon my website where I was writing about my plans to cycle along the Eurovelo 5. He had been sufficiently interested in what I was doing to get in touch and I had been in regular contact with him, via the blog, for many months. Iain's approach to cycling was a more rigorous one than mine; he knew all about the technicalities of a bike, fine tuned his machines and had even built his own. Learning how to repair Reggie was one of those things that I had always intended doing but never quite got around to. I could change an inner tube and, well, I could change an inner tube. I was praying that heading south I would not have any major technical problems and that if I did, I would be within spitting distance of a repair shop. Basil, my friend who had provided breakfast the previous morning and who would hopefully do so again when I arrived in Puglia once told me that '...if a job's worth doing, it's worth paying somebody to do it for you', and to my shame, when it came to servicing and repairing my bike, that had certainly been my philosophy. It's the kind of sentiment which would have horrified Iain.

We seemed to get on well and the conversation eventually turned to my decision as to whether I would take him up on his offer of accommodation or not. The last time I had stayed in someone's house on the night after having met them was when I went to France on a school exchange at the age of 14. It just wasn't something that I had never made a habit of doing. Iain, however, seemed like a nice chap; he had never given me reason to suspect anything otherwise during our online exchanges and here he was in person presenting himself as the epitome of a gentleman. He had cycled all the way from work (in Folkestone) to meet me. My lurking suspicion that he was anything other than genuine found no evidence to back it up in what I could see sitting in front of me in the café. So I said yes.

We still had plenty of daylight remaining in which to cycle the twenty-five kilometres to Deal and, travelling light, Iain acted as a useful pacemaker as we whizzed up and down the undulating and stunningly beautiful Kent countryside. The early evening sun seemed to be providing the perfect amount of light to make the final leg of the day the most enjoyable of the trip to that point.

Iain lived with his equally charming partner, Carly in a modern house on the outskirts of Deal. There was a little bit of me which wanted to pitch the tent in their garden and camp – I didn't want to get out of the habit of doing so after just one night under canvas! – but after taking a shower and given the opportunity of seeing a bed again, if only after barely 48 hours on the road, I wasn't so stupid as to turn down the offer.

Having showered and rested for a short while, the three of us drove down into the town and sat outside The King's Head pub on the seafront. I could have eaten my lasagne three times over and if I had been on my own, I may well have done so.

Deal was a little gem of a town with a clean, pebble beach, placid sea, long, simple but elegant pier and seafront that hadn't been blighted by the kind of commercial activity that has ruined many such places around the coast of Britain. As we walked along the pier, it was a genuinely satisfying thought knowing that I had cycled all the way from Reading to the English Channel, had met up with a couple of people who until a few hours previously were strangers and felt completely comfortable in their presence. They were both interesting as people and interested in me and my little adventure. If nothing else they had boosted my confidence that yes, I could strike out across the continent and perhaps make it all the way to Brindisi and for that I was eternally grateful.

Cycling Day 3

Tuesday 20th July: Deal to Boulogne-sur-mer, France

3 hours 3 minutes in the saddle, 57 kilometres

If day two of the cycle had been an invigorating and genuinely satisfying end to cycling in England, day three, my first day on the continental mainland would be ultimately bizarre.

Iain gave my bike a quick once-over in a way only he could and I couldn't. He miraculously made squeaks disappear and panniers stop rattling with the twist of an allen key and turn of a screwdriver. In such circumstances, I usually resorted to a thump of the fist. I watched carefully, took note and I bid him a genuinely fond farewell.

My first stop was Dover, probably one of the best-known least-known places in the country. Most people arrive in the town, at speed, by car via the M20 and A20 which funnel drivers directly towards the Eastern Docks and then directly onto a waiting ferry. My approach from Deal gave a completely different view of the town. Cycling first through the picturesque village of St. Margaret's and then, via the coastal road to Dover itself, all I could see of the town were the north-facing walls of the castle. Many people won't be aware of the fact that Dover even has a castle but it does, and when viewed from the east, it paints a fearsome picture of solid isolation. That's probably because of its size – it is after all the largest castle in England – and its location perched on top of the hill overlooking the modern-day ferry terminal.

I couldn't see anything of the town until I poked my head over the hill and was rewarded with an almost bird's eye view of the ships coming and going out of the walled harbour. I paused to take in the view for a few minutes before descending around the back of the castle and into Dover town to join the cars along a busy but for me, mercifully short stretch of the A20.

I felt quite privileged as I cycled through the formalities of customs in the open air rather than cooped up in a car or coach and joined the line of other cyclists queuing for the ferry to Boulogne-sur-mer. The wait for the boat was quite long and I fell into conversation with two more elderly New Zealanders. What is it about their pensioners? This time it was two women in their seventies and they were just as enthusiastic about their travels as the gentleman I had met at the campsite back in London. And boy! did they put me to shame with their cycling adventures. They seemed to have been everywhere and done everything on the back of their bikes but weren't in the least bit condescending about my own trip which to them must have sounded like some kind of Sunday-afternoon jaunt. As they clearly had more experience than me in taking a bike onto a ferry, I followed them when we were allowed to board and when they lashed their bikes to one of the mooring points on the car deck of the ship, I followed suit leaving Reggie to the mercy of any passing truck driver who didn't like the look of him.

Once upstairs I made my way outside onto the open deck and sent a last few text messages to friends and family while I could still do so at a reasonable rate. Should they have wished to do so, they could have followed my progress across the channel via my satellite tracker that I had detached from Reggie and brought up from the car deck with me. Every ten minutes it sent a message to the spy in the sky which then beamed my location to a server which in turn plotted my progress across the continent on a website for all to see.

The reason I was choosing to deviate slightly from the route of the Eurovelo 5 (which would normally have taken me to Calais) was because of Alain, the second of my online contacts. His face wouldn't be quite as unfamiliar as the others I would meet en route as we had already encountered each other in Reading thanks to the website warmshowers.com.

The website, whose name gave some of my colleagues at work much cause for innuendo-laden sniggering, is actually a social networking site for cyclists seeking accommodation en route. As its name implies, it enables cyclists wishing to offer a room and place to wash in their house or a patch of grass for a tent in their garden to contact other cyclists in the hope of one day the gesture being reciprocated albeit not necessarily by the same person. And that's how it was going to work with Alain and me although in our case, it was a mutual arrangement. He had already stayed a night in my flat earlier in the summer while making his way back to Boulogne from a friend's birthday party in Wiltshire. It happened to be the night when England was unceremoniously ejected from the World Cup in South Africa by Germany. We watched the game with a couple of friends and a crowd of increasingly disgruntled England supporters in a pub in Reading. Alain was the only one who seemed to be having a good night. Today was the day he was going to welcome me to his house in the countryside a few kilometres from Boulogne itself.

Boulogne-sur-mer, a town I had grown to know well after having escorted many school trips to the area over the previous ten years – indeed I had been in the town only the previous week, twice, with large numbers of excited 11 year olds – is further down the coast than Calais and the ferry journey a little longer. I spent most of the time on deck taking in the view, descending back onto the car deck after we arrived in the French port to collect Reggie – still in one piece – and cycle off the ferry. I wished the New Zealanders bon voyage and they responded similarly and just as enthusiastically.

Compared to busy Calais, the ferry terminal at Boulogne was almost too quiet, contained within a deserted expanse of concrete surrounded by what appeared to be empty industrial units. I had not been in contact with Alain since leaving Reading when we agreed to meet at the port at 3 o'clock shortly after the expected time of arrival of the ferry. By the time I had made it off the boat however, it was nearly half past and when I bumped into Alain who was waiting for me just outside the perimeter of the terminal area, I could sense that he was already a little concerned as to how we were going to pack into the afternoon everything that he had planned. I wondered what that might be.

Alain had spent much of his working life in Britain – he was even familiar with the little corner of West Yorkshire where I myself had been born and brought up – and had an English wife as well as a son who lived in England and a daughter in America so his English was more than fluent. However, we were now in France and he kindly chose to speak in French instead. Although I am a French teacher, it can take a little time to change gear back into real French rather than the French of the classroom so to be obliged to do so with a sympathetic companion was very useful.

The plan, as far as I was aware, was first to cycle to Alain's house just outside town, have something to eat and then meet some of his friends. Perhaps in a local bar? I wasn't sure. The following day we were to cycle together to Lille and stay overnight with his cousin who lived in the city and then the day after that we would go our separate ways; me south towards Luxembourg and Alain east towards Anvers in Belgium where he had planned to meet up with a friend for a few days cycling.

Just as Iain had acted as a pacemaker in Kent, Alain was doing the same job justice in the Pas de Calais as we made our way across some quite hilly terrain. After about thirty kilometres – I was only expecting it to be ten – we arrived at Alain's renovated house in the country. What had once been a simple rural dwelling was now an extremely comfortable home on two levels with a large outdoor area and a sizable chunk of land around the back. Which was a good job because although it was just Alain and me staying the night – his wife was in England visiting relatives – we did have to share the property with a cat, two extremely large dogs and two donkeys. The latter gave the whole place a very distinctive odour, especially at the rear of the house where they lived. It was clearly a full-time job looking after them and keeping them fed as within moments of us arriving, Alain disappeared into the field at the back to tender to their every need. I was left in the house to shower and rest but once finished I wandered out to see what he was doing. This was not the right thing to do and Alain quickly told me to stay behind the fence. Clearly these were not the kind of donkeys that took easily to visiting cyclists.

I hadn't expected to be spending the night with a couple of donkeys and certainly could not have foreseen what came next. Alain returned from the field, showered and announced that we were going to be spending the evening ballroom dancing. Yes, you did read that right; ballroom dancing.

Dressed in matching blue short baggy trousers and equally baggy shirt, Alain looked more like a brightly-coloured kung-fu instructor rather than a ballroom dancer but you couldn't fault his enthusiasm for the evening's entertainment. I wondered if he could detect my distinct lack of stuff.

We drove some distance to the smart hall where the event would take place but on arrival it was deserted. I was dearly hoping that Alain had got the wrong day and that we would be obliged to spend the evening in a local bar after all. Damn! Somebody else arrived. And then a few more until we were about a dozen dancers in total. We all shook hands or kissed and I was introduced as a cyclist from England. Alain didn't make it clear that I wasn't a ballroom expert and I wondered if any of them were expecting a demonstration from an overseas professional but I think they read the unease on my face quite quickly and drew their own conclusions. Actually it was more like a baker's dozen and that meant we were one person short when it came to making up couples. Again, I thought this may be my way of escape but fear not, the resourceful Alain simply suggested that we regularly swapped partners and that one of us would step off the dance floor for a few moments so that we would all get to have a go. I volunteered to be the first not to dance but it was only delaying the inevitable.

Alain teamed me up with a lady called Nicole. She was in her mid-fifties and looked at me quizzically. Once positioned by the firm hands of the master himself, the music started – a waltz – and I started to rotate. Or rather, I was rotated as I don't remember having any choice in the direction that we happened to be going. After a few moments, I tried to relax and, literally, get into the swing of the thing. There are times in life when you have simply got to persuade yourself that the chances that the people who are watching you at that particular moment are never going to come back into your life ever again to taunt you with the memory so, what the hell! I'll make a fool of myself! Following the waltz came the paso doble and after a while I have to admit that it was quite a bit of fun. Bizarre, but fun. Alain seemed very keen on taking a photo of my efforts for the blog but after a short wrestle with my iPhone, he thought better of the idea. I retired after about twenty minutes leaving the dancing to the experts and wandered outside to take in a few moments of the still, warm evening albeit with the dulcet tones of an Argentinean tango band in the distance.

It's difficult not to admire the French when you come to a place like this. The building where the dancing was taking place was in a small village but was relatively new and must have cost at least several hundred thousand euros. The signs in the entrance hall detailed the busy schedule of activities that were taking place on each night of the week and clearly it was a valued piece of infrastructure for the local community. It was clean and had a smart, tarmac car park, neatly tended garden around the perimeter of the building and proudly displayed the local shield above the door. There was no graffiti, no litter and no pile of cigarette butts outside the entrance. Now imagine a similar community resource, if you can, back in the UK...

The day was not over. Alain and his dancing chums eventually appeared from the building and after a little chatter outside – they were all very complementary on my efforts to cycle to Italy but never mentioned my dancing – we headed off in our separate directions. Our direction was back to the village where Alain lived and that elusive bar that I had been looking forward to all day.

Although having only cycled barely half the distance of the previous two days, I was still famished. Perhaps I was still trying to catch up. The bar-restaurant was a simple establishment and had the obligatory television blaring in the corner which, of course, nobody seemed to be watching. It being a Tuesday evening in July, the place was very quiet. The only other table taken was a party of three, one of whom was English. We exchanged pleasantries and the owner of the café remarked how they rarely saw one English person speaking French let alone two who were speaking French to each other.

Alain, being the consummate host that he was, had already phoned ahead to say we were coming. He clearly wasn't worried that we wouldn't get a table, but he did want to ensure that they had prepared the dish we were about to indulge in; steak tartare. Eating raw meat – which is what steak tartare is – is a practice from which many in Britain have an automatic recoil. The old joke about the steak still mooing at the table is one that says much about our reluctance to put into our mouths anything that is in the least bit bloody, or appears bloody. What you see when you cut into a rare steak is not blood but simply the juices of the meat coloured red by the protein in the muscle. Biology lesson over. That said, although I have had some delicious rare steaks in France in my time (the best by far being the thin piece of meat that I was served up 'bleu' by the mother of my French exchange partner back on the trip when I was 14), I had never eaten steak tartare and I didn't realise that we would actually have to prepare the dish for ourselves.

We were presented with the ingredients – fresh (I hope) minced beef, chopped onions, capers and a raw egg. There was also Tabasco sauce and salt. Following Alain just as carefully as I had followed Nicole back on the dance floor, I proceeded to mix the ingredients until they were well and truly integrated. The result was delicious. It was useful to have the ingredients in front of us so that we could then modify the mixture slightly if required to do so. There weren't volumes of the stuff although more minced beef did arrive from the kitchen after we had polished off the first lot but it did fill me up in a way that the lasagne failed to on the previous evening. Note to self: eat more raw meat!

If Alain ever gets to a point in his life where he is at a loose end (which is highly improbable as he seems to have many fingers in many different pies), he could do much worse than open up his house to paying guests wishing to experience an authentic cultural immersion into life in the French countryside. That is what I experienced on that first day in France. Thoroughly enjoyable, unexpected and yes, bizarre but all the better for it. Merci Alain!

Cycling Day 4:

Wednesday 21st July: Boulogne to Lille

5 hours 32 minutes in the saddle, 114 kilometres

I was a little concerned about getting out of the habit of camping. Although I had been away from home for three nights, I had only camped once. I was now waking up in Alain's house and the following night would be spent at his cousin's flat in Lille. Although this was very useful, I was wary of my own self-discipline. Would I get so used to the comfort of a mattress, or rather, would I not get used to the discomfort of my ultra-light (hence ultra-thin and ultra-ineffective) camping mat and sneak off to a hotel at every opportunity I was given? I love the freedom of camping; the fact that when you wake up in the morning (for the final time!), you are but a zip of high-tech material away from the outdoors. No key card to remember, no lighting system to figure out, no lock to fathom, no lift to operate, no breakfast buffet to be tempted by and no receptionist at the entrance to be pleasant to. Not all of those are bad but it's all part of the little charade that you need to be involved in when staying in a hotel. In comparison, campsites are beautiful in their simplicity. And most don't have donkeys.

For that is how I was waken, quite early, by the brays of Fred and Ginger outside. They weren't called Fred and Ginger but they were clearly involved in some kind of morning sing-song that only donkeys can appreciate. As I lay in bed, slowly extracting myself from the mist of sleep that had be somewhat aided by the quality red wine that had helped the steak tartare slip so comfortably into my stomach on the previous evening, I wondered what adventure Alain had planned for today. Was his cousin the mayor of Lille and would our night be spent in some grand chateau at the expense of the French taxpayer? Was she an opera singer with tickets waiting for us at the door of the opera house in Lille (if it has one). Probably not, but after the previous day, I was open to any eventuality and it certainly made for a fun existence not knowing what lay ahead.

What I did know was that it was about 100 kilometres to Lille, the regional capital. Heading to Lille actually meant cycling more east than south but by doing so, it did put me back on the track of the Eurovelo 5 and would 'correct' the deviation that I had taken by going to Boulogne rather than Calais. It also meant another night of free accommodation.

Panniers packed and deposited back on Reggie we set off. Alain was the master of travelling light. He would no doubt have utter respect for those credit-card audax boys that I had come across in my planning. I had four full panniers and a tent. He had one pannier, half empty. He also cycled using open sandals. He told me this was because he found them more comfortable, especially in the hotter weather. I was still sticking to my clipless pedals and the cycling shoes I had bought to use in conjunction with them but did wonder if my sandals – the only other footwear I had with me – would be more appropriate as well, especially as it became hotter and hotter as I made my way south. I would keep the situation under review.

Just as Kent must suffer from people racing through the county to get to the channel ports and generally ignoring its merits, the Pas de Calais, its Gallic equivalent must surely suffer from the same plague of ignorance. Hoards of British tourists blindly heading off to the beaches of the Vendée in the west and the sun and style of Provence and the Côte d'Azur in the south, ignoring all but the service stations of this little corner of France. I include myself in those hoards so if nothing else, today's cycle would be an interesting one.

From what Alain had told me about our route, I was expecting a day of tortuous ups and downs but it turned out to be more flat. Climbing out of Boulognais country where Alain lived was hard work but after a few kilometres, we started to descend and descend. It never really seemed to stop. When I consulted the map we were actually heading slightly north as well as east; this was a deliberate decision on Alain's part as he wanted to make sure that we got the opportunity to climb to the top of the hill upon which the small town of Cassel is built.

Travelling much lighter than me, we occasionally split up from each other, Alain further ahead although I wasn't worried as the route was relatively straightforward and I knew we were heading for Cassel. When I arrived, I assumed that Alain had already done so. I also assumed that he had paused here for lunch – it was, after all, about midday and would seem the most appropriate place to get off the bikes and rest for a while. However, it wasn't immediately apparent where Alain was. I followed the centre ville signs and eventually found myself in a small park at the very top of the town. There was a windmill, a statue of Maréchal Foch on a horse (we were, after all, now in Flanders and the heart of World War I territory), but no Alain. I pushed Reggie around the perimeter of the park but he certainly wasn't here. I began to wonder if he had just cycled on and was waiting beyond Cassel at some unknown (to me) location. Had I perhaps said something to offend him – my comment about the donkeys earlier in the day? - and as a result he had decided to leave me to my fate in the midst of the French countryside? Was my paso doble more twist than tango and as a result had he waltzed off on his own?

Pondering what faux pas could have left me in this situation, I gazed out over the spectacular view looking north and back towards the English Channel. Should I continue to Lille or should I see if there is a more appropriate destination that allows me to make progress southward as well as eastward?

"Ah! Andrew, tu es là ! J'attendais dans la place au centre ville !"

I wasn't sure if Alain was annoyed or not. Clearly my logical place to find my travelling companion – at the very top of the town – was a bit different from his in the main square. However, if he was annoyed, he didn't show it in his actions and produced from his pannier some home-made sandwiches, a couple of bananas and some yoghurts. My goodness, he really was travelling light as that seemed to be the entire contents of the bag!

We chatted over our lunch and spent a few moments consulting the detailed table d'orientation which told us what we were looking at. It pointed us to Lille, still some 50 kilometres away in the far distance but at least we were half way there.

The afternoon was a flat and uneventful ride albeit a pretty one in nice cycling conditions. We finally arrived in Lille at about 5 o'clock and made our way to the city centre. Alain had been born in the city and spent his formative years there which was the reason why he still had family in the area. He must have taken up cycling in later life as I cannot imagine how anyone who was born in the centre of Lille would ever do it out of choice.

Cobbles. My pre-trip research had warned me about the cobbles that I would encounter in the Alps and Lille gave me an opportunity to practice cycling upon them in a big way. Doing so is hard work at the best of times. Try doing it with four full panniers and a tent and you will realise just what a bone-shaking experience it can be. Not that it should have come as a surprise. There is an annual cycling race from Paris to Roubaix – the town sandwiched just between Lille and the Belgian border – which has a reputation for being one of the toughest cycle races in the world. Why? Because of the cobbles! It's been taking place for well over 100 years and of the roughly 260 kilometres from Compiègne in the Parisian suburbs to Roubaix, about 50 kilometres are on cobbled road the bulk of them at the Roubaix rather than the Paris end. Spectators line the cobbled sections to watch the small pieces of rock take it out on the poor riders and to rub it all in, in recent times the winner has been given one of the little buggers mounted on a plinth as a trophy! The most miraculous thing is that the cyclists manage to complete the entire course in just over six hours at an average speed of well over 40 kilometres per hour. On my own journey from Boulogne to Lille I could barely manage an average of 20 kilometres per hour and that, until I hit them in Lille itself, was keeping well off the cobbles. The race is nicknamed L'Enfer du Nord or The Hell Of The North and it wasn't difficult to see why.

Alain's cousin, mercifully, lived in a modern apartment block just outside the city centre on a gloriously cobble-free tarmac road. It was only a few minutes before we were at the foot of her building slightly laden-down with wine that we had purchased from the supermarket around the corner. Her name was Anaïs and she was a gentle lady who had recently retired from working as an accountant. It was all oddly reminiscent of arriving at that house of my French exchange partner. We carried our bikes up to the raised first floor of the building and Reggie found a comfortable place to lean on his stand in the middle of the front room. Whatever you do, don't drip! I could see that Anaïs had already very kindly blown up an inflatable sleeping mattress for me which took up a large area at one end of the living room. She was slightly on the frail side so I wondered if she had been doing it in instalments over the previous few days. With Reggie in the middle, the mattress at one end and a large dining table taking up most of the rest of the available space, it is a wonder any of us were able to navigate our way around the room. But we did and Anaïs turned out to be the perfect host providing us not only with a meal but also an opportunity to do our washing (so that's how Alain manages to travel light!) and consult online maps for the journey I would have to take the following day.

It wasn't late when we decided to turn in but as I lay on the mattress, Reggie standing sentry (albeit a slightly leaning sentry) to my side, it was a real effort to keep my eyes open as I tapped out the day's events onto my iPhone for the blog. I was the most tired that I had yet been. I had been cycling much greater distances than I had ever planned (or not planned) to do and I wondered if that was down to having to meet people in certain places at certain times as well, of course, of having Iain and Alain as pacemakers for much of my journey from Canterbury. They had both been excellent company and had given my trip a fantastic start but I was looking forward to the following day when I would be striking out on my own, at my own pace and with only my own deadlines to meet.

Cycling Day 5:

Thursday 22nd July: Lille to Maubeuge

5 hours 50 minutes in the saddle, 115 kilometres

To the extent that I had pondered over maps prior to my departure from England, much of the time had been spent trying to work out a route from Lille to Strasbourg. I dearly wanted to go via Luxembourg for the simple reason that I had never been there before. However, to visit the Grand Duchy was the downside of 'removing the Belgian kink'. By avoiding Brussels and taking a route that straddled the Franco-Belgian border, Luxembourg had become a slightly inconvenient detour back towards the east. That said, I was on holiday after all and saw no reason for simply choosing my destinations because they were the most convenient ones at which to pause overnight. The same was true for Strasbourg. But whereas nice tourist destinations were dotted all along the Eurovelo 5 from Strasbourg south to Brindisi, they were a little thin on the ground between Lille and Luxembourg and then again between Luxembourg and Strasbourg, especially if you have an extra requirement of them being nicely separated between eighty and a hundred kilometres apart.

Ideally, Lille to Luxembourg was a four-day cycle, but try as I might, I could not divide that part of northern France up into four stages. It seemed to be devoid of any decent-sized settlements that linked the two cities with three overnight stops. Even the great minds of Alain and Anaïs with local knowledge on their side failed to solve my conundrum so I eventually decided that the best tactic was to grit my teeth, try and complete the trip in three days rather than four and stay overnight in the towns of Maubeuge and then Charleville-Mézières before having a well-earned rest holed up in a nice hotel in Luxembourg.

Now be honest, have you ever heard of either Maubeuge or Charleville-Mézières? No, I hadn't either and you are reading the words of someone who lived for nearly five years in France trying to teach the French how to speak English. The French love to celebrate what they call their patrimoine. Patrimoine is all the stuff that makes the French the French; the food, the language, the history, the beautiful architecture, the countryside and in this case those little out-of-the-way places that most countries just quietly forget about. I guarantee that if you switch on the lunchtime news bulletin on the main French television channel, TF1, you will see Jean-Pierre Pernaut (I have just checked and he is still there; he was reading the lunchtime news when I lived in France 15 years ago and he's still at it!) introduce a short film about some forgotten place in the middle of the French countryside. They can't get enough of it. But, despite the best efforts of Jean-Pierre and his mates at TF1, Maubeuge and Charleville-Mézières were still unknown quantities to me, Alain and Anaïs and I was beginning to understand why the European Cyclists' Federation had sent the official route of the Eurovelo 5 via Brussels.

Alain and I left Anaïs' flat at about half past eight. We were both heading for the town centre; Alain for a meeting with a solicitor to discuss some inheritance problem that only the French legal system could have devised and me for a coffee in order to spend more time worrying over my direction of travel. We arrived at the point where Alain needed to branch off to see his legal advisor and I needed to suffer the bone-shaking torture of the cobbles of central Lille once more. I thanked him for all he had done in the previous couple of days and we cycled off to our respective destinations.

This was it. This was the point where I had to stand on my own two feet, or rather balance on my own two wheels and continue my journey south without the assistance of a local guide. The next familiar face I would see would be that of Claus, my German friend who I was due to meet in Strasbourg in just over a week's time. I was on my own. Quite a sobering thought.

I sat down and slowly sipped my strong black coffee in the Place du Général de Gaulle , the main square in central Lille. Where would I be sleeping tonight? Would I find a campsite in Maubeuge or would I have to resort to a hotel? Would Maubeuge have a hotel? My guide book made no mention of the place so I was travelling blind. Would I have to wild camp? I really didn't want to do that. Nervously contemplating my short-term future I started to wonder what I had got myself into...

"Ah! Andrew! Tu es là!"

Hadn't I heard that before somewhere? I looked up and it was Alain.

"Mais qu'est-ce que tu fais ici ?" I replied, somewhat surprised and just a tiny bit disgruntled. Although I was genuinely anxious about my day of cycling, I was actually looking forward to striking out on my own across the verdant grasslands of north-eastern France.

The solicitor hadn't been in the office so Alain had changed the appointment for a later date. He suspected that I was still in the city and as he was heading in the same direction as me en route to Anvers, for the first part of the day at least, he had come to find me. Chouette!

It was strange trying to crank the conversation back up with someone you had said farewell to only a few minutes previously but after we had finished our coffees, we headed off together in the direction that we both needed to travel. Actually, that was one of the things I had been pondering over my coffee - which route out of the city? – and it was to be a constant problem for me as I set off on most mornings throughout the journey, so to have Alain guide me was no bad thing.

We spent the morning together. Sometimes I would lead the way, at other times it would be Alain. When it was me, I got the distinct impression that he was keeping watch over me as would a protective father over his son, ready to take up the reins of direction should I falter. He was testing me, checking that I was able to find my own way along the country roads. I worried that if he wasn't confident in my abilities by the time he needed to turn left for Belgium and Anvers, I might have a cycling companion for the next five weeks, all the way to Brindisi.

We stopped for lunch – would it be our last meal together? – in a small town called Condé. It was deserted, as all French small towns always seem to be (where does everyone go?) and we sat outside the red-brick Brasserie Au Bailleul munching steak-frites. Our conversation was by now almost exhausted and I think that even Alain himself was ready for us to go our separate ways. Which is what we did, re-enacting the scene that we had acted out earlier in the day in Lille city centre.

Although already having nominated Maubeuge as my destination for the day, my mind was still open to persuasion and if some other, eminently more suitable town were to present itself as I cycled through the lower reaches of the département du Nord I would have no hesitation in stopping there instead, especially if it had a campsite. There wasn't a direct road from Condé to Maubeuge so I picked my way across the countryside crossing off unsuitable stopping places as I went. My route included my first quick excursion into Belgium.

Every time I have been to Belgium I wonder if it exists simply to make the British feel a little less ashamed that they live in a scruffy, run down country. But at least we have the English Channel to help us forget memories of our unkempt and litter-strewn towns and by the time we arrive on the continent, the difference is not so stark. When you cycle from France to Belgium the transition is abrupt and you do wonder why the Belgians haven't made a special effort in these border areas at least. I cycled through the frontier town of Quievrain thinking I'd been teleported to the Wild West, or Blackpool on a bad day. Even the residents seemed somehow more "earthy" with the majority of the men between 17 and 25 passing me in shiny, black, souped-up, tinted-windowed... errr... Renault Twingos. The look is not a good one. The roads were just as poor as the local lads' taste in cars and one section consisted of slabs of concrete reminiscent of that medieval section of the M62 in East Yorkshire. Horrible to cycle on as the movement from one slab to the next causes anything passing on top to jolt as it jumps the small gap in between. It was no surprise that Reggie's rattles returned and we both sighed with relief on re-entering the civility and quality roads of France.

We arrived in Maubeuge at about 5pm and made the quick decision that it probably didn't have a campsite. In fact on first appearances, it wasn't the kind of place that had a tourist office where I could have checked. It was a modern town, or at least it would have been when the majority of its buildings appeared to have been built during the 50s and 60s. I later discovered why; Maubeuge was devastated during the Second World War with the greater part of the town centre being flattened by bombs in 1940. It had, however, started to smarten up its act in more recent years and as I approach the area around the Gare SNCF there was a cluster of very modern buildings including a Holiday Inn and a multiplex cinema. I reasoned that after three nights of free accommodation, the budget could afford a night in a hotel but I didn't opt for the simplicity of the Holiday Inn, I chose instead the Moulin Rouge.

OK, I admit, it wasn't actually called the Moulin Rouge, but it should have been. It was named the rather more prosaic Grand Hôtel and it was just down the road from the Holiday Inn. What initially attracted me was the large blue sign on the side of the building (circa 1965) that informed me that they had chambres à partir de 44€. Great; that was my kind of price range for a hotel. I wheeled Reggie to the front entrance and inspected the more detailed price list posted outside to check that it was only the building that dated from the 1960s and not the sign (which would, if you think about it, have been very bizarre in that the Euro only came into circulation in 1999...). No, I was in luck and the price was indeed from 44€ for a single room for one night. Leaving Reggie parked outside I went in and asked if they had any rooms available and yes, they did. So far so good. They even had free Wi-Fi. 'What about the bike?' I asked; would I be able to take him with me into the room? To a French person of course, me referring to Reggie as a living, breathing person doesn't sound in the least bit odd. Everything in French is either male or female and as le vélo is male, it wouldn't have sounded odd. That said, they do also have la bicyclette, which is of course feminine. I suppose you pay your money and take your choice.

"Non, c'est pas possible, je suis désolé..."

I thought back to Mary Bryant's advice about taking the bike into the hotel room. Was this the kind of town where Reggie would be safe away from the clutches of his master? I enquired as to where I might put my bike overnight, if he couldn't join me in my room. The gentleman on reception indicated a corridor adjacent to the kitchen. It was the best I was going to get and after stripping him of his panniers, I left Reggie to be watched over by the cooks of Le Grand Hôtel; he could look after himself just as he had already done with the lorry drivers on the Dover to Boulogne ferry. Meanwhile I made my way to my room, or should I say boudoir on the first floor. Welcome to the Moulin Rouge.

If I were ever to open a hotel, I would probably furnish it with items from IKEA. Fresh, light, clear, simple, tasteful... Perhaps there wasn't an IKEA in the local area; there was certainly no evidence of it in my room. It was a riot of deep reds and floral patterns that would put the Chelsea Flower Show to shame. Everywhere there was some kind of ostentation. Nothing was plain. Every surface needed to be punctuated with a swirling frenzy of activity, which gave me a headache. Was I in Pigalle? I needed to escape.

I found refuge in the pizza restaurant just opposite the hotel. Served with a glass of wine that was equal in size to the giant pizza I was eating, I soon began to forget the horror of my room. My first day of real independence along the Eurovelo 5 had been a successful one and I couldn't now fail, could I? The sun was shining, the sky was blue. What could possibly go wrong?

Cycling Day 6:

Friday 23rd July: Maubeuge to Charleville-Mézières

7 hours 2 minutes in the saddle, 132 kilometres

Waking up in my bedroom at the Moulin Rouge, sorry Le Grand Hôtel, I peeped out from below the crimson (what else?) bed sheets to see a sea of clutter on the floor below me. Camping is a very efficient way of travelling and it forces you to be economical with how you treat your belongings; if it's not needed, it stays in the bag. There simply isn't the space. Even staying in people's houses, which is what I had done for the previous three nights forces a certain discipline upon you in terms of tidiness. Get to a hotel however and it's party time! Empty the bags, chuck the clothes here and there, tip the contents of the wash bag next to the sink in the bathroom, open the maps and leave them open... I groaned and slowly raised myself to a standing position, moved towards the window and flung open the curtains in a style that befitted the curtains on the stage of a Parisian nightclub. It wasn't the Boulevard de Clichy in front of me however, it was a rather dull backstreet scattered with cars, wheely bins and rubbish. On my right was a long row of lock-up garages. Ah, the glamour of the Eurovelo 5 I thought.

The 44€ price for the room didn't, of course include petit déjeuner so once packed, an activity that clearly took some time, I made my way downstairs to find Reggie (who had survived his evening with the cooks) and went to explore downtown Maubeuge and search for a boulangerie. It didn't take long and I was soon tucking into a couple of croissants and a pain au chocolat while sitting on the sill below the bakery's colourful window. I looked at the map and could see that Charleville-Mézières stood at more or less the halfway point between Maubeuge and Luxembourg on a loop of the meandering River Meuse. It was perhaps a hint that water would be a key theme of the day ahead.

Route 5 is a bit of a Cinderella in the Eurovelo network. I know this because in my research prior to the trip I was never able to find a definitive detailed description of it and here I was just making the whole thing up for myself. At no point during the journey south, not even in the cycling signpost heaven that is Switzerland did I pass a sign indicating that I was on the Eurovelo 5. Some of the routes however have hit the big time. I've already mentioned routes 6 and 12, The Rivers Route and The North Sea Cycle Route respectively and this morning, shortly after leaving Maubeuge I was to cross another of the big boys, route number 3, The Pilgrims Route.

Aren't you on the Pilgrims Route? you are probably thinking. Well yes I am, but I'm on the one from London to Rome and beyond, The Via Romea Francigena. The other, more famous pilgrimage route is the Way of St. James the one that leads all the way to Santiago de Compostela in north-west Spain. It should really be renamed the Ways of St. James because although the route along the northern part of Spain is common to most of the 'ways', once it hits France it fans out across the continent in a network of pilgrimage paths. So why the powers that be at the European Cyclists' Federation chose for their Pilgrim Route, Eurovelo 3 to start in Trondheim in Norway and follow a path that takes in Sweden, Denmark, Germany, Belgium, France and of course Spain is anyone's guess. I suppose they had to start it somewhere. Anyway, back to Maubeuge or rather to Rue Victor Hugo in the small town of Ferrière-la-Grande about three kilometres from my starting point. It was rather an exciting moment when I saw, from a distance, the small blue square with a white number in the centre surrounded by a circle of golden stars. This was the signage symbol for the Eurovelo network and was the first physical evidence I had seen of the routes actually existing in anything other than a eurocrat's imagination. I couldn't quite make out the number. Was it a five? I wondered as I approached the junction where it was placed. Highly unlikely when I thought about it and remembered that I had unceremoniously chopped most of Belgium off my route. I hadn't actually been cycling on the Eurovelo 5 since I left Dover although the official route and my variant of it were destined to meet once again in Luxembourg at the end of the following day. It was a three. I paused and took a photograph of this important symbol of European integration. Goodness knows what the locals thought of a bloke on a bike taking pictures of signs in their town centre. A sign spotter perhaps? No sooner had I packed away my camera than it started to rain.

Rain. Such a small, inoffensive word, but one that has the potential to change a summer's sun-bleached cycle into a tedious trudge. Here's another four letter word: hail. Yes, the hard bits of ice that fall from the sky. That's how the rain set in, with hail! But I tried to be positive. So far, the weather had been OK. Not quite uninterrupted blue skies, but it had be fine and warm. I couldn't really expect to cycle 3,000 kilometres across a continent and not expect at least some inclement weather.

When I arrived in Trélon, at the very end of the finger that is the département du Nord, I stopped and cowered under a very large ornate podium in the main square which seemed to have no purpose apart from giving potted plants something upon which to hang and passing cyclists somewhere to shelter in wet conditions. Perhaps this kind of weather was not all that uncommon. I waited in the vain hope that the downpour would abate but it didn't. I stood and dripped.

People sometimes ask me how I commute to work if it's raining in the expectation that cyclists abandon their means of transport at the merest hint of a drop of precipitation. If you are overly worried about getting wet when cycling, you really should consider alternative methods of transport in the long-run. And with this philosophy in mind, I pushed Reggie out from under the glorified plant pot and once more set off. If everything you are wearing is wet and every inch of your skin equally moist, it can't get worse. You cannot get more wet. But I think I did.

The countryside was reminiscent of my part of northern England, West Yorkshire. Darkly-coloured stone barns, green rolling hills, Friesian cows and fat woolly sheep. You could film an episode of Last Of The Summer Wine here and no one would spot any differences until a car came into shot on the wrong side of the road. Even then, that would be put down to one of the idiosyncratic antics of one of the cast.

I ploughed on through Chimay in Belgium and then Recroi back in France where I had lunch. I paused at one of the customs posts that still stand on every route linking the two countries. How strange it must have been for locals to have to regularly produce papers to get to the other side. The buildings themselves, still usually sporting their douane signs on the wall seem to have found a variety of new purposes. The one where I stopped had been transformed into a local tourist office.

Recroi was an interesting little walled town in the shape of a star, the kind of place in which, if it hadn't still been raining I might have spent a bit longer. The main square where I had lunch had roads leading off it in all directions which didn't make life easy on leaving. That said, the fortress walls blocked most roads so I ended up cycling back in the direction from which I had arrived.

As I continued to cycle, I wondered if perhaps I was turning into a sign spotter after-all. The following bizarrely-named places were sign-posted along my route; the village of Mon Idée (My Idea), Mont Malgré Tout (Despite Everything Mountain) and, rather forebodingly, the Vallée de Misère (Valley of Misery) which interestingly, is where the drama began.

When I had spotted the River Meuse on the map earlier in the day, I had worked out that for that last part of the cycle, along the long winding path of the river all the way to Charleville-Mézières, I was in for a nice, gentle ride downhill following the Meuse as it made its way along the valley. What wasn't particularly evident from my map – a compromise 1:200,000 scale Michelin job giving me sufficient detail without requiring me to carry dozens of the things (I actually had ten which covered the length of the entire journey and I jettisoned them one by one along the route as they became surplus to requirements) - was that there was a large difference in height between the area around Recroi and the valley bottom. I've never seen a Wagner opera, but I know what it would sound like and if my journey were ever to be set to music, you wouldn't find a better composer than Wagner himself to provide the background music to what happened next.

Suddenly the clouds blackened and my road descended steeply into the valley. It was almost as if Mother Nature herself had told her minions to put on a show to impress. And I was. As I cycled the road the rain pelted down. Arriving in the valley bottom there were flash floods with me struggling to cycle through currents of water. It was great! And so was the scenery; the bland rolling hills had been replaced with one dramatic steep sided valley with a monster of a river in the bottom; The Meuse, my new best friend which didn't fail to impress as I continued my ride along its banks all the long, winding way to Charleville-Mézières itself. I later posted a sentence to the blog that summed up what an invigorating end it had been to a very, very wet day; The adventure started today!

Along the river I had been cycling La Voie Verte Trans-Ardennes, a cycle route that starts in Givet further up the valley and continues for 85 kilometres all the way to Charleville-Mézières. I had joined the path at a curve on the river where the town of Revin had been built. There are plans to extend the route further south into the Ardennes département and if they make it only half as good as the bit that currently exists, they will be doing a fine job. Its beauty, apart from having a magnificent setting, is that is not a shared space between cars and bikes. It's just for bikes and pedestrians. It looks a bit like a road as there is a white line down the middle and you need to keep to the right as there is cycling traffic coming in the other direction. The name voie verte, incidentally or green track is well chosen and increasingly used in France to describe purpose built cycle paths that are not simply a cordoned off strip along a normal road. Well done to the French!

I stumbled upon the municipal campsite in Charleville-Mézières without really having to look for it. It was conveniently placed next to the river on a particularly tortuous loop creating a green and pleasant presqu'île just to the north-east of the town itself. It was only my second night under canvas on the trip so far and I still wasn't completely at ease with the etiquette of being a cycling camper but I seemed to work the whole thing out successfully as within a matter of minutes I was sitting on a patch of ground surrounded by a little hedge bang in the middle of the site.

Looking back over the whole trip and knowing where I did stay on each night, the municipal campsite in Charleville-Mézières would rank somewhere in the middle. It had everything I needed, was well-kept, had friendly enough staff and was located quite near to the town centre. The Wi-Fi was a bit dodgy and to get a signal I had to sit outside the wash block despite the receptionist having reassured me that my pitch was well within the Wi-Fi zone. Technical issues aside, my main problem was that it didn't really cater for people travelling with small tents and bikes, either push ones or motorised ones. The best campsites were the ones where an area of land had been set aside for people with small tents and no car and in which you just picked your own spot; under a tree if you wanted shade, in the open if you didn't, next to the interesting looking people if you fancied a bit of conversation, next to the fat ones if you didn't have time to go to the supermarket and fancied having a slap up meal at someone else's expense. You get my drift. On the other end of the spectrum – and this is where the municipal site in Charleville-Mézières was I'm afraid – at some sites you were allocated a pitch the size of an average house in Surrey and were expected to fill it with a tiny tent and something on two-wheels. It just didn't look right. What's more, the hedge around the perimeter of the emplacement, presumably grown with large, noisy families in mind, didn't do anything to encourage idle chat with your neighbours.

Anyway, I had at least found a place to rest my weary and still wet head for the night. Once the tent was erected and Reggie relieved of his bags, we set off into the town centre. Now, remember I mentioned earlier that I had never heard of Charleville-Mézières prior to seeing it on a map in Alain's cousin's flat? Well, shame on me as it is actually the capital of the Ardennes département and quite a smart little place. It is built to a square plan in a loop of the Meuse (isn't everything around here?) and at the centre of the grid is a very attractive square with lines of cafés and restaurants set up along each side. I picked one of them, ordered a beer and settled down to read my copy of The Rough Guide To The Eurovelo 5.

If only such a publication actually existed! Prior to my departure it didn't. I didn't want to carry, sorry for Reggie to carry, three heavy guidebooks all the way to Brindisi. So I improvised. The bookshop back in Reading had Rough Guides on offer; three for the price of two so I bought the Rough Guides to France, Switzerland and Italy and set about making my own personalised copy. I carefully removed the sections that I would need to refer to en route, put them in order of when I would visit them, removed the cover from an old 2004 copy of the Rough Guide to Europe to wrap around the sections, asked my colleagues in the woodwork department back at school to drill holes down the left-hand side of the book and wound a shoe lace through the holes to keep the whole thing together. It worked a treat and I was able to sit in Place Ducale in the centre of Charleville-Mézières reading all about the departmental capital of the Ardennes..

I learnt that the Place Ducale itself was modelled upon the Place des Vosges in Paris, that it is a 'major international puppetry centre' and that its most famous son is, or rather was, the poet Arthur Rimbaud who comically ran away from the place four times when he was young because he hated its 'provincialism' only to be returned to his home town after he died. 'Probably the last place he would have wanted to be buried' notes the Rough Guide wryly.

It had been another enjoyable, if rather wet day on the road to Puglia and only one more day before I could enjoy my day-off in Luxembourg. I felt good.

Cycling Day 7:

Saturday 24th July: Charleville-Mézières to Luxembourg

7 hours 45 minutes in the saddle, 150 kilometres

Braying donkeys or Michael Jackson? Which would be your alarm clock of choice? I'd already experienced the one on four legs, or rather eight legs when Fred and Ginger were duetting back in Alain's garden. The term duetting should of course be used to refer to birds communicating with each other; how nice that sound would have been to lure me out of my slumber. Now it was the turn of the King of Pop himself. Fear not! He had not risen from his grave and come to give an impromptu concert at the municipal campsite in Charleville-Mézières, but he was being played at very high volume through the speakers of a car that was parked on the road next to the campsite at 5.30am. I assumed that they were late night, well, early morning revellers on their way home. Why they had chosen to break their journey just fifty metres from my soundproof-less tent, I shall never know. What I do know is that once you wake up in a tent on an ultra-thin mat, you don't get back to sleep unless you happen to have knocked back a bottle of scotch on the previous evening. I'd only had a few beers back in Place Ducale so that wasn't an option. It was Michael's 1987 album Bad to which we were all being subjected and we had just started to listen to Leave Me Alone when, ironically, the car drove off. Perhaps the joke was on us.

As I lay in the tent, I knew I had a long day ahead of me. Estimating the number of kilometres I had to pedal every day was always to be a difficult task. The best I could really do was to measure the distances on the map using the gap between my outstretched thumb and forefinger as a guide. In a dead straight line it was already over one hundred kilometres from Charleville-Mézières to Luxembourg so by the time I had taken into consideration the twists and turns of the route that I intended taking, which I was never able to do with any kind of accuracy using the finger and thumb method, I knew it was probably going to be the longest day yet in the saddle.

At which point it might be a good time to broach a subject that had amused so many friends and relations prior to my departure; saddle sores. It is the stuff of legendary innuendo, probably because of its association with Vaseline a substance which must have caused more mirth in the mind of your average Englishman than an entire box set of Fawlty Towers.

In a very accessible and well-written paper, a certain Dr. Patrick Kortebein of the Mayo Institute in Rochester Minnesota, describes saddle sores as 'skin-related disorders of the area of the body in contact with the bicycle seat'. He explains that they are caused by a combination of four factors; pressure, shear (or stretching force), moisture and temperature and goes on to list six possible ways of preventing saddle sores developing in the first place; stand up once every so often to increase the flow of blood, check your positioning, gradually increase mileage, wear clean, dry shorts (with no underwear and consider slapping on some 'petroleum jelly'), maintain good hygiene and consider changing seats.

So, was I at risk? Let's look at the evidence...

I rarely stood up. If I did it was usually to, err... 'readjust' things rather than because of anything else. My position on the bike, as far as I could feel was good, certainly comfortable, but it should have been. Before placing an order for Reggie back at the bike shop in Reading I was measured up for him like a three-piece suit. Measurements were taken of parts of my body that have never been measured before nor indeed since. Reggie, as a result, fitted me like a glove. As for gradually increasing mileage, well, I had progressed from a daily commute of 12 miles to averaging something around 70 miles per day so it had increased but clearly not gradually. Were my clothes clean and dry? I had two pairs of Lycra shorts and whenever I could, they were washed and only rarely did I have to resort to pulling on a damp pair in the morning (although on days like the previous one, becoming drenched was all but inevitable). My hygiene was good; I washed everything that mattered in a shower on almost all days of the trip and I had no reason to change my seat as it was perfectly comfortable. I did at one point in my two-years of preparation consider changing to a Brook's leather saddle which apparently moulds itself to your backside. I can't help wondering however if proponents of the Brook's have ever considered that it might be their buttocks that are moulding to the shape of the saddle, rather than the other way around. Check next time you see someone cycle past with a large, brown leather saddle although if you get arrested in the process, don't quote me...

So, Dr Kortebein, not perfect, sorry, but not bad either.

The proof of the pudding is, of course, in the eating or in this case the cycling and although I was a little sore on some days, it was nothing that made me walk like John Wayne off a horse, and all I did was continue cycling regardless, albeit after a liberal dose of Vaseline between the thighs. Snigger, snigger.

Back in Place Ducale, after wolfing down my regulation continental breakfast quicker than you could say pain au chocolat, I was to be found yet again poring over my maps trying to decide which route to take out of town. Eventually, I decided to continue to follow the Meuse but it was a ride that was nowhere near as dramatic or picturesque as the one from Revin to Charleville-Mézières had been on the previous day. The wide meandering mammoth in a steeply wooded gorge had now morphed into just another river in a very pretty but relatively flat valley.

As I neared the town of Sedan my route was increasingly dotted with forceful reminders of World War I; pillar boxes and poignant monuments dedicated to the dead fighters. Sedan was a point of enormous strategic importance; the railway that the Germans were using to supply their armies in France passed through the town. In late 1918, the Americans were close to Sedan helping to increase the pressure on the Germans to sign the armistice and by so doing signal an end to The Great War. On a memorial to the dead located just to the south of Sedan it was shocking to see listed the number of names of American soldiers who were either killed or lost in action. The striking white pillar at the top of a flight of steps marked the furthest point of advance of that nation's soldiers in those dying days of the war.

Shortly after pausing to consider the sacrifices made by people far younger than myself taking part in adventures far more frightening and meaningful than my own, I decided to cycle over into the next valley, away from the Meuse and towards Belgium for the third and final time of the trip. As I entered the country, predictably the road surfaces took a turn for the worse and the towns were just as shabby as they had been further north compared to pristine France. The scenery too had jumped back to what I had been experiencing prior to my meeting with the Meuse on the previous day.

I had been trying to keep to the minor or at least secondary roads - the white and yellow ones on my Michelin map - as much as I could, but occasionally it was necessary to take on the major ones coloured red on my map. I purposefully use the imagery of a fight as this is what it felt like after the quiet, often deserted roads of most of my trip so far and certainly of the bike-and-pedestrian-only voie verte I had made use of along the side of the Meuse. This was definitely the case in Virton which, despite being only a medium-sized town just over the border into Belgium, felt like urban hell as lorries thundered past me on the relief road and also as I neared the Luxembourg border at Aubagne some twenty or so kilometres further on.

Three countries meet near Aubagne in Belgium and the area was full of industry which, even on a Saturday afternoon equated to lots of traffic. At times it felt like a two-lane motorway and I did question whether I should have been on the roads in the first place. The occasional concession to cyclists with a short piste cyclable told me that I was not breaking the law but it didn't make for the most pleasant of journeys.

Things improved dramatically as I entered Luxembourg however. It was almost as if the Grand Duchy wanted to take me to one side, massage my shoulders, unfurrow my brow and give me a long, lingering hug. The road surfaces were even better than in France – silky smooth – and although there were no encouraging cycling signs until entering the capital itself, most roads had an unmarked band of tarmac to one side which I was able to use as a de-facto cycling lane. Wealth was evident everywhere you looked; the country was clearly one of money and the cars and houses told their own story of financial success. To a certain extent, it was a bit like Disneyland; very colourful, very neat, very clean. But in one key way it was different; it clearly had a bit of history.

Now, if you give your capital city the same name as the whole of your country (although I'm sure if you are a pedant you are sitting there telling me that the country is called the Grand Duchy of Luxembourg – the only one left in the World apparently - and the capital is Luxembourg City), it's hardly surprising that people who hear about 'Luxembourg' on the news, occasionally read about it in the newspapers but crucially, have never been to the place, imagine that it is just another big European urban sprawl surrounded by the tiniest bit of greenness before you hit the border with Belgium, Germany or France. You couldn't be more wrong (or, if you are that pedant, probably right). Before I arrived anywhere that could remotely be described as 'urban', I had to cycle a good twenty kilometres from the border. That's twenty kilometres of fields, farms, cows and crops. And you need to bear in mind that my destination – the capital – is in the south of the country. There are another sixty kilometres worth of fields, farms, cows and crops north of Luxembourg City. I really should have paid more attention in geography lessons at school.

The long, straightish N5 was my route into the capital and was predominantly an uphill slog. I had read in my guidebook that it had been built on top of a plateau but I expected that to be just the very last bit, sticking out of the ground like a bolt on a piece of metal. This plateau had clearly had the builders in to construct a disabled ramp all the way from the Belgium border. Up, up, up. Well, most of the time. There were some annoying downhill sections (annoying because you knew you were losing all the height that you'd just gained through the long, slow slog up the other side) which rewarded me with some high-speed descents. I managed to record a stunning 63.5 kilometres per hour (very nearly 40 miles per hour) at some point down one of these slopes which was to be the highest speed achieved at any point of my journey along the Eurovelo 5. Great fun. I wasn't the only one speeding along however; the Luxembourg police were laying in wait at the bottom of one of the slopes, radar gun poised to trap any unwitting speeding motorist. One of them smiled as Reggie and I whizzed past in a blur of blue. One part of me wanted to be stopped and be fined, if only to have a good tale to tell. I wasn't and cycled on albeit more slowly as I hit yet another hill.

As I approached the capital, my mind turned to where I was going to sleep. After one night at a cheap hotel, two-nights in the tent and three nights in people's houses, I was open to spending a little bit more to celebrate the end of my first full week of cycling. But would that be in the centre of the city or further out? Logic says that hotels near the city centre are very expensive, those in the suburbs, cheaper. I had already noted the opulence of the country (certainly compared to neighbouring Belgium) so things weren't looking good for my chances of finding a room to call my own within a short walk of whatever there was of interest in the capital itself.

Following the well-identified cycle paths, I found myself in Place Guillaume II, plonked myself down on the terrace of a bar and ordered a beer. As I glanced around the square, I could see I had managed to find, without even looking for it, the very conveniently located main tourist office which was only a few metres away on an adjacent side of the square.

My first impressions were of being in Germany albeit with lots of different languages being spoken on the street. From what I could hear French was prevailing, although it was by no means the only language I could identify in the general hum of human noise surrounding me. German, definitely, Flemish (or perhaps Dutch, probably both), interspersed with a regular dose of English, but not always from the tourists.

The massaging effect on my brain of the mix of languages that I could understand and those that I could not combined with a second beer and 150 kilometres on the clock, was beginning to make me feel sleepy. I realised that I had better make an effort to find a bed for the night before I dozed off in the café only to find myself woken by the waiter at closing time telling me to move on. It was already six o'clock and I needed to crawl over to the tourist office before it closed.

Luxembourg City Tourist Office (as the large sign informed me above the doors, in English) was on the bottom floor of a handsome red-stoned building with a small flight of steps leading up to the entrance. Despite our training session back in the tunnel under the Thames in London, they were too much for Reggie, or rather me who would have to push him so I left him, unsecured in the square. Mark Beaumont would have been proud! The young woman I spoke to inside was charming although she did have that annoying habit of identifying my nationality even before I could open my mouth and welcomed me in crystal clear English. It's a moral dilemma being a languages teacher and being spoken to by someone in a tourist destination in English. You can understand completely why it's being done – because the majority of British people who turn up in that particular place won't speak the local language – but by not insisting on speaking French, am I just perpetuating the myth that 'the English don't do foreign languages'? As I pondered this question, I suddenly realised that it was me who was supposed to be doing the next bit of the 'tourist office role-play' and explained that I needed to find a hotel, not too far from the city centre and not too expensive. In English. Shame on me. I refrained from using the word 'cheap' as from the evidence so far – the price of the two beers had already shocked me to the point of requiring a third – Luxembourg didn't do cheap. I'm always a bit suspicious about under-the-table deals between hotels and tourist offices when it comes to recommendations for rooms, but putting my suspicions aside for a moment, my tourist office lady whipped out a flyer, showed me a price that didn't cause me to fall back down the stairs and straight into a startled Reggie, phoned the hotel and booked me in. Deal done!

I picked up some more beer and some nuts from a small supermarket en route and only half an hour after being in a bar wondering where on earth I would be staying that I night, I had found myself a modern, very comfortably furnished room on the fourth floor of the Hotel Parc Plaza located within a few minutes' walk of the city centre. Sigeric was smiling upon me once more. The room even had an Ikea Poang chair. What more could a weary cyclist ask for? The Parc Plaza was not the kind of hotel where you would even dare ask if you could take your bike in the room with you, so I didn't and Reggie spent the night on his own, in a small parking place in the locked garage, five levels below me as secure as I was contented. For a few moments at least.

Once my panniers were emptied with the same reckless abandon that I had displayed back at the Moulin Rouge, I stepped into the shower and stood motionless while leaning again the temperature dial in front of me. The forceful jets of water massaged my body in a way I hadn't experienced since I had left my own power shower back in the UK and whereas back at home I rarely needed a massage, I certainly deserved one today.

Campsite washrooms don't have shiny floors; neither do most people's houses. The Moulin Rouge certainly didn't. Decent hotels, however, have them in abundance and when combined with a moist foot and, let's be honest, two beers in a café and another can of the stuff while testing out the Poang chair just before my shower, they can be lethal. At some point in my fall, I was probably in contact with nothing in the bathroom, gliding through the steam like a refuse skip off the back a careless driver's truck. And then I hit the ground, or rather my right foot hit the ground. The rest of my body slumped vertically onto the floor. Ouch. I picked myself up and wandered back into the room only turning to see that the carpet had developed a new red polka dot pattern. I sat on the bed and blood poured from the heel of my foot.

Several bloodied towels later, I slumped back in the chair, beer in hand, too drunk to care about the irony of my first cycling injury being inflicted by the shiny floor in a business hotel in the centre of Luxembourg City. I switched on the TV, rocked backwards and forwards on the chair and looked forward to my day off in a still largely unknown city. Albeit probably with a slight limp.

Rest Day 1:

Sunday 25th July: Luxembourg

I was concerned that when the cleaners came in to tidy up and change the sheets, they would freeze and immediately call the police to report gruesome events having taken place in room 426 overnight, the evidence being the once pristine white but now very red towels and a blood-stained carpet. So my first task on waking on my day-off the saddle in Luxembourg was to find someone who worked for the hotel and inform that I hadn't murdered anyone. Job done (from their reaction they had clearly seen worse!), I hopped down to the restaurant to tuck into a breakfast. This was a hotel where there was no separate charge for the first meal of the day so it would have been churlish not to fill myself to the brim and I certainly did.

Belly more than full and foot bandaged I made my way into the city centre and back to the café in Place Guillaume II which had served me well the previous evening. It was so nice not to have a destination in mind for the first time on my trip. I sipped the coffee and took out my guide book in order to have a leisurely read through the entry for Luxembourg and to formulate at least a tentative plan for the day. But there was a problem. My Heath-Robinson Guide to the Eurovelo 5 didn't have an entry for Luxembourg; it only contained sections for France, Switzerland and Italy. The offer at Waterstones had only been for three, not four for the price of two. Damn. I did at least have the tourist office to my right so I contented myself with further sips of coffee and a view of the still very quiet square in front of me.

Most of the city is built on a plateau with the Rivers Alzette and Pétrusse cutting their bendy paths through the rock to create "haute" (high) and "basse" (low) towns. Most of the albeit limited action on a Sunday morning was in the high town and one of the first places which I stumbled upon was the Musée d'Histoire de la Ville de Luxembourg. What a fantastic place to start my day as it did exactly what it said on the tin. It was a classic case of buy one get one free as by providing me with a history of the city, it was difficult not to do the same thing for the whole country. As the museum was so deserted, it felt like a private visit. There were certainly no screaming kids pushing the buttons on the interactive exhibits to the point of destruction. Although built inside old buildings the museum was very modern – opened in 1996 – and consisted of three upper floors and two lower ones. My interest was underground as it was here that I found the story of the town.

Luxembourg seemed to have been administered at some point or another by most of the powers who have ruled in or around Western Europe over the course of the last two thousand years from the Romans to the Germans who did so twice in the twentieth century – in 1914 and then again in 1940. The latter of these two invasions from the east was the most fascinating. The Treaty of London in 1867 established Luxembourg as a neutral and independent country. It wasn't part of any political pact and had no army to speak of so when the Nazis came to power in Germany in the 1930s and knowing what had happened some twenty years previously, the Luxembourgers were rightly worried about what could take place. Their anxieties were well placed as the Germans did indeed invade, en route to France, on May 10th 1940. The ruling Grand Duchess of Luxembourg, Charlotte had left the country the previous night with her cabinet of ministers and spent the war years in exile in London becoming an important symbol of national unity. No resistance was offered by those who were left behind and the Germans imposed martial law, renamed the area Gau Moselland and integrated it into the Third Reich. A campaign of germanification then started but in a referendum organised by the Nazis in 1942, 98% of the population stated that they didn't want to become German. It's curious why the invaders actually chose to ask. Needless to say the result didn't go down too well and brutal reprisals took place followed by forced conscription into the German army. Although there was some armed resistance, it didn't start to gain momentum until the Allied invasions of Normandy in June 1944 with the Americans arriving to liberate the country later that year in September. The infamous Battle of the Bulge caught the liberators by surprise in December and once again, Luxembourg had German soldiers on its soil but this was mainly in the northern part of the country and the capital itself remained free. Once the bulge had been repelled, liberation came for a second and final time in February 1945. The story of the remainder of the twentieth century mirrors that of the reintegration of Europe as a whole with Luxembourg playing a full role in the creation of the European Economic Community, now of course the European Union. And should the Germans ever get big ideas again, the population of the Grand Duchy can be reassured that they now have an army and are no longer militarily neutral being paid up members of the NATO club. The problem might be their number however; well under a thousand and they are still working on the navy…

There is a curious footnote to this potted history of Luxembourg; the Grand Dukes and Duchesses are very keen on retirement, so much so that the last three have all abdicated before their time was up. Since 1815, there have been seven of them and first to abdicate was William I, the first Grand Duke in 1840. More recently, Marie-Adélaïde stood aside for her older sibling Charlotte in 1919. Mind you, she hadn't done herself many favours by getting a little too close to the Germans on their first visit to the country during World War I. She went for reasons of popularity. Charlotte herself gave way to her son Jean in 1964 to enjoy almost twenty years of retirement and he in turn passed the job to his son Henri, the current Grand Duke in the year 2000. Grand Duke Jean is still around to see his son hard at work. What a civilised way to administer succession!

The excellent museum had given me a perfect context in which to explore the city which is exactly what I did for the remainder of the day, wandering around both the high and low towns aimlessly. At the bottom of the cliff, below the ramparts and just next to the Musée d'Histoire Nauturelle I found a smart cultural district which at some point of the week must make for a lively destination but on the Sunday afternoon that I had chosen was closed up and almost empty of people. Have they not heard of the principle that states you should exploit visiting tourists at every opportunity you can?

A lift inside the rock brought me back up to the haute ville of the city to indulge in a local Bofferding beer (great name!) while watching and listening to Luxembourg's equivalent to Roy Castle in the Place d'Armes; the street entertainer changed instrument and musical style after every song in his repertoire.

I was in a good place to find somewhere to eat as the square offered plenty of choice. It ranged from the obligatory McDonalds to more up-markets affairs. I was tempted by the fast food option as it would have given me instant and generous satisfaction to my growing hunger. Although I had not been cycling, I had been chewing up the miles in and around the capital and needed to eat. I plumped for somewhere in the middle of the restaurant spectrum; a pizzeria.

One of the downsides of travelling alone is having to eat alone but you either do it or starve so it's Hobson's choice. There are a few things that you can do to overcome the potential discomfort of being the only single person in a restaurant however. Taking something to read is a popular choice but I didn't of course have my guide book to delve into in Luxembourg. Another popular method which Bill Bryson seems to do a lot on his travels is to get drunk. That was a possibility but it does take time. I often went for the third option; write something. On a previous trip around Europe I had written a very detailed and informative diary. On this trip south, technology had caught up and I was able to send my thoughts to my blog. As I sat on the terrace of my chosen restaurant in the Place d'Armes, I tapped out a blog entry with the title '24 Hour Eating';

I'm facing 12 on the terrace of Pizza Hut in central Luxembourg City. Behind me at 7 are three Americans in their early 20s, full of tall stories and tales of their European adventures. They speak English to the waitress without hesitation. True to type, everyone can hear them but few are interested. At 9 are a young Spanish couple who couldn't fathom the restaurant's insistence upon using English words to describe the size of the pizzas. They don't look that happy... She lit up a cigarette even before the meal arrived and stubbed it out (to finish later) when the "medium" was delivered. They too spoke automatic, albeit limited English when ordering their food. They figured out the meaning of "medium" by examining mine. At 11 are two blokes who walked in smoking, are probably still smoking and will do so for dessert. One is wearing a shell suit and both look as though their cars have tinted windows and unfeasible loud exhausts. There is probably a warrant out for their arrest. At 3 are a middle-aged German couple. They look a little disappointed as they clearly turned up for the Luxembourg leg of "Drink this country dry". Both are in the running for a medal position. It will be fun watching them stagger away. They had a confusing conversation with the waitress where neither party could really figure out which language to speak. At the hub of it all is me. Eating alone in a restaurant is the worst part of travelling alone (outweighed by the advantages I have to say). The waitress spoke to me in English and I replied resolutely in French. Everyone else is probably thinking "what is that bloke typing on his iPhone?....". They will probably never know.... If the blokes at 11 find out, I'd better run for it.

Cycling Day 8:

Monday 26th July: Luxembourg to Metz

5 hours 11 minutes in the saddle, 98 kilometres

Apart from giving me something to do as I waited to be served in restaurants, the blog had been invaluable in allowing me to make contact with people who were interested in my trip and very often able to offer advice through their own experiences. One topic of conversation that I had thrown out into the ether of the Internet a few weeks before setting off was the question as to which items I would take with me but would end up depositing in a bin in Strasbourg as they had proved themselves to be surplus to requirements. Well, I was only in Luxembourg but after a week on the road I had already come to the conclusion that certain things were going to be of little value. They were mainly to do with the camping element of my trip. I suppose I always imagined rolling up at a campsite, erecting the tent, getting a little stove out, boiling some water in order to cook some pasta, rinse my cycling shorts (although not in the same water I hasten to add) and hang them on a line that I had tied up between the tent and a nearby handy tree. It wasn't quite working that way. OK, I had only spent two nights in the tent so far but it was fairly clear that faced with a camp-site bar and a nearby town full of cafés and restaurants, my cooking kit was just not going to see much action. Neither was the washing line; there are many things upon which any self-respecting camper can drape his wet shorts. So the small gas bottle, screw-on burner, set of nested pans, plate, pack of spaghetti and washing line went. Or rather stayed in the hotel room when I departed Luxembourg. Goodness knows what the cleaners thought when they found the small pile in room 426 but I hope they were able to put them to good use and if you are ever wandering the suburbs of Luxembourg and happen to spot someone hanging out their smalls on a lurid fluorescent green washing line, you can probably guess where they work.

One day off the bike had made me eager to climb back on and reacquaint myself with Reggie. Luxembourg had been a fascinating little stop-over but I was on a cycling mission and needed to make progress. For the first time since Dover, I also needed to reacquaint myself with the Eurovelo 5; I was now back on it and would stay on it all the way to Brindisi; no more 'Belgian kinks' to iron out. My next day-off would be in Strasbourg where I had planned to meet up with a German friend, Claus who was going to drive over from nearby Stuttgart. That was pencilled in for Thursday or Friday and it was now Monday morning so I had three to four days to make it to the capital of Alsace. I reckoned on overnight stops in Metz and then, well... something would turn up. The bit between Luxembourg and Strasbourg was another section of my route plan that contained towns called '???'.

The first day back on the Eurovelo 5 was a bit clearer however and relatively straightforward as it involved cycling first to the bottom right-hand corner of Luxembourg and then following the Moselle from eponymous Schengen to Metz and a municipal camp-site. I expected a fairly flat ride along the river after a gradual descent from the Luxembourg plateau. I would worry about the towns of ??? later.

I was correct about the gradual descent but I hadn't countered on having to cycle directly into a cold wind that was trying to push me back to the capital of the Grand Duchy. It more than compensated for the gradient of the road and it was a relief, finally to arrive at a point where I could look down upon the River Moselle in the knowledge that I would soon be changing direction to head south and hopefully out of direct conflict with the gusts of wind. The Moselle Valley was exactly how I expected it to be; steep-sided with vineyards carpeting each incline leading up from the river, one in Germany, one in Luxembourg. Have you ever knowingly drunk any Luxembourg wine? The chances are you haven't because the vines are only grown in this one, thin strip of land, 42 kilometres in length from Wasserbillig further north on the eastern bank of the

Moselle to Schengen. Vines are not allowed to be planted anywhere else in the country apparently. In his Essential Wine Book, Oz Clarke tells us that "Luxembourg... produces a delicate, steely, green Riesling, quick to age to petrolly austerity, but absolutely straight and unmistakeable" which unfortunately only leaves me more confused as to whether I should try and spot a bottle down at Tesco's.

I descended to the valley bottom through the smart rows of vines and as I did, the temperature rose. Or was it simply that down here there wasn't a wind chill factor? It wasn't long before I arrived in the centre of Schengen, a place made famous by a bit of paper. If you are not familiar with it, the Schengen Agreement is the bit of European legislation that allows people to travel from one country to another without having to show their passport. Border controls are maintained if you are travelling into the agreement area which is why, when travelling from the UK to continental Europe you still have to flash your passport at a stern looking official as the UK never signed up, but within the area itself all the controls have been removed. It was this piece of international co-operation that had enabled me to travel backward and forward between France and Belgium without ceremony and at will in the previous week and see all the abandoned border crossings in the process.

I wonder if there was ever any kind of bidding process to bring the signing of the agreement to little Schengen in the same way that cities bid for the Olympics or countries for the World Cup. Prior to 14th June 1985 when the document was signed, presumably no-one apart from a few wine growers in that corner of Luxembourg had ever heard of Schengen. Now it appears to live off the association. Certainly the modern quay next to the river had benefited from a makeover which is where I parked Reggie and read the perspex plaques retelling the story of the signing. It actually took place on a boat in the middle of the river at the exact point where Luxembourg, France and Germany meet and the politicians came back in 1990 to sign it again. Perhaps the original hadn't been spell-checked.

Just as Schengen has its agreement, Lorraine has its quiche and that was the region I entered when I crossed the border back into France. There was another voie verte to follow alongside the Moselle but it was a pale imitation of the one by the Meuse and disappointingly, the very promising Moselle Valley as observed from the vineyards back in Luxembourg all but flattened out after just a few kilometres in France. The Moselle meandered through unremarkable country dotted with sporadic bits of industry. The visual highlight of the morning was a large power station.

The economy of Thionville, the town where I paused for lunch about half-way between Schengen and Metz, is based around heavy industry which probably explains why the power station was situated so close. The heavy industry consists of an iron and steel plant, a chemical plant and a cement factory. Now fear not, I didn't rush to the Thionville tourist office on arrival (if it indeed exists) and demand a list of the main employers in the area, I just looked that up now while writing. But it doesn't surprise me in the least and if I had chosen to dwell upon such a question as I was sitting in a bar in Rue Georges Ditsch, drinking a 3,20€ glass of Diet Coke, I would have probably guessed along the right lines. It was all just a bit drab. The weather wasn't helping as it was starting to rain again, off and on, but even the people seemed a bit disgruntled with life (although I have no good reason to assume that people who work in heavy industry should be any more glum than the rest of us). The barman who served me acted surprised when I asked for the menu; they didn't do food so my large investment in the glass of cola had been in vain. I pushed Reggie through the increasingly wet streets to find somewhere that did have the temerity to serve something to eat but could only find a branch of Subway. I was hungry so I ordered a sandwich in the only chain of food outlets in the world that has turned ordering a quick snack into something akin to finding the Higgs Boson particle. Why make it so complicated boys?

I must have looked a real sight as I rejoined Reggie outside in the street. Not only was I sodden from head to toe but I had managed, unknowingly, to cut my leg quite badly when dismounting from him at some unknown point earlier. Blood covered the lower part of my right leg. Perhaps that's why the guy back at the bar had told me they didn't do food; he just wanted rid of me and my bleeding lower body.

As I had suspected, the voie verte didn't continue after Thionville or if it did, it was keeping itself well hidden so I was forced back onto the roads. What's more, the wind had returned and once again seemed to be working against me. The rain not only continued but got significantly worse. It was horrible, boring rain that depresses you, not the Wagnerian stuff that I had found so invigorating just a few days previously. I sheltered at a bus stop at one point until realising that there was no logic to my actions; I was thoroughly drenched already and with not a patch of blue sky around me, staying put was only delaying the inevitable. All in all, it made for an afternoon ride that I can only describe as a trudge.

Arriving in Metz itself was such a relief; it must have been as I didn't even mind the cobbled streets of the city centre. Although I knew Metz had a camp-site, I hadn't seen any signs so I popped into the tourist office which was at one end of the long square alongside the Cathédrale de Saint-Etienne. The lady who served me was wearing a badge upon which had been stuck four flags indicating the languages she could speak. One was a Union Jack of course, but I was in more of a mood for a linguistic tussle than I had been back in Luxembourg so I spoke immediately in French and, to my surprise and delight she replied in French, we continued in French and we ended in French! Her parting question to me, in French, was where I had come from - "pour les statistiques" she explained – and I was delighted to reply "je suis anglais". I left the building feeling rather proud of myself for not being so obviously English. Perhaps her flags simply indicated where she had recently been on holiday.

It had now stopped raining and even the sun threatened to shine at one point. I made my way to the Camping Municipal Metz where to my relief I was allocated to a patch of ground without any dividing hedges preventing me from fraternising with the neighbours should I choose to do so. I didn't but that misses the point. Tent pitched on my bit of very brown grass very close to the edge of the river, I wondered if the lack of green in the grass provided evidence of the sun being a regular visitor to these parts or was it just that the groundsman had run out of lawn restorer. Who cared? It was at least dry.

I sat for a few moments by the tent, watching the river drift by behind the sporadic trees growing on the bank. There was even a bit of blue sky up there. The scene was a pretty one from that angle and I tried to ignore the fact that if I were to turn and look behind me, my view would be of the municipal swimming pool cleverly disguised as a nuclear power station. But sticking to the positive, my first impressions of Metz had been generally good so I decided to have a shower and head back into the city centre.

Once there, my energy levels dropped and all I did was wander slowly around the sombre interior of the Cathedral before plonking myself down for a drink. It was still just as quiet as Thionville had been earlier in the day. I thought for a moment and realised that it was of course Monday, the quietest day of the French working week and the reason why so many shops and restaurants were closed. That, combined with the wet weather had presumably made your average Mr or Mrs Metz stay at home in front of the TV. I slowly made my way back to the campsite (worryingly passing a sign barely fifty metres from the gate informing me that I had pitched my tent in a 'zone inondable' or an area at risk of flooding), went to the lively bar-shop-restaurant, ate some chips and a packet of biscuits and hit the sack.

Cycling Day 9:

Tuesday 27th July: Metz to Dabo

6 hours 8 minutes in the saddle, 120 kilometres

We've had quite a few history and geography lessons so far, so let's broaden the curriculum and have a maths lesson.

Think of a right-angle triangle with the right angle (the one that is 90 degrees or square for those of you who struggled in your GCSE maths class) at the bottom left hand corner. The triangle is longer than it is tall (like a widescreen TV – this is differentiated!). Hopefully you have in mind the same image as me. If your shape has more than three sides then please stop reading this book immediately and go and watch something unchallenging on TV. At the top left-hand corner of the triangle is Metz and bottom left is Nancy. Bottom right is Strasbourg. If at this point you are expecting me to tell you what is top right, please refer to the end of the previous sentence. The distance from Metz to Nancy is about half the distance from Nancy to Strasbourg so the easy thing to do would have been to break down the rest of the week into three journeys, the first from Metz to Nancy, the second to half way between Nancy and Strasbourg and the final one to Strasbourg itself. However, there was of course the alternative of cycling along the hypotenuse (nothing? – reconsider the TV option) for three shorter journeys but with bugger all on the map which resembled a decent-sized town at which to stop overnight. I lay in the tent pondering the situation, but I couldn't decide what to do so instead, I got up and did the next best thing; ignored the fact that I had to make a decision pretty soon.

The sky was blue. On a long cycling trip, that was one of the best ways to start the day, especially coming the morning after a very wet day in the saddle. I took down the tent, carefully packed my panniers and lowered them onto a patient Reggie who was waiting by my side. I was now getting into the swing of the morning camping routine so it wasn't too long before I was back at the campsite reception changing the dressing on my injured foot.

Just outside the entrance to the site was a large car park filled mainly with white camper vans (why are they always white?) from different corners of Europe. It is often the case at camp-sites that people travelling in these comfortable metal boxes arrive after dark, spend the night in such a holding area and then check-in to the camp-site itself first thing in the morning. This is what Jean-Jacques had done and the reason why he happened to be standing in a slow moving queue just next to where I was administering first aid to myself. He was the first to speak and it was to compliment me on how meticulously I had packed everything up and loaded it all onto Reggie a few minutes earlier. He had been watching my every move from a distance and from the detail he was able to recount he either had a photographic memory or was dictating notes to his wife as he watched like a policeman on a stake-out ("08.15: The suspect has now shaken the tent three times and is beginning to roll it up while gently brushing off bits of wet grass..."). I thanked him for his comments and genuine interest explaining that it was quite important to try and get a balance on the bike. He contrasted my efforts with his own which could be summed up as 'throw everything in the back and drive off'. I was in no rush – I was continuing with the long, fiddly job of patching up my heel – and the queue wasn't moving so we continued to chat and a remarkably wide-ranging conversation ensued. We discussed languages (his wife was an English teacher and he himself spoke Breton - he even gave me a short demonstration), comparative political centralisation in France and the UK, the up-coming cycling event in Verdun (involving a remarkable 12,000 cyclists of which he was going to be one), his career as an insurance salesman and how it had taken him to the six corners of France (remember this is l'Hexagone), his travels around the UK (especially in Scotland), his daughter's time spent working in Bournemouth and Edinburgh and, of course, my own trip to the south of Italy. Just before we finally went our separate ways, he asked how old I was. He told me that it was the perfect time in life to do what I was doing.

It was such a nice way to start the day. Remember that one of my main concerns in the initial days of planning the journey had been that I would be lonely on a solo cycling quest. Here was a man who I had never seen before and who I will never see again but we were chatting like two old friends in a café. It was brilliant. Just brilliant.

It also put me in a very carefree frame of mind so when I was once again studying the maps over coffee in a deserted square in the centre of Metz, I wasn't in the least bit concerned that I hadn't yet made up my mind where to stay that evening. I did, however, need a direction of travel and I went for the hypotenuse option. I didn't really want to replicate the previous day's cycling along busy roads towards Nancy so I would head out into the wilderness of Lorraine and towards the Vosges mountains. If I got as far as Sarrebourg good, if I didn't so be it. Jean-Jacques had been a walking Prozac tablet and I had swallowed him in one big gulp. No stress.

One of the perks of being a languages teacher (we don't get many so the ones that do present themselves at our interactive whiteboards are worth milking for all you can), is the opportunity for a bit of foreign travel in your job. OK, in the great scheme of things, it's not the kind of foreign travel that some employees get to do jetting off for conferences in California or bonding weekends in Bali but it is nevertheless foreign travel. I've already mentioned that I had been to Boulogne-sur-mer for the day, not once but twice in the week prior to setting off along the Eurovelo 5 (I have been there so many times over the past ten years that my heart no longer considers it as 'abroad' and I have no sense of excitement whatsoever about returning each year), but I also get to spend a fun weekend in Paris with a group of thirty or so 15 year olds every May. It's a residential trip of course which means that most evenings are spent trying to prevent the students smuggling alcohol and cigarettes from the local corner shop into their rooms and then later trying to smuggle themselves into rooms containing members of the opposite sex, but it does give us a quality amount of time to explore the city and one of the cultural gems of the French capital is the Pompidou Centre.

What's all that got to do with cycling to Brindisi? I hear you cry. Well, they have just built a second Pompidou Centre in Metz. The Pompidou Centre in Paris is famed as much for its architecture as the works of art it contains. It was one of Richard Rogers' 'inside-out' creations with as much as possible of what you would normally find inside a building (pipes, escalators, air-conditioning etc...) on the outside in the hope that the interior space would be maximised. Viewed from the hill of Montmartre, it is still a striking addition to the Paris skyline. The same certainly goes for the Pompidou-Metz which, although closed on the Tuesday I was in town (perhaps it was where everyone had gone on Monday) was still worth a visit just to look at from the outside.

Following the signs from the city centre, I was led to an area behind the Gare SNCF. You didn't need to read the board which said 'Bienvenue au Centre Pompidou-Metz' to figure out that you had arrived. I parked Reggie in the vast but deserted car park and sat on one of the many flat benches to examine what I could see. Supported on a lattice of wooden stilts, the roof resembled the fresh dough of a pizza in mid-air having just being flung there by the chef, curving up and down around its edge. A drunken stingray comes to mind as well. Puncturing the roof was a tall flagpole sporting the French tricolour. Very impressive and well worth the minor detour. But it was time to get cycling along the hypotenuse so Reggie and I set off in a south-easterly direction towards the as yet unnamed town of ???.

The morning's ride was very pleasant; rolling countryside, the odd little climb to keep me awake, a mixture of sun and cloud to heat me up but then cool me down once I got too hot and some increasingly attractive towns and villages through which to cycle. I stopped for lunch at Morhange, some fifty kilometres from Metz. By this time it was looking more than likely that I would be in Sarrebourg that evening. Morhange wasn't a bad little place and I bought a sandwich jambon-fromage from a small take-away place in the main street. The town had everything your average Frenchman would want; a bank, a bar, a baker, a greengrocer, a post office, a hardware shop (called strangely the Crack Bazar – was it a cover for something more nefarious?). But it had something missing. What was it? Ah yes... people! Apart from me and the woman who had served me in sandwich bar, the lengthy main street had not a soul on it. Was there going to be a high-noon gun battle and everyone had taken cover? We weren't in siesta territory, not yet surely. How do places like this in France survive? In Britain, everything would have been shut down years ago. I know that I had arrived between the hours of twelve and two but even so... The café down the road was just as quiet. The French economic miracle at work (i.e. they never appear to do any but still live very comfortable lives).

I reached an important milestone soon after Morhange. Well, milestone doesn't seem an appropriate term as I was celebrating the completion of one thousand kilometres along the Eurovelo 5. Only another two thousand nine hundred to go and they started with the afternoon's cycle to Sarrebourg which was very much in the same positive vein as the morning's cycle to Morhange and there were tantalising pieces of evidence that I was making progress south; a lavender field, the noise of cicadas, white-washed houses and a more mountainous landscape. However, it was all still very ephemeral and some places were still securely fixed in a more granity northern France. As I made progress towards Sarrebourg, I could see the Vosges Mountains looming in the distance. That would be tomorrow's challenge I thought and pedalled on.

I had no preconceptions about Sarrebourg but was hoping for the kind of quiet, picturesque place you find nestling in the Dordogne with a campsite (with no hedges) and a couple of bars in which to while away the evening. I was in for a bit of a disappointment. It was an inconsequential town with a penchant for drabness. It was only remarkable for being unremarkable. I asked at the tourist office about campsites and the helpful woman gave me a list of five, none of which were close to the town itself. Keeping positive, news of the non-existence of a campsite in Sarrebourg came as a blessed relief; it meant I would not be staying in the town overnight and the ones that were listed were all east of the town which was good as that was the direction in which I was travelling towards Strasbourg. On closer inspection, one of them appeared to be more ideal than the others as it was on a direct route to Strasbourg; the site in Dabo.

There was only one problem; Dabo was another 20 kilometres away and up a big hill. Not just any hill but one the hills I had seen earlier; the Vosges Mountains. I looked at my watch; it was only 4pm. Plenty of time to ride 20 kilometres albeit in an upwards direction. Jean-Jacque's Prozac vibe from earlier in the day must have still been working so I set off east towards the first real cycling challenge of the trip. It was certainly that as the route wound its way backward and forward up the slope towards the village. But I didn't stop once; I just plodded along, one rotation of the pedals after another, up and up. After a couple of hours of gentle effort I arrived in the village of Dabo and paused to get my bearings. There was a cluster of shops and a sign for a tourist office which, once I had located, tucked behind the town hall up a couple of flights of steps was, much to my surprise, still open. The elderly gentleman who was on duty explained that the campsite was just a couple of kilometres further along the road but that it didn't have a shop or bar so I would need to buy something to eat and drink in the village.

I felt almost French as I reappeared out of the little Casino supermarket clutching a large triangle of Camembert cheese, a fat baguette and a bottle of Bordeaux Supérieur red wine. The price of the latter did not reflect the lofty pretentions of the label but I was sure it would do just fine. With my Gallic feast packed into the panniers, bread protruding from the top, I continued my journey and, just as the old man had said, the campsite was on my right after a couple of kilometres. I was welcomed by the charming lady who ran the whole place. She explained that there would be no staff on site after about 9 o'clock but I looked around and although far from packed there were plenty other happy campers preparing their evening meals. This included a group of children from one of the big cities who were on a colonie de vacances organised by their local council. They had one large marquee and a series of smaller tents in which they slept. The sky was still bright, but it did have something about it that suggested we may have rain at some point, so I chose a patch of ground not too far from the large marquee to pitch my own tent. It may come in useful, I thought if there was going to be a downpour.

It was a beautiful wooded setting. I had found my little corner of the Dordogne in Lorraine after all and I tucked into the bread, cheese and wine as the sun set in the far distance. By coming so far I had managed to get myself within only half a day's cycling of Strasbourg itself. I would cycle down the other side of the mountains in the morning and have a leisurely ride across the valley and towards the banks of the Rhine. At that point, in that camp-site on that evening, eating that food and with that view I was the happiest I had yet been. And just as the day had started with a lengthy chat to a stranger, so it was to end when Michael and Jeanette pulled up in their Crazy White Elephant. It was the name they had given to their camper van. A bit less smart and flashy than Jean-Jacque's earlier in the day but just as white. They were heading back to Heidelberg in Germany where they lived after a few days of touring around France. We shared good conversation and average wine. Michael was infectiously enthusiastic about life; I told him he should abandon his life as an accountant and become a teacher. He said he would consider my suggestion carefully. I wonder if he ever did.

An idyll in south-east London: Abbey Wood camp-site

Iain & Carly, my welcoming hosts in Deal, Kent

My first evening on the continent... ...ballroom dancing

Alain, my guide through the Pas de Calais

Your author, sheltering from the rain

The magnificent Meuse: cycling heaven

My old friend Claus in Strasbourg

Philippe & Paul, my wine advisors in Eguisheim

My first view of the Rhine & Switzerland

Sharing gripes about the weather with Carl & Nick, English motor bikers in Sursee

A grey day over the unpronounceable lake that has been sensibly renamed Lake Lucerne

Finally! A blue sky on the morning of the big climb to the St. Gotthard Pass

The cobbles en route to the St. Gotthard Pass

The physical & emotional high point

The unforgiving old road down from the
St. Gotthard Pass

Emergency repairs for Reggie in Airolo

A bit of elegance in Lugano

Simone & Alan (his bike!) in Como

Cycling Day 10:

Wednesday 28th July: Dabo to Strasbourg

3 hours 14 minutes in the saddle, 65 kilometres

Cycling down the mountain from Dabo and the Porte des Vosges could have been the most enjoyable ride so far; the long descent through deeply forested hills, opening out onto a plain full of colour, both from the crops in the fields and from the pretty villages with their brightly painted houses and window boxes and finally a dedicated cycle route along disused railway tracks and an overgrown canal which brought me right into the centre of Strasbourg itself.

Unfortunately for all but a few cherished minutes as I started to cycle along the canal, it rained heavily all morning. I had hung around the campsite that morning as long as reason dictates that a passing shower might stop but it was no passing shower so I plunged head first into the watery cycle that was waiting for me. A field of sunflowers summed up my mood; their heads were hung, facing the ground having given up on their search for the sun in a depressing reflection of the morning's weather. I paused my journey for breakfast in Romanswiller where I cowered under an awning outside the boulangerie wondering where the sunny summer weather had gone.

Strasbourg is a city I had wanted to visit for many years. Tucked away as it is on the far eastern border of France it is a destination in itself (unless you happen to be cycling along the Eurovelo 5 that is) so I had never happened to stumble upon it in my numerous years of criss-crossing France. About the only thing I knew about the city was that it is home to the European Parliament. Well, one of them at least, and to be fair, it was the first one. Here is not a place to debate the utter stupidity of there being two but as a European taxpayer I'm not going to let the opportunity pass to do just that. The parliamentarians wanted to be closer to the heart of power but the French were having none of that so they lobbied successfully for the original parliament in Strasbourg be retained and it is now enshrined in European legislation that twelve plenary sessions lasting four days each must be held there every year. To seal the deal in stone and mortar, or rather glass and steel, the former French president, Jacques Chirac had a replacement parliament building built at a cost of 300 million euros. It continues to incur 'duplication costs' of 200 million euros per annum. According to a BBC report shortly after the building was opened in 1999, door frames had to be removed to move the office furniture into the building (although it doesn't make clear who was to blame; the people designing the doors or those ordering the furniture), and luxury showers fitted into the MEPs' offices costing over 8,000 euros each were never used because the politicians are not allowed to stay overnight in their rooms for security reasons. If you think these were just teething problems, in 2008, part of the ceiling above the debating chamber collapsed. No one was in there at the time (unlikely if you think about it as twelve sessions of four days each leave the place empty for 317 days a year), although if they had, the damaged ceiling would have fallen on the heads of eurosceptic MEPs. You couldn't make it up! And I'm a fully-paid up member of the European Union fan club.

Back to the cycling. To be honest I was a little disappointed on arrival. Clearly a time of biblical downpours is not the best moment to arrive anywhere and the suburbs looked drab and dirty. I meandered my way into the centre following signs for 'centre ville' whenever I could see one. There was an extensive system of cycle paths but as in many French cities there was also an extensive system of improvement works taking place (where do they get the money from?) so following the cycle routes was a bit hit and miss.

I eventually found myself in Place Kléber which appeared to be the central square, plonked myself under the canvas of a covered terrace in front of one of the numerous bars in the square and dripped. Two demi pressions later, I decided that I better make an effort to find somewhere to sleep. Although I had passed a campsite in the suburbs, I had always planned to use hotels when in big cities, as I had done back in Luxembourg and saw no reason to not do so here. My guide book mentioned a few interesting establishments, which, had I not been feeling as though I had been through the rinse cycle in a washing machine, I might have investigated. As it was, I just wanted to dry off and as soon as I saw a sign for the budget hotel Ibis and a reasonable price advertised outside, it was a done deal. Reggie was allowed to join me in my room and as soon as we were both inside and the door shut, I slumped on the bed and dozed.

I woke around an hour later and showered without managing to slip on the bathroom floor (Ibis don't do shiny floors in bathrooms thank goodness). My next task was to sort myself out with some clean clothes. The lady at the reception desk sent me off in one direction to find a laundrette but when I arrived there the place was boarded up so I returned to the hotel just a little dejected. At least it had stopped raining. The same lady then sent me off in the opposite direction to find another laundrette which was about twice as far away as the first. And it started to rain again, chats et chiens, as the French don't say. I must have passed for a tramp as I swam along the streets wearing a pair of shorts and a white t-shirt that was anything but white and which was destined for the bin once I had alternative clothes to wear and with a pull string bag slung over my shoulder containing all my dirty clothes.

Laundrettes don't tend to be in the most fashionable parts of town; I couldn't see a Gucci or Prada down the Boulevard de Lyon; there were however quite a few kebab shops, a dodgy hotel with an official accreditation from 2002 but with the stars taped out and lots of shifty looking characters who kept popping into the fishing tackle shop next door to the laundrette. None of them came out with anything resembling a fishing rod. My initial poor impression of Strasbourg was not being enhanced. However, on the positive side of things, the laundrette ticked all the boxes or perhaps more appropriately pushed all the buttons. I whiled away the time reading the numerous signs and instructions that you find in laundrettes worldwide and before you could say "we accept no responsibility for loss or damage to your clothes" (in French of course), I had a dampish pile of freshly laundered clothes. Fantastic! Even better, it had stopped raining again.

As I made my way back to the hotel, I forced myself to try and see a different, more welcoming side to the city, and I began to spot it through the sporadic glints of sunshine. My mood was also improved as I quickly found and bought a new white t-shirt and blue polo shirt for an amazingly cheap 15€ from H&M in the shopping centre next to the hotel, hung all my other clothes around the room to dry properly, put on my new outfit and set off into town to explore.

The Ibis Hotel was just next to the canal on the north-west side of the city. Apart from the European Parliament being housed in the city, I did actually know two other things about Strasbourg; that it was on the Rhine and that Germany was on the other side of the river. Well, I was correct about the Germany bit but not quite correct about Strasbourg being on the Rhine. The heart of the city is actually some four kilometres east of the river and is built on a kind of island formed between the canal and the River Ill. My map indicated that the area around the Cathédrale de Notre-Dame might be worth exploring so I headed there, back through Place Kléber and towards the south-east. It was late afternoon so I guessed that I would be better off exploring inside the cathedral the following morning when I had more time. So instead, I simply sat below the rose window opposite the main door of the cathedral and had a coffee. As I looked up at the building looming above me I could see two remarkable things. Firstly the building itself. Bathed in the evening sunlight it had taken on a strikingly orange hue and the whole facade was a riot of detail and intricacy, especially the long thin columns that supported the balconies under each of the arched windows. It looked a bit lopsided however. Well, more than just a bit. The cathedral only has one tower, the one on the south was planned but never built. And here's a fascinating fact; for over two hundred years, from the mid 17th century to the late 19th century, the tower that I was looking at was the tallest building in the World. The other remarkable thing that I could see? The deep blue sky behind the cathedral itself. Not a cloud to be seen. Was this a good omen for the days to come?

I exchanged messages with my friend Claus in Stuttgart and we arranged to meet at midday the following day on a bridge over the canal in the area called La Petite France. With my day's work done, I slowly made my way back to the hotel and ate in an adjacent restaurant looking out over the canal. My second full day off the saddle beckoned.

Rest Day 2:
Thursday 29th July 2010: Strasbourg

Breakfast was an ad-hoc affair eaten en route back to the Cathédrale Notre-Dame on the other side of town. The weather was OK. Well, it wasn't raining which was the main thing. Having seen the cathedral from the outside, I wanted to explore the inside and also the viewing platform which was at the point where they had decided not to build the second spire so it should, I thought, give me a good view of the rest of the city and perhaps, weather permitting, beyond.

As I entered the Place de la Cathédrale, I could see lots of activity taking place just in front of the main entrance to the cathedral itself. A podium was being set up, crash barriers erected along the side of the square and an inflatable arch had been blown up and positioned at the end of the main street out of the square. I took a seat outside the same café that I had visited on the previous evening, ordered a coffee and watched the developing activity all around me. Some moustachioed men had now set up trestle tables just to one side of the podium upon which they were spreading out their documents and a public address system was being tested. My little grey cells were working overtime trying to figure the whole thing out. I reckoned it was some sort of sporting event, a marathon perhaps? But surely I would have noticed lots of activity elsewhere in the city if that was the case. A cycle race? Too late for the Tour de France; that had finished in Paris the previous Sunday and if it had been la Grande Boucle, I wouldn't have been able to move, let alone find a table on the terrace of a café, even at that early hour. Just as I was finishing the last few sips of my coffee, a van pulled up and out jumped a small band of enthusiastic (and brightly-dressed) young people. They immediately started to dress the podium, crash barriers and even the inflatable arch (don't use drawing pins!) with publicity material for the Tour Alsace 2010. I had been correct; it was a cycle race albeit a relatively local one. In fact it was the second stage of a five étape event which had started in Colmar (my destination incidentally for the following day) on the previous day and would end the following Sunday in a curiously-named place called Ballon d'Alsace. Today's destination, after an invigorating cycle of 153 kilometres mainly around the Vosges Mountains would be Bischoffsheim, a small town south-east of Strasbourg. How exciting! Unfortunately for me, the time of departure was set for midday, the same time that I had arranged to meet Claus in La Petite France so I would miss seeing any racing but it was still interesting watching the build-up and gave what would normally have been a quiet Thursday morning in the square a bit of a buzz. The French love their local sporting events. The old guys with moustaches had probably watched the Tour Alsace (or something similar) as kids, gone on to perhaps race in the event themselves and then taken on the mantle of organisation later in life. Not that it was just a parochial affair involving the local Alsatians; teams from Switzerland, Germany, Belgium, Norway, The Netherlands and even one from the USA were listed as taking part. And never let it be said that the French have bowed before the altar of political correctness for not only does the Tour Alsace have a (male) cycling champion, it also has a (female) Miss Tour Alsace and in 2010 that had been a certain Claire Siffert, 20 who was a languages student described by the Tour Alsace publicity machine as une jolie brune. Eric Morley, eat your heart out!

Coffee now well and truly sipped, I made my way into the relative calm of the cathedral. As you might have guessed from the knowledge that it had spent two centuries at the top of the list of tallest buildings in the world, it was impressively lofty inside. It has to be said that many cathedrals are much of a muchness. Ouch! That's a terrible thing to say isn't it? Well, they all have their particular points of interest – this one having its astrological clock that chimes midday at the wrong time and its Vitrail de l'Europe or stained glass window dedicated to European unity and designed by Max Ingrand replacing one blown out by an Allied bomb in 1944 – but they all have the same blueprint. You'd think God might have been a bit more impressed if the architects and stone masons of the Middle Ages had gone for something a little more, dare I say, unorthodox. With this sacrilegious thought in mind, I made my way to the entrance of the staircase leading to the viewing platform and a penitential climb of 332 steps. The spiral stairs to the top were encased within the same thin columns that I had been admiring from the square the previous evening; they really were that delicate and would have found a more suitable home on a wedding cake rather than in the structural support job they were doing here. Beautiful nevertheless. Only two-thirds of the wall space sweeping around the stairs was taken up with the elegantly supported windows. The remaining third was stone wall where the stairs were attached to the cathedral and these walls were covered in graffiti. It was the prosaic 'Claudi + Alex 26.05.2006' or 'Je t'aime Shi Yeng!' kind of stuff written in black marker pen and what I could only guess was bright white correcting fluid that you tend to find on many a large expanse of wall but come on, this was a place of prayer and devotion to God! The last time you visited a cathedral, did you take either a black marker pen or correcting fluid with you? Me neither. At least you can't fault Claudi, Alex and Shi Yeng on their planning. The graffiti problem got worse towards the top and then when the stairs opened out onto the large panoramic viewing platform, the wall of the tower that had been built was also completely covered. But there was a twist. Whatever attempts the cathedral authorities had been making to clamp down on the graffiti, they had not been effective for quite some time; there was one piece that had been indelibly scrawled on the wall and it read 'Hervey 12 Oct 1773'. It had been 'written', quite ornately, with a chisel. Now when was the last time you took one of those with you when you visited a cathedral?

But I'd come for the view and so I turned my attention away from the vandals of the 18th century and peered over the edge. It was quite hazy (it was no doubt approaching rain clouds) so I couldn't look back upon the Vosges Mountains that I had successfully conquered the day before. I concentrated my gaze upon the town of Strasbourg which I could see much more clearly and looked down upon the small maze of streets and buildings in the older part of town between the cathedral and La Petite France. It was an unmistakably Germanic view consisting of three- and four-story houses with large shuttered windows topped off with steeply-sided red roofs containing rows of small dormer windows. Immediately below me of course were the ongoing preparations for the Tour Alsace and I watched as they moved around with the organisational efficiency of worker ants. At which point it started raining again so I darted back down the spiral stairs and within a few minutes was back with the ants in the square.

The time was approaching to meet my old friend Claus so I walked briskly through Place Gutenberg, pausing briefly to examine the statue erected to the man who gave his name to the square. Gutenberg was at the top holding a piece of paper (what else?) but on each side of the plinth was a detailed fresco depicting what seemed to be every luminary that had ever lived up until 1840, the date when the statue was erected. I made it to La Petite France with only moments to spare and looked for the bridge where we had agreed to meet. The only problem was that there were about three of them. I called Claus who told me he was also on 'the bridge' so I looked down the canal and could see a bearded bloke with a phone in his hand; we were only one bridge out.

Claus is also a languages teacher and we trained together back at university in the UK where we first met. A few years after qualifying he decided that his future lay back in the fatherland so returned to Stuttgart and a very comfortable life teaching English and music to German teenagers rather than their British equivalents. He has many talents; he is above all an excellent linguist speaking English like a native and also has an enviable ability to play the piano without sheet music. If you hum it, he can play it. It is very impressive I assure you. To every yin however, there is a yang and if Claus' yins are languages and music, his yang is most certainly his love life. He had only just finalised what sounded like an acrimonious divorce from his wife and on the evening we met in Strasbourg was planning to go on a date with a 'borderline schizophrenic' (his words, not mine) who he had been chasing. For his sake I was delighted to hear later that it hadn't worked out.

We spent a good three hours on a café crawl around the pretty La Petite France district chatting, reminiscing and trying to fathom Claus' love life. The half-timbered houses dated from the 16th and 17th century and used to be the homes and workplaces of fishermen, millers and tanners. Now of course, these kinds of places are the homes and workplaces of waiters, chefs and pickpockets. I don't think this latter description will read quite so well in a guide book in three hundred years time.

Being a fellow linguist, I asked Claus to explain the language situation in Alsace. I had been speaking French of course to everyone; we were in France after all and anyway, I spoke no German. People replied to me in French so clearly the language was the main language of Strasbourg and Alsace. In addition, everything that I saw – signs, posters, shop names, books, notices in laundrettes(!) – were all written in French and just French. But that didn't tally with what I was frequently overhearing in bars and cafés. Why were lots of people – young and old – speaking what sounded to me like German? He explained that actually, what I was hearing wasn't quite German, it was a dialect called Elsässisch. It's spoken by about 40% of the Alsatian population although its usage is skewed to the older age groups and only around a quarter of children are able to speak it. That said, it is the second most spoken regional language in France. Occitan, the language of the south is at number one and to my surprise at least, Elsässisch is spoken by more people than Breton, the language of Jean-Jacques back at the gate of the Camping Municipal de Metz. Regional languages have been a big issue for the French state over recent years as the constitution of the Fifth Republic (they like them so much they have had five of them!) states, in article two (so it's up there with the big boys) that 'La langue de la République est le français'. President Chirac (who is such a good European that he made us waste all that money on another European Parliament building), refused to change the constitution which would have enabled him to sign the Council of Europe's charter supporting minority languages. According to a 1999 article in the Times Educational Supplement, ratification of the charter '...would have reinforced pupils' rights to a bilingual education in their own regional language'. However, things have now moved on, as has Mr Chirac and in 2008 the French constitution was changed and now includes the simple line 'Les langues régionales appartiennent au patrimoine de la France', or 'Regional languages belong to the patrimoine of France'. We mentioned 'le patrimoine' earlier if you remember; it's all the stuff that makes the French the French and it's good to know that even if you only speak Elsässisch, you are still part of the French happy family courtesy of article 75-1 of the French Constitution. Just don't expect a Christmas card from former President Chirac.

I escorted Claus back to his car, wished him luck on his date with the borderline schizophrenic (but had my fingers crossed behind my back), shook his hand and bid him farewell. It had been great to see a familiar face and to a certain extent forget about the cycling for a few hours which, however much I was enjoying it, was not the only thing I was capable of talking about or indeed wanted to talk about.

Heading back to the hotel, I made a detour via the Place de la Cathédrale where by now, all that was left of the Tour Alsace were a few advertising flyers strewn on the cobbles. That little carnival had moved on elsewhere. But I hadn't come back to see the bright Lycra; I had returned because in one corner of the square was the Strasbourg Office de Tourisme and I needed some information about the Rhine Cycle Route. The cycle route is one of those upon which the Eurovelo 5 piggy backs as it makes its way south although it starts, as it logically would, in

Rotterdam. I would be following it all the way to Basel in Switzerland at which point I would pick up the Swiss National Cycle Route 3. Now you would think that a tourist office that is situated in a square which had just hosted a significant, if minor cycling event, might be eager to help a touring cyclist who happened to be passing through their town. Not one bit of it. They were polite but knew nothing of the Rhine Cycle Route. Even a translation into French - La Véloroute du Rhin – didn't jog any distant memories so I left empty handed hoping that it would simply be very well sign-posted. I contented myself with the supposition that it wouldn't be difficult to follow a cycle path that itself follows a river.

Back at the hotel with an impromptu buffet of food spread around me on the bed, I studied my map carefully and noticed a very thin red line heading south. A thin green line on the Michelin 1:200,000 series of maps indicates a cycle path, but this one wasn't following the river, it was following Le Canal du Rhône au Rhin, a linking channel that starts in Strasbourg and heads (initially at least) due south. It ran in a series of dead straight lines all the way to Colmar, my planned destination for the following day. I reckoned that I must have found the Rhine Cycle Route.

I put the maps to one side, lay back on the bed (trying to avoid the remnants of my meal) and switched on the TV. It happened to be the weather forecast which told me that although it would probably rain the following day, Friday, I could look forward to some sun at the weekend. Perhaps, at last, I was about to cross that imaginary line of latitude after which blue skies, sunshine and baking temperatures would be guaranteed. Or had I already fallen asleep and was I dreaming?

Cycling Day 11:

Friday 30th July: Strasbourg to Colmar

5 hours 43 minutes in the saddle, 105 kilometres

Trying to find a way out of the town or city in which I had stayed the previous night was often the greatest cycling challenge that I had to overcome each day. Urban areas are built for cars and in France, the standard practice when exiting a town centre in any form of motorised vehicle is to follow the 'Toutes Directions' ('All Directions') signs which will, if you are patient, eventually take you to the road you need and send you off in the direction you want. The problem that I encountered time and time again on my journey south was that I wasn't driving a motorised vehicle and let's face it, I wasn't that patient. In a car, in an unfamiliar place you are more than happy to be sent off on a circular route around the town until you get to your particular exit road. You probably don't even realise that it's happening. On a bike, that's not the case and it was a source of ongoing frustration that I seemed to spend many, many minutes, literally going around in circles trying to find the right road out of town. Today however was stress free, or at least it was on leaving Strasbourg.

The Canal du Rhône au Rhin was directly linked to the canal over which the Hôtel Ibis looked. All that was required of me was to make sure that I had a channel of water beside me and the sun in the sky to my left. It worked a treat and I gleefully ignored all the 'Toutes Directions' signs that I passed. Within a few minutes I had found the unmistakably dead straight canal that I needed and I headed south. I decided that rather than have my usual continental breakfast in the centre of Strasbourg, I would wait a few minutes until I was on the Véloroute du Rhin and then pause briefly at the first boulangerie that I passed.

The southern suburbs of Strasbourg were just as grim as the ones that I had encountered in the west on my arrival in the city but at least they weren't drenched in water. Indeed the sun flashed like the bulb on a paparazzi's camera as it was repeatedly hidden and then exposed by the avenue of trees that lined the banks of the canal. I couldn't really go wrong that morning. The Véloroute du Rhin was indeed well sign-posted; I just had to watch out for the occasional transfer of the route from one side of the canal to the other. There was only one slight problem and that was the complete lack of boulangeries or supermarkets at which I could stop and buy breakfast. I could have made a slight deviation and headed into one of the villages on either side of the canal, but once I was out of range of Strasbourg, these seemed to become more and more distant from the canal so although my hunger was building, my motivation for making an increasingly long detour was diminishing.

The canal had three kinks in it; one at Eschau, a second at Boofzheim and a third at Marckolsheim and it was here that my hunger had to be quelled so I left the security of the canal and headed into the town centre. I had made astonishing progress having cycled 60 kilometres in less than three hours but that was entirely down to the simplicity and flatness of my route. The buildings in Marckolsheim were even more Alsatian than they had been back in the old part of Strasbourg; high roofs, shuttered windows, many timber framed and even more painted in pastel shades of yellow, blue, cream and red. It was undeniably very pretty. And of course, being a small French town, it was almost deserted. Fortunately, the owner of the rudimentary patisserie had seen the light and decided to stay open in order to entice into his establishment any passing trade, or indeed passing cyclist who might be ravenous. I bought a baguette and a large slice of wobbly tart which I devoured with the table manners of a hyena while sheltering in the very large and ornate bus stop on the other side of the main street. I say sheltered because, you guessed, it had started to rain once more. As I munched away watching the shower develop into something more substantial, the local church clock rang out twelve bongs to indicate it was midday.

I successfully fought off the temptation to return to buy a second slice of the tart and perused my map for a while. I wasn't too far from Colmar, my destination; it was only another twenty kilometres or so along a different canal – the Canal de Colmar – that took a sharp right turn heading west away from the Canal du Rhône au Rhin just after Marckolsheim. The rain, to my great delight and surprise, had decided to stop so I saddled up onto Reggie and sauntered out of town on my little trip to the not-so-wild west. Before I had got more than a couple of hundred metres however, I noticed a sign for something called Le Musée Mémorial de la Ligne Maginot du Rhin. I was up for a little lunchtime diversion so I temporarily abandoned my plans to trek west and instead headed east along the Route du Rhin and towards the museum. Even if the museum turned out to be closed I thought, I might get to see the majestic River Rhine which, despite having followed a cycle route named after it all morning, I had yet to even glimpse.

There was no sign of the river but the museum was open. Well, I don't think it ever actually closed as most of the exhibits were in the open air just set back from the road at the other side of a large gravel car park. There was no security, no barrier or hut at which to pay an entrance fee, just a swing gate that Reggie and I managed to negotiate without too much trouble. On the left was a large fortified bunker with the name of the museum written in square, white letters on one side. It reminded me a little of the correction fluid graffiti back at Strasbourg Cathedral. Perhaps Shi Yeng had managed to turn an annoying anti-social habit into a career. On the grass to the right of the building was a small collection of military vehicles and heavy duty weaponry dating back to the Second World War including an American Sherman tank, a Russian cannon and one part of a Bailey bridge. I wandered in between the various exhibits hoping not to step onto any unexploded ordnance before climbing the short flight of stairs that allowed me to access the summit of a small mound next to the bunker.

The place was riddled with retrospectively ironic health and safety signs from the post war period; 'danger zone: access forbidden', 'do not climb on the roof' and the most inappropriate which was accompanied by an arrow pointing at the main door saying 'entrance' in three languages, including of course German. I'm sure any invading Nazi would have been appreciative of the advice.

Explanatory panels drew me away from my frivolous thoughts and back to the seriousness of conflict. What I was visiting was the number 35 fortified gun emplacement of the third line of defence of the Maginot Line. Maginot was the French minister of war in the early 1930s and he persuaded the government of the necessity of building a defensive barrier along the course of the Rhine to stop the Germans invading. Tragically, when the Germans did decide to invade France, they marched through Belgium instead and in the words of the historical blurb at the entrance to the museum, after entering the country in May 1940, the Germans "...were at the gates of Paris by June 14th". Almost to prove how ineffective the line of defence was, the Germans did send troops over the Rhine in June 1940 in the process destroying 80% of the town of Marckolsheim. I thought about the buildings that I had been admiring only an hour or so previously. All but a few of them must have lain in rubble only seventy years ago. A sobering thought and a testament to the abilities of the local post-war architects and builders who had managed very successfully to rebuild their town.

A twenty-kilometre reflective cycle is what was needed which is handy because that's what I got, all the way to Colmar along the Canal de Colmar. On arrival I didn't spend too much time in the town itself. I wandered around aimlessly for a short while to admire the views and soak up the atmosphere (and two Leffe Blondes). I was very suspicious of the Rough Guide's description of the campsite in Colmar. It had used two adjectives; acceptable and inexpensive. Hardly a ringing endorsement but they would have probably got my business had my cousin (who was no doubt following my progress via the satellite tracker) not sent me the following message earlier in the day;

'If you have any trouble in Colmar I would unhesitatingly recommend the campsite in the pretty little village of Eguisheim, a mere 5 km SW and supper in the tavern in the square by the fountain, which serves generous jugs of Alsatian wine.'

That endorsement was ringing more loudly than the church bells back in Marckolsheim so I set off for Eguisheim. At this point you may want to refer back to the first paragraph of this chapter of the book where I talked about how easy it had been to leave Strasbourg that morning. The contrast with my attempts to find the correct route to Eguisheim was stark. I initially wriggled my way through the suburbs of Colmar, and what interesting suburbs they were! A fascinating mixture of 19th century 'grand' houses in both the French and English senses of the word, interspersed with lots of very modern, architecturally interesting houses. I eventually found what I thought was the correct road out of the town but after a few kilometres of things not adding up, particularly at the point where I had to pause for a train to pass at a level crossing that, according to my map, really shouldn't have been there, I realised that my confidence was misplaced. I knew that the further I pedalled along the N422, the greater would be the rectifying lurch back to the east and the D30. Good fortune intervened. I decided to take one of the small tracks to my right in the hope that it would lead me to the road that I should be taking and after a couple of kilometres of what at times was verging upon off road cycling, I was back where I wanted to be.

Eguisheim had never been part of the plan. Until earlier that day, I had never even heard of the place so I had no idea what to expect on arrival. The camp-site was well sign-posted but didn't take me through the centre of the town; I skirted around the edge but was soon at the entrance of Camping Des Trois Châteaux.

First impressions are important so it would have helped if the owner (or at least the woman who seemed to be in charge at the reception) had been on the training course that involved learning how to smile. You would think it would be the first thing you'd do if you were in the tourist industry, no? And with it being the most expensive camp-site that I had visited so far – a shocking 13,50€ – I would have expected her to throw in a few jokes for good measure! I was allocated a patch of ground with barely any grass on it and was left to fend for myself.

What the camp-site lacked, the town and the people who inhabit it more than made up for. Famed for its wines (more of those in a second), it was a walled town built to a pattern of concentric rings. The tightly-packed houses were predominantly timber-framed (not the kind of place to choose to live if you have a reputation for not getting on with your neighbours) and painted in shades of blue, orange and yellow. Hanging baskets adorned most of the windows and the cobbled streets finished the whole thing off perfectly. Reggie was less keen of course on the cobbles so I pushed him around so that we could get a good look at the place, eventually pausing in the square at the centre of the concentric rings of streets to observe lots of fevered activity. It was time to play the guessing game again. I wondered what event I had stumbled upon this time. Surely not the Tour Alsace! Fear not, they were sensibly keeping their bikes well clear of the cobbles of Eguisheim. Lots of long tables were being set up, four booths being built, a stage readied with speakers and microphones and lots of crates being unloaded from small vans. It was clearly some kind of food or more likely, wine festival. I resolved to come back a little later when whatever it was had kicked off.

Rather than return to the tent and sit in a patch of mud, I stayed in town and found a bar in which to catch-up on some planning for the following day's journey to the Swiss border. No sooner had I sat down than I was joined by a British thirty-something couple who were travelling on motorbikes and were slowly making their way in the opposite direction to me back home.

Probably not that slowly come to think of it as the size of their bikes indicated they might get a few tuts from the local residents of Eguisheim should they decide to set off too early the following morning. We passed the time chatting, mainly about how disappointing the weather had been before they excused themselves to go and eat and I headed back into the centre to see if the mystery festival had livened up.

It certainly had and the square was now so full that I found it quite difficult to push Reggie through the crowd. We needed to find a corner where he could lean on a wall and where I could ask someone what was going on. I attached him to a drainpipe and lingered next to one of the booths that had been built. Many of the boxes had been unpacked and bottles of wine had been lined up on the table at the back. This was indeed a wine festival; La Nuit des Grands Crus: Eichberg et Pfersigberg. Try saying that after a few glasses. A chap in his early 40s was stood at the bar knocking back a glass of white wine. He seemed like a likely candidate to fill me in on the details so I asked him.

His name was Paul and I had chosen well as he seemed to be very well-informed. He first explained that I was lucky to be experiencing the wine festival on that evening; it had actually been scheduled for the previous Friday evening but the whole thing had been rained off. No surprise there I thought. Rather than just shrug gallicly and look forward to next year's festival, the organisers did the sensible thing and decided to try again the following Friday which nicely coincided with my arrival in town. Paul explained that the two wines being tasted that evening ('tasting' in the broadest sense; there was no spitting taking place here!) were from the two local Grand Cru areas of Eichberg and Pfersigberg. Both were white wines and to be honest, that's all I can really remember about what he told me. The rest of the detail is lost in a happy mist of alcohol. I do remember being introduced to his mate Philippe who was working behind the bar next to where we were standing. Philippe worked for ones of the vineyards in the area and he explained the system that I needed to follow in order to taste some of the wine which involved paying at one point, receiving some tickets and then exchanging them for glasses of wine at the different booths. I must have understood this very well as I merrily chatted away for the next couple of hours to my new wine advisors while quaffing the local produce.

I can't specifically remember arriving back at the tent but I got there, with or without Reggie's assistance. That was about the only night of my journey when my ultra-thin, ultra-uncomfortable camping mat seemed to work perfectly well.

Cycling Day 12:

Saturday 31st July: Colmar to Huningue

4 hours, 39 mins in the saddle, 99 kilometres

The cycle from the Canal du Rhône au Rhin to Colmar and then Eguisheim on Friday meant that the first thing I had to do on Saturday morning was to spend an hour or so cycling back along the Canal de Colmar to hook up once again with the Véloroute du Rhin. It did however have its advantages; I was cycling directly into the rising sun which helped me not only warm up after a night in the mud patch but also sober up after the evening at the wine festival. I felt like a meerkat as I tried to sit up on the bike and make the most of the restorative rays of light. And what rays they were! For the first time my morning ritual of slapping on a thick layer of factor thirty sun cream didn't seem to have been in vain.

I had left the camp-site quite early, despite having woken up with a spinning head. Some thick black coffee combined with a couple of croissants eased me back into the real world at a café in the centre of Colmar. My phone, a vital link to my followers on the blog, was in desperate need of sustenance too and I spent more time than I would have normally liked examining the maps over breakfast while it was being recharged behind the bar. When we were both replenished, I headed to the Canal de Colmar to do my meerkat impression.

The plan was to head south to Basel, just over the border into Switzerland by continuing to follow the Véloroute du Rhin. Paul, who had so eloquently advised me on the qualities of the wines of Eguisheim (I think), had described Basel in a less positive way. I vaguely remembered him telling me that it was 'une ville industrielle' and nothing else before getting back to his pet topic of the relative merits of the two competing grands crus. He didn't seem that impressed with the Swiss city but the views of the waiter in the café in Colmar were much more complimentary and informative telling me it had an old quarter and a lively atmosphere. I supposed that I would find out for myself later that day. Perhaps they would both prove to be correct. My chatty serveur also pointed out that the following day, the 1st August, was the Swiss national holiday and that there would be fireworks tonight. What a great way to be welcomed into a new country; I could at least imagine they were in my honour.

Arriving back at the Canal du Rhône au Rhin I turned right and kept going, the flat ride along the canal being very much a continuation of the kind of cycling that I had experienced the previous day along the northern section of the Véloroute du Rhin. There was still no sight of the Rhine itself which lay beyond the fields on my left. I just continued to pedal following the signs which depicted a yellow cyclist on a rudimentary bike consisting of two wheels of twelve golden stars. How very European! The scenery became increasingly stunning as I made progress south, especially on the German side of the still unseen river where the hills had developed into mountains. The industrial might of Germany had also begun to rear its head. And it wasn't an ugly one from my perspective on the French side of the valley; it mirrored the landscape behind it, and added to the drama of the view rather than detracting from it. I might have had a different opinion of course if I had been cycling on the other side of the Rhine, nearer to the fumes, traffic and noise of the factories and chimneys.

It seemed appropriate, while passing through the town of Ottmarsheim to stop at a big red sign that instructed me to do just that. It was actually for the benefit of drivers approaching on an adjoining road just after a blind bend but as it was around lunchtime, was positioned next to a small supermarket and had an area just to one side complete with bench, flower beds and a church bell on a plinth, I stopped anyway for something to eat and a rest. The sun was continuing to shine in the middle of a deep blue sky so after having purchased a sandwich and some savoury snacks from the shop, I positioned myself on the plinth so that the bell was protecting me from the sun and munched away. This was what I had come to find; great cycling, interesting, out-of-the-way places, freedom from the rat race and above all, sunshine. I was happy! My mind wandered lazily and I could quite easily have shut my eyes and dozed off had I not been conscious of keeping one eye open and on Reggie who was leaning silently on his stand just to my side. I examined the detail of the bell in a way that it didn't really merit. I couldn't understand the inscription but I managed to conclude that they - there was another one of the other side of the road - were from a long-destroyed church as they were covered in intricate religious imagery. The one I was leaning against had a large crack in its side so it must have sounded a bit flat; perhaps it had just been replaced with a newer, more tonal instrument... I was very, very relaxed. Sun, quiet, food in my stomach, lingering somnolence from the Eguisheim wine, bell trivia on my mind. Reggie would survive if I snoozed...

I could have been there, sleeping like an itinerant tramp (albeit one with an expensive bike to his name) for quite some time had I not been jolted back to life by the stark tones of a message arriving on my phone. It was from a couple of friends who had been reading up on my journey so far on the website and had decided to send me a message expressing their disbelief that I had actually cycled as far as I had. Smiling at the thought that people back home were increasingly aghast at the progress I was making, I decided that I had better crack on with the cycling lest they be disappointed the next time they looked me up online so I dragged myself off the bell, stumbled a little, stretched, yawned, reacquainted myself with Reggie and cycled out of town. Switzerland here we come!

Well, not quite. My plan had been to make it to Basel and stay somewhere in the Swiss city that evening. That would probably have been a hotel but the more I thought about it, the more I wondered whether this was an appropriate thing to do. On approaching the French town of Huningue, I paused at a small tourist office next to the canal for some advice and guidance. The lady behind the desk warned me that the centre of the city would be extremely busy due to the fireworks. It didn't escape my attention that they seemed to be celebrating a day early; this was, after all only the 31st July and not the 1st August but who am I to question the wisdom of the Swiss, the masters of organisation and home to what I hoped would be the greatest cycle network on earth. It was recommended that instead of a hotel in Basel, I stayed in Huningue that evening and cross the border the following morning. What's more, there was a campsite on the banks of the Rhine in the centre of Huningue. Yet again a not-so-well-laid plan seemed to be coalescing in front of me as I chatted.

Huningue was modern, clean and tidy. It seemed to be one of those places that makes its living from being close to another country, or in this case, just like Schengen, being close to two other countries. The canal I was now following – the Canal de Huningue – cut its path through the centre of the town, emptying out into the Rhine just opposite the point where Switzerland meets Germany meets France. It was gratifying to see evidence that the River Rhine did actually exist and a little ironic that the first time I had seen it, despite having followed the Véloroute du Rhin all the way from Strasbourg was here at the very end of my journey along its path. I gazed across the wide stretch of water in front of me and took in the view of Switzerland beyond. It was a view of power, industry and wealth. It was also a view of the unknown. Cycling in France had been easy; although I had never travelled in the east of the country, the language, culture and people were all very familiar to me. I could understand the signs and have a conversation in the street with few problems. What I was looking at was a country I had only visited a couple of times before and on the one occasion when I had spent more than just one night in the country, it had been in the relative cultural security of the French-speaking west. I knew precious little about the culture of everyday life in the larger German-speaking area. It was a country, however, that I would be cycling through for the next week or so. I wondered to myself what little adventures lay ahead.

Camping au Petit Port was not difficult to find and what a find it was. It was the kind of camp-site that every town in the world should have; compact, informal, friendly and most importantly, no bloody hedges! The place seemed to have been designed with the cycling camper in mind and it had certainly attracted them in their droves. I cycled down the short drive that lead towards the reception building. It was very quiet which wasn't surprising as the reception didn't open until 5 o'clock. I looked around me; a one-story timber-framed hut on my left, a shelter with barbeque and table to my right and beyond, a large open space that was refreshingly devoid of mud. What a contrast to the previous night's accommodation. I must have been spotted because suddenly the door to the reception was flung open and I was invited in by a bearded gentleman who was keen on chit-chat. If he was doing it to vet the quality of his customers then I seemed to have passed with flying colours as I was soon being given instructions as to where I could pitch the tent, how I could access the shower block, when the snack-bar would be open and what would be happening that evening with the fireworks. The only question that wasn't answered before it was asked was as to why I had never considered camping here in the first place. I'll put that down to the usual excuse; lack of forward planning back in the UK.

As I pitched the tent, I was not the only one in the process of doing so; there was a Dutch contingent on the far side of the free-camping area who were doing exactly the same thing. Between us was a haphazard collection of small tents and bikes. Reggie had found his spiritual home but whereas he could feast upon the view of his new found metallic friends from the Low Countries, I needed a more practical feed. The camp-site facilities would not be opening until a little later in the evening so instead of waiting, I reasoned that it couldn't be too far to the nearest shop or café in town where I could find something to eat and drink. Dragging Reggie away from his new two-wheeled mates on the camp-site, we went to explore Huningue.

After cycling around for quite some time I decided it would be a good idea to ask someone where I could find a shop that sold food. Huningue, or the bit of it where I was cycling, didn't seem to have a café to its name let alone a restaurant or even the smallest of supermarkets. I spotted a lady with a brown paper bag which looked as though it might be full of food so it seemed logical that she would be able to fill me in on the secret that would enable me to solve the riddle of the location of Huningue's food suppliers.

"Est-ce qu'il y a un supermarché ou un café près d'ici mademoiselle ? " I enquired

"Il faut aller en Allemagne" she replied.

That wasn't really the answer I was expecting – I had to go to Germany! It's not every day that you get directed to another country simply to buy a bit of bread and cheese, but then again, most of us don't live in towns that sit on international borders.

My helpful passer-by pointed me in the direction of a footbridge that spanned the Rhine. It was an elegant piece of engineering that I had seen from the banks of the river next to the camp-site and had something of the Sydney Harbour Bridge about it but much thinner, more delicate and just a little bit more squat. It also lacked an opera house to one side but would, I thought, make an interesting foreground for the fireworks that would be springing up all over the city of Basel beyond its long arch later in the evening. In that respect it would be fulfilling the same role as its antipodean big brother on New Year's Eve.

I cycled over the bridge and into my fifth country of the trip; Germany. OK, it was only a very brief visit but the contrast with sleepy Huningue was stark to say the least. As I reached the eastern bank of the river I was suddenly plunged into a Germanic frenzy of people, cars and shopping. Welcome to the town of Weil am Rhein! It was overwhelming, and just a little bit bizarre. In a matter of moments I was seeing as many people as I had encountered during the entire day up to that point. On my right was a gigantic shopping complex complete with fast food outlets, a four star hotel and a supermarket called Marktkauf. If this was what neighbouring German-speaking Switzerland would be like, I was in for a roller-coaster ride in the next few days. I hunted around the vastness of the shop trying to find a few familiar items upon which I could dine al fresco back at Camping au Petit Port. I eventually succeeded but it was far from easy; this was a supermarket that catered for the family and everything seemed to come in boxes, packets, tins and cartons that you only normally see in the back of people carriers full of children. The young woman at the check-out spoke no French or English but I was saved by my familiarity with the single European currency and the digital display telling me how much I had spent. I walked quickly back to Reggie; he was cowering next to a bunch of teenagers who had taken up position well within his comfort zone, placed my provisions in the pannier, unlocked him and escaped back over the border and into the relative tranquillity of France. As I did so, my heart was beating just a little bit faster.

The supermarket had been no busier of course than your average supermarket on a Saturday afternoon anywhere in the World. The noise had been no greater, the hustle and bustle no more frantic and the teenagers no more hostile or threatening. In fact they could very well have been discussing the virtues of the latest work of Günter Grass for all I knew. What had been bewildering was the immediate contrast between the two countries and the two cultures divided only by a short stretch of water.

Back at the campsite I started chatting to one of the Dutch cyclists who called himself 'Bob'. This was not his real name but an adopted one as he assured me that his birth name was unpronounceable if you didn't speak Dutch. After some persuasion he did tell me what it was, I tried to repeat it and failed so was happy to stick to plain, simple Bob. Bob was heading in the other direction to me and had come from Siena so we passed quite a considerable amount of time looking at his maps. He didn't seem that interested in my maps and my journey and I could soon see why he was travelling alone as he had yet to learn the ability of having a two-way conversation. I had falsely assumed that he was travelling with the other Dutch people who I had seen earlier but this was not the case. In fact the other two had left the camp-site already having decided they would be better off in a hotel. I wondered if Bob had played any role in their decision to do so. That said, despite his complete lack of interest in the lives of others, he was affable enough company and it did allow me to hear about some of the places I would be visiting over the few weeks to come.

At around 10.30pm Bob and I wandered down to the footbridge to watch the fireworks but we couldn't see that much. The crowd around us didn't seem to be dwindling however; perhaps they were easily pleased. There were a few coloured explosions in the far distance but it was nothing to get too excited about. If I had been Swiss and desperate to celebrate my Swissness, I might even have described the event as disappointing. After some time had passed and it was heading for midnight, I suggested we return back to the campsite so we left the locals to their star gazing still scratching our heads as to why they weren't heading off home themselves. On arrival I said good-night to Bob, thanked him for his company and hit the camping mat.

I was on the verge of nodding off (which in the tent could often describe the entire night's sleeping efforts), when suddenly there was an almighty series of very loud bangs and shrieks. The inside of the tent lit up with the bright flashes in the sky. Either one of the three countries has just declared war on the other two or, more likely, it was the start of the real fireworks, the ones everybody had been patiently waiting for. Bob came back over to my tent and asked if I wanted to go back down to watch them but I acted as if I was asleep and didn't reply. It was never an easy procedure undressing in the tent, climbing into the sleeping bag and trying to get comfortable and I had just spent a good five minutes or so doing just that. The thought of having to do it all in reverse and then repeat the exercise later when the real fireworks had finished was too much to contemplate so I stayed in the tent and missed out on the display. The party continued with very loud music emanating from across the border until 3am. Needless to say, I didn't sleep a wink. Welcome to Switzerland! Almost.

Cycling Day 13:

Sunday 1st August: Huningue to Sursee

6 hours 14 minutes in the saddle, 103 kilometres

Switzerland is great for what it isn't. It's not part of the European Union which in my mind at least, makes it just a little bit more exotic than France, Spain, Germany or any of the other twenty-four members of the big continental club. Now as I've said before, I'm all for the EU and have benefited in many ways from its existence but I also like the drama of a good border crossing where you show your passport, try not to look shifty and play it cool. Leaving the U.K., we Brits do this all the time thanks to our government not having signed the Schengen Agreement as I noted earlier, but most of the rest of the population of the EU saunter from one country to the next, just as I had been doing on Reggie for the first two weeks of my journey, without a care in the world let alone a passport in their back pocket.

So approaching the Franco-Swiss border, passport poised ready to flash it at a surly border guard, buttocks clenched for fear of intimate searches, I was just a tiny bit apprehensive. What I hadn't realised is that the Swiss, despite their long-standing love for independence and neutrality, have also signed up to the Schengen Agreement and I was able to cycle across the border with the same nonchalance that I had crossed every border since leaving Dover. How disappointing! The only difference between cycling from France to Belgium and cycling from France to Switzerland was that the Swiss hadn't turned their border posts into tourist offices or florists. Indeed the border crossing at Basel was brand spanking new, or at least looked that way. It was also completely and depressingly for me, empty. 'Come on boys, strip search me!' I thought but didn't shout as I cycled over the white line in the road.

Just as I had felt on my foray to the German supermarket on the previous evening, I found myself, within seconds, in unfamiliar territory trying to fathom signs in a language I didn't speak. The streets of Basel were deserted apart from a few drunken or hung-over stragglers from the festivities of Saturday night. Nothing was open but I did find a cash machine and immediately took out 200 Swiss Francs although I wasn't quite sure how much that was or how long it would last me in the notoriously expensive country I had entered. The bank notes were alarmingly colourful and made the euros I still had in my wallet look rather dull and drab in comparison. Not that I could find anywhere to spend them. None of the shops were open – it was after all Sunday morning in a country that still values Sunday as a day of rest – so I gravitated to the only place that is guaranteed to offer a welcoming embrace to any passing traveller on any day of the week; the train station. I followed the signs for bahn and after only a few minutes of cycling, dodging trams and trying to make sure that my tyres didn't get lodged into the rails in the road (there were plenty of comically visual signs warning me of what could happen if I did), arrived beneath the elegant white facade of the Bahnhof SBB. I pushed Reggie through the entrance and looked for somewhere where I could buy breakfast.

Having the ability to speak another language is a wonderful skill. It not only allows you to gain first-hand understanding of another culture and people that remains hidden to those who don't speak the language, but it is good, simple fun. My knowledge of French enabled me to do this effortlessly in France, Belgium and Luxembourg despite the occasional frustration of people in tourist offices insisting upon speaking English all of the time. My limited but functional knowledge of Italian would allow me to at least have fun experimenting with that language on arrival in Italy. In German-speaking Switzerland however, it was another thing altogether as the flip-side of speaking one or two languages fluently is (in my case at least) extreme frustration when in a country whose language I have never grasped. And I have never really got to grips with the German language. It's all those consonants together in a long line; my eye wanders before I get to the end of the word ensuring that my mouth collapses into a heap of linguistic nonsense. So here was my first linguistic challenge in Switzerland; buying something to eat and drink for breakfast.

I spotted a likely purveyor of food and perhaps even coffee. I approached, Reggie in one hand, luridly-bright bank note in another and hovered over the counter with only a pane of polished curved glass between me and a sumptuous early morning feast. The lady behind the desk finished serving the person to my side and looked me in the eye. The linguistic scoundrel inside my head uttered those infamous words of last resort;

'Sprechen Sie Englisch? ' I enquired

'Nein' she replied.

So I pointed at a cake below the counter;

'ein'

The lady looked at me, half in pity, half in disgust but it did the trick and, after a few moments of excessive wrapping she presented me with the unnecessarily-boxed pastry. My green credentials had to be suspended for this transaction; I wasn't going down the 'don't bother with the packaging' route in German if I could barely manage to utter a simple request that I wanted to buy one of the cakes in the shop. I was on a roll however and the word 'coffee' did the trick. I was handed a steaming paper cup full of black liquid. Job done! As I sat outside the entrance to the station eating and drinking, I wondered if the next week would be a string of similarly stressful linguistic encounters.

Basel was not really what I expected. A grimy, dark city surrounded by industrial areas, much as Paul back in Eguisheim had told me. I had hoped for something more southern European, lighter and more airy. However it reminded more of Brussels that it did of Rome and was quite a brutal reality check that perhaps Switzerland wasn't going to be the walk or rather cycle in the park that I had thought it might be. I needed to find

Cycle Route 3 so I cycled east and out of the heart of the city centre in the hope that at some point on that side I town I would bump into it. Much to my surprise and delight, I did, in a leafy suburban street. There it was on a sign and I was so startled and delighted that I stopped to take a picture. The sign informed me that I was not only on Route 3 (the Nord-Süd Route), but also on Route 2 (the Rhein Route), Eurovelo 6 (the Atlantic Route), the Dreiland-Radweg (or three countries route) and the Südschwarzwald-Radweg (or Black Forest route). You wait for one cycle path and then five come along all at once! If I had wanted to, I could have chosen to continue to follow the Rhein Route; its destination was Andermatt, high in the Alps which was where I was heading but the route of the Rhine took that cycle path first east as far as Lake Constance and then south and west through a long curve back to Andermatt. My Route 3 was much more direct slicing Switzerland in two from top to bottom.

Unfortunately my delight was not to last. Back at home in the UK, I had dreamt of cycling in Switzerland; beautiful roads, sign posts at every turning and polite drivers all with a backdrop of stunning Alpine vistas... The reality of that first day didn't really meet those wild expectations. The roads were on a par with France but were not of the luxurious standard to which I had briefly become accustomed in Luxembourg. The cycling sign posts were good when they were there but all too often I would arrive at a junction which was devoid of any indication as to which way my Route 3 was going and I was left scratching my head. The normal road signs didn't give distances (mildly annoying in a car, infuriating on a bike) and were nowhere near as frequently placed as they had been in France.

Within an hour of rejoicing at the sight of my first Route 3 sign, I was almost ready to jump on a train as I became increasingly frustrated at my inability to follow the on-street directions. I was looking sufficiently bewildered in the far eastern suburbs of Basel that a middle-aged couple pulled over to ask the question, in English "Are you lost?". Perhaps I wasn't the first to have been beaten by the idiosyncratic signs of Route 3. They pointed me in the correct direction and I was able to escape the clutches of the city and breathe some Swiss country air for the first time. It tasted sweet.

I persevered and eventually started to make good progress along Route 3. I successfully climbed the most arduous hill of the journey so far, to Schafmatt at 810 metres (Basel had been at 266 metres) and stopped for lunch at a hilltop restaurant called the Berghaus Schafmatt where I tucked into a long, fat wurst that did the business perfectly. The Swiss flag was hoist high on a flag pole just in front of the restaurant, the scenery was half-way to being stunning and I was slowly beginning to forget my first impressions of a cyclist in Switzerland forged back in the suburbs of Basel. The real fun of the day was still ahead of me however.

It was a leisurely ride down towards Aarau, my destination that day. Despite my extremely annoying screechy brakes, I arrived in the town in good spirits looking forward to pitching the tent and settling down for some evening grub on a nice Swiss campsite.

In retrospect Sunday had not been the best day to arrive in Switzerland. On any normal Sunday the town of Aarau would have been very quiet. If you arrive in Switzerland on a Sunday that also happens to be the Swiss national holiday, you may as well try finding life on the surface of the moon. Aarau was a ghost town. I rattled the door of the tourist office in vain; no one was at home. Or rather everyone was at home and no one, not even the tourist office employees were at work. I scoured the map to find reference to a campsite; nothing. Even the hotels – my second option - appeared to have closed their doors. Bugger! I sat on the steps of the tourist office pondering my options. They were limited. I could stay in Aarau and redouble my efforts to find a hotel but I wanted to avoid that simply because of the cost involved and there hadn't seen an abundance of cheap Ibis-like establishments on my route so far. I could wild camp. That was a scary option, not least because I wasn't in a wild area. I would probably discover in the morning that I'd pitched the tent in someone's back garden. The third option seemed like the only reasonable one; continue to cycle to the next town where I was certain there would be a campsite. I knew that was in a place called Sursee but I also knew that Sursee was another thirty kilometres further south. It was all very reminiscent of the day I had cycled from Metz only to be forced to extend my cycle by an unexpected slog into the heart of the Vosges Mountains in the early evening because of the lack of a camp-site in Sarrebourg. But if I had done it once, I would do it again. I could at least comfort myself with the thought that the following day's cycle to Lucerne would be but a short hop and I would, in effect, have a half day of rest before I started the climb towards the St. Gotthard Pass and over the Alps.

I stuck to the main roads from Aarau to Sursee not even looking for the Route 3 signs. I knew that I needed to eat up the kilometres and was keen to avoid the twists and turns of a cycle route that would probably take me away from the traffic of the roads that I was using but would be much longer. It was with great relief that I entered the gates of Camping Sursee. On the outskirts of the town, it was the perfect place to unwind after what had been by far the most stressful day of the journey to that point. It even had a patch of ground for free camping. The reception was housed on the upper floor of the main building and as I climbed the stairs I found it difficult not to smile as I realised that yet again I had somehow managed to bring the end of the cycling day to a satisfactory if miraculous conclusion. Perhaps the lack of planning had something to say for it. 'When I return to school in September, should I just stop planning all my lessons, throw caution to the wind and see what happens?' I wondered. On the Eurovelo 5 that strategy seemed to be working just fine.

I bought some beer from the reception to celebrate my good fortune and descended back to the grass to pitch the tent and relax. No sooner had I done so than there was a loud roar of an engine approaching or to be precise there were two loud roaring engine sounds. It was British father and son bikers Carl and

Nick who were on their way south to Argelès-sur-mer on the French-Spanish border to meet up with the female side of their family who had taken the easy option and flown south instead. They were good company for the evening and we swapped stories in a way that Bob back in Huningue would have found incomprehensible.

As we chatted and the sun set, the sky darkened and a storm approached. By the time we crawled into our respective tents, rain drops were falling and they had no intention of stopping for quite some time to come.

Cycling Day 14:

Monday 2nd August: Sursee to Lucerne

2 hours 0 minutes in the saddle, 35 kilometres

In their wisdom, the owners of Camping Sursee had placed the free camping area next to a long, wooden, open-fronted shed. This was a perfect place in which to sit and watch the rain fall. Carl and Nick joined me when they crawled from their sodden tents. They hadn't invested in quality tents but had gone for the circular ones that unzip and pop up in a matter of seconds. These must be great on a Mediterranean beach but perhaps weren't the best option for a stormy night in Switzerland. There was even room for Reggie in the shed and he had taken on the role of a clothes horse draped in t-shirts, cycling shorts and a quick-drying towel. The four of us were joined by two German cyclists who had arrived after we had gone to bed. They didn't seem in the least bit bothered by the heavy rain and continued their morning routine regardless. We three Brits just used it as an excuse to sit and moan.

I was now into my third week of cycling and Reggie Ridgeback Panorama (to give him his full name) seemed to be holding his own. In the first few days of the journey, I had been a little annoyed with rattles, squeaks and vibrations but they now seemed to have disappeared. I put that down to having started the trip on British 'boneshaker' roads although the minor service he had received from Iain back in Deal had clearly helped. The predominantly good quality roads on the continent were treating him with much more respect but I was concerned that that might not last when we left Switzerland at the end of the week and had to start cycling on the infamously pot-holed roads of Italy. I was over using the middle front plate or cog as it was occasionally starting to slip, especially when setting off with the chain in that position but apart from this minor problem, he was in good shape. And so was I if you were asking. Apart from a nagging twinge in one shoulder which had started shortly after the ballroom dancing episode in Boulogne, my injured foot from when I had slipped in the hotel bathroom in Luxembourg and the cut on my leg which had bled so profusely in Thionville, I too was holding up well. I had now stopped bandaging my foot in the morning and had taken to cycling in my open-toed sandals instead of the 'clipless' cycling shoes so as to not put pressure onto the wound. I was beginning to understand why Alain in Boulogne used them all the time for his cycling as they were much more comfortable. The cycling shoes would, I thought, only be used in future on long, arduous climbs starting with the big one up into the high Alps in a couple of days' time. Gulp.

Carl, Nick and I debated whether it is cyclists or motorcyclists who suffer more in the rain. The speed of the motorbike makes getting from A to B quicker but the intensity of the raindrops smashing against the visor of the helmet makes the whole process a more violent one. On a push bike you can at least choose to wear the minimum amount of clothing and as long as the raindrops are not being thrust in your direction by a strong wind, you simply get very, very wet.

Eventually the storm did pass and we were able to escape from under the protective shed to shake down our tents and pack them away carefully, or in the case of Carl and Nick, shake and zip in the blink of an eye. I was, however in no hurry whatsoever as I only had a short cycle ahead of me, around the northern side of the Sempachersee lake and then south towards Lucerne itself. As the crow flies it was only about twenty kilometres so I could take my time. Once packed, Carl and Nick roared off towards the Alps; one of the reasons they had chosen the route they were taking was to experience driving up and down switchback mountain passes. I wasn't envious that they would be able to do so by simply turning the handlebar throttle and receiving instant power from their engine although I was open to the suggestion that I might change my mind later in the week when I was half-way up some relentless Alpine road.

The whole of cycling day fourteen would be at a leisurely pace. Breakfast was courtesy of a patisserie in the centre of Sursee where I laid back on a flat concrete bench nibbling away at some delicious but unknown cake. The bench was remarkably comfortable or was it just that I was now getting used to sleeping on my ineffective camping mat? An early lunch was taken in a small square in a town called Rothernburg where I sat on the side of the fountain admiring the pretty chalets that bordered the main street and from there it was only a short hop over the infrastructure of the valley bottom to Lucerne itself. In a country that is split four ways by its four languages, it is hardly surprising that many larger towns have several names from which to choose. Here I could pick from Lucerne (French), Luzern (German), or even Lucerna (Italian and Romansh). In English we tend to use the French spelling (which is strange as the town is well and truly within German-speaking Switzerland) so I'll stick with that convention and called in Lucerne.

Lucerne was quite an important stopping off point on my route. My cycling through Switzerland so far had been through rolling valleys, nothing too mountainous. As I approached Lucerne however, I could see in the distance the mighty Alps and somewhere up there was the St. Gotthard Pass which would be my gateway to Italian-speaking Switzerland and beyond that, Italy itself. Geographically, Lucerne sits at the north-western end of the Vierwaldstättersee which, for understandable reasons I will call Lake Lucerne. You can perhaps guess why the name never really caught on with English speakers. The lake has a ghostly shape to it with Lucerne sitting on the head, Alpnach and Küssnacht at the tips of the fingers and Altdorf at the feet. That would be my destination the following day after a cycle around the southern shoreline, a ferry to Gersau and finally a cycle on the northern shoreline to the hometown of William Tell. More of that later.

For the moment, I was in Lucerne and had arrived in the early afternoon. The waterfront was striking. Split into two halves by the river that ran through the middle of the town like a torrent, one side was what you would expect a Swiss lakeside town to look like; pretty (and pretty expensive) hotels with terraces and balconies overlooking the water. The other side was much more modern with the railway station resembling an airport terminal with taxis pulling up at the front in an orderly 'drop off zone' and a very large, modern black building with an immense overhanging roof. I wasn't quite sure what this place was but made a mental note that it would be worth investigating later in the day.

A large overhanging roof would have come in quite useful at Camping International Lido Luzern, my home for the evening some three kilometres or so out of town to the east. The rain had kicked in again as I arrived in Lucerne and this time had it had no intention of stopping. By the time I had cycled along the shore of the lake to the camp-site, it was bucketing it down and was in the process of rapidly transforming the tent pitches from nice patches of grass and dust into a paddy field of mud. This really was no longer fun.

There was a long queue of people at the reception desk; were they checking in or out? Logic would dictate that they were all as fed up with the bad weather as I was and were moving on elsewhere to escape the rain, but the reality was that they too were just arriving and looking to the sky for any positive sign that there would be an improvement sooner rather than later. When I got to the front of the queue I was given a choice of pitches upon which to erect the tent but they were all just as soggy and muddy as each other. I chose one next to a tree in the hope that it might shelter me from at least some of the raindrops but the thick buttress roots prevented me from pushing the pegs into the ground so I was forced to use more open ground anyway. The two German cyclists who had also been at the camp-site at Sursee the previous night appeared and we exchanged weary nods although mine seemed just a bit more weary that theirs.

I unburdened Reggie of his panniers, stowed them away inside the tent and with only a waterproof bag containing just the essentials of a trans-European traveller, we headed back into the town centre where my primary intention was to find a bar and drown my sodden sorrows. I would normally shy away from British or Irish-styled 'pubs' in a place like this but as the weather was being so English, I saw no reason why I shouldn't stop and have a pint of beer at the Mr Pickwick Pub. I didn't quite go all the way and sell my soul to the tourist trail devil making sure that I ordered a pint of Swiss beer rather than a pint of Fosters which was also on offer. I sat outside next to the fast-flowing River Reuss on a green plastic chair at a table upon which had been placed a menu offering 'traditional pub grub', under a parasol advertising the Australian beer I had chosen not to drink and, of course, it continued to rain. In fact it was getting worse not better. All around me sat miserable tourists who were not getting the holiday experience they had paid for. At least they hadn't just cycled nearly 1,500 kilometres from the U.K. to not get it. It was a low point in my journey south to say the least. In northern and eastern France I put the continuing bad weather down to latitude and bad luck. Here, in the middle of Switzerland, it was beginning to be cruel.

To forget the weather, I delved into my guide book to read about what a wonderful place Lucerne was when it wasn't raining. I learnt that the name of the town comes from a Celtic word lozzeria meaning 'a settlement on marshy ground'. It still was back at Camping International Lido Luzern. The town only really started to grow when the Gotthard Pass was opened at the start of the 13th century; merchants would sail from here down the lake towards Altdorf from where they would start their long arduous trek up the mountains. Queen Victoria came to Lucerne in August 1868 although she clearly wanted to keep it quiet as she used the title Countess of Kent for the duration of her visit. Prince Albert had died back in 1861 so you would have thought the black outfits might have been a bit of a giveaway. One of her day trips was to 'climb' Mount Pilatus, the mountain that sits just to the south of the town. It is 2,132 metres high which is just a fraction more than the St. Gotthard Pass. Obviously a mountain is a mountain and a pass a pass (the bit between two mountains) but I could see it clearly from my plastic chair at Mr Pickwick Pub and tried to contemplate the enormity of the cycling job I had to do over the next few days. Queen Victoria, sorry, The Countess of Kent hadn't really climbed it. She had gone up on the back of a mule but if she could do that as a podgy fifty year old monarch, surely I could do something similar as an active forty-year-old cyclist.

Anaesthetised slightly against the weather by two pints of beer, I decided that I needed to explore more than just the terrace of a British pub so braced myself against the weather and went for a wander. There were a few interesting bits and pieces to investigate including a wooden bridge called the Kapellbrücke which spanned the River Reuss diagonally. Most of the structure burnt down in a fire in August 1993 and I couldn't help thinking that it must have been a blessing in disguise to the tourist officials as the history of the bridge burning down and what they did to replace it was far more interesting than the story of its previous 700 years of existence. Having crossed the bridge, I made my way to the large black structure I had seen on arrival. It turned out to be the town's new art museum – the Kunstmuseum Luzern - plus café, shop and all the other places in which people spend more time than actually staring at paintings. A market of some description had just taken place and workmen were in the process of cleaning up, removing all the market stalls and generally making lots of noise so it didn't make the best place to sit and admire the view but I did anyway and stared out and along the lake towards the mountains. The dark clouds which shrouded the tops of the highest peaks added a touch of menace. No turning back now I thought.

Reggie and I trudged back to the camp-site taking a path that was as close to the lake as possible. On our left were the exclusive terraces of the high-class hotels with women dressed in cream dresses and men in dark suits and unnecessary sunglasses. Goodness knows what they would have thought of me if they had chosen to glance in my direction, every piece of cloth on my body dripping wet. I chose to push Reggie rather than ride him; the gravel path made cycling difficult and anyway, I was in no rush. Every so often I paused and took another brooding picture of the lake and the landscape beyond.

If nothing else, my weather-affected day would allow me to put some meat on the bones of my plans for the following few days so on arrival back at the camp-site, I went immediately into the large room next to the reception to spread out my map and consider the options. The room was busy with other campers sheltering from the elements; some were chatting, some were preparing food using the small kitchen in one corner, some were watching TV, some were using the two desktop computers in the corner of the room catching up with emails (and no doubt updating their Facebook statuses with caustic comments about the rain), some were playing chess and some were planning their next move, just like me. My phone was running low on energy so I located a socket behind the television and plugged in the charger which was attached to a continental adaptor. It didn't slide in as smoothly as it should as it wasn't quite the right fit but with a small amount of pressure, I was able to force the male and female parts together. This was not a good move. Suddenly the room was plunged into darkness, the TV went blank, the fridge stopped whirring, the computers shut down and everybody in the room stared at me. I stood and stared back. It would have been a good thing to learn a few key phrases of German before having entered Switzerland, but I hadn't so I stuttered in English 'I'm sorry...' Could my day get any worse?

I walked over to the reception and explained what had happened. I was hoping for a reaction along the lines of 'don't worry, it happens all the time' but the girl called her supervisor over and neither of them looked in the least bit impressed. He went off to investigate what had happened and I returned to the room where all the people were probably expecting some kind of reassurance that they could get back to the electronic activities momentarily and that their frozen ice-cream wouldn't soon be soup. I couldn't give any reassurance so I sat down and smiled nervously, praying that suddenly the lights would flicker back into life. Eventually, much to my relief, they did and I was able to see my maps once more. The rest of the room returned to their respective activities diplomatically ignoring my presence.

The plan was this; the following day, Tuesday, I would cycle to either the campsite at Flûelen or Altdorf. The journey would be mainly flat as it was around the lake and, as mentioned earlier, at one point involved taking a ferry. I had telephoned a chap at the camp-site in Altdorf earlier but he didn't speak English or French and I, as you well know, didn't speak German so I wasn't sure whether I had booked myself in or not. He hadn't seemed interested in noting down my name so I suspected that I hadn't. None of the sites so far en route had turned me away but, I reasoned, I was now heading into a high valley where alternative options would be increasingly limited. I decided to do what I had done on numerous occasions so far on the trip and simply ignore this triviality. On Wednesday I would cycle from Altdorf to Andermatt. There it would have to be a hotel as there was no campsite. It would also mean cutting the main ascent up to the pass into two. On Thursday I would climb from Andermatt to the St. Gotthard Pass itself. It wasn't far horizontally on my map but it would be around 700 metres vertically. I would love to spend the night at the top but it would be dependent upon two things; the weather and also, more practically if I was able to do so. Camping up there would be fun but there was no site and the top of a mountain is not the greatest place to make your first ever foray into the world of wild camping. It would have to be a hotel or a hostel. Would I need to book that in advance? If I had to wait a day in Andermatt for better weather for the last bit I was prepared to just that. It would be a disappointment to get to the top and not to have a view to look down upon. The following day's cycle would be the last predominantly flat one for some considerable time.

Cycling Day 15

Tuesday 3rd August: Lucerne to Andermatt

7 hours 8 minutes in the saddle, 112 kilometres

It rained all night long. It never stopped or if it did, it happened to coincide with the very brief periods when I was actually sleeping. It wasn't so much a case of waking up as deciding when to stop making an effort to fall asleep and I arrived at this point at about half past seven when I proceeded to pack everything into the panniers while still inside the tent itself. This was far from easy as I could barely sit up inside my little moveable home but I persevered and just before eight I was ready to unzip the door, load the bags onto Reggie and escape soggy Lucerne. And at that precise moment, the rain stopped.

Following Route 3 from Lucerne to Altdorf would, I thought, be a relatively straightforward task as there was really only one road to take and that was the one which lead all the way around the lake. Until I found the ferry, all I had to do was to ensure that the mountains were on my right, the lake was on my left and Route 3 was both in front of and behind me. Once on the other side of the lake, I would simply swap over the position of the mountains and the water and continue as before. If any of them were not in the place they should be, I would pause and consult the map. Problem solved even before it had presented itself.

This strategy worked fine until I arrived in the town of Stansstad about 10 kilometres into my journey. The civil engineers of Switzerland had clearly got fed up of slavishly building their dramatic road next to the lake and had decided instead that a short-cut was needed. The road moved inland towards the town on Stans, alongside an airport (presumably Stansstad Airport although I couldn't spot any low-cost airlines...) only to join up once more with the lake at a village called Buochs. This might have thrown me had the cycling signs not been playing ball but they were now coming up with the goods at every turn. Indeed one lamp post just outside Stans had a total of twelve cycling, walking or rollerblading signs attached to it. It was verging on directional overload but I wasn't complaining. It informed me that I had already cycled 20 kilometres from Lucerne and it would be another 32 kilometres to Altdorf.

As I was admiring this celebration of cycling signage, a little old lady came up to me. I think she assumed that I was lost. She spoke to me half in German, half in English and from what I could understand, she was trying to tell me that there was a much more direct route if I followed the main road. The sign for Altdorf was encouraging me to take a quieter back road (as cycling signs tend to do). I smiled and from somewhere dragged up the expression 'Ich liebe' while moving my hand from one side to another like an eel moving through water. I wanted to indicate to her that on this occasion I didn't mind going around the houses. She probably just thought I was an English weirdo with a fish fetish. As she walked away, she was still chuntering happily to herself.

Just outside Buochs, I noticed a small log cabin with a tourist information sign on the roof. Although I knew that at some point along this stretch of shoreline I had to jump on a ferry, I wasn't sure exactly where that was so I took the opportunity of asking. After a few minutes of conversation with the elderly chap inside, I was beginning to get the impression that the Buochs tourist information cabin didn't get many visitors. He spoke impeccable English and he kept milking the conversation for all he could. All I wanted to know was where I could find the ferry and at what time the next one would be leaving but my helpful tourist information officer had clearly spent most of his working life in some sort of sales job. I'm sure that if I had not made some fairly abrupt comments about wanting to get the next ferry, it would only have been a matter of time before he had me signed me up for a three-week stay in one of the shore side hotels, full board! It is sometimes possible to be too nice. When, eventually, I was able to continue my cycle along the side of the lake, I dare not look behind me for fear that he may have jumped into his car and be pursuing me down the road with a bunch of leaflets in his hand.

For everyone's sake, this was not the case and within a few minutes I arrived at a slipway turning left off the road. I noticed one of the now familiar blue squares containing a small Swiss flag and a large number 3; it was comically pointing straight into the lake. I concluded that I had found the ferry. To be honest, there wasn't much concluding to do as the boat itself was sitting in the water at the end of a wide ramp. It was a fairly rudimentary ferry compared to the giants that ply their trade across the English Channel and of course, it was much smaller. It also lacked the hoards of English men drinking pints of lager at 10am. The boat consisted of a large open deck with space for perhaps twenty or so cars and an upper deck with a few bright red park benches and a flag pole sporting the Swiss flag. I suppose if you are a land-locked country, you need to take every opportunity given to sport your ensign. I lashed Reggie to a railing on the port side of the vessel (I feel obliged to use the nautical terminology even though it's difficult to 'lash' something with a bike D-lock and the 'port' side was actually in the case at the rear of the vessel) and climbed the stairs to the upper deck to take up position at the front, one eye on Reggie, one eye on the mountains on the other side of the lake.

The ferry was very quiet with only myself, Reggie and a few other cars. One of them was being driven by a German couple in their late fifties. The husband joined me on the bench on the upper deck while his wife stayed on the car deck looking out over the lake and we struck up conversation. After I had regaled him of my story, he told me of his which was a strikingly touching one. His wife had visited the area around Gersau, our destination, on many occasions when she was a child with her parents. The second of her parents had recently died and she was coming back to rediscover a place which must have held many happy memories for her. They even planned to sleep in the same place where she had stayed with her family all those years ago. It was no wonder she was standing on the car deck, alone, looking at the shoreline beyond.

Wiping a tear from my eye (or was it the fierce lake wind?), I glanced down at my cycling computer which I had taken off Reggie lest he be the victim of crime on the car deck. In retrospect this seemed unlikely when I looked around at the car drivers who were also travelling across the lake but you can never be too careful. I scrolled through the different statistics that it was able to furnish me with every evening and noticed that the total number of kilometres that I had cycled since leaving my flat in Reading was exactly 1,500. How strange, I thought. A rationalist would say of course that this was no more significant than me noticing that I had cycled 1,426 kilometres from Reading to Lucerne the previous day but then again rationalist don't get all teary-eyed by a couple of Germans reliving past holidays. Or indeed write travel books about journeys with bicycles called Reggie

After about half an hour or so, the ferry arrived in Gersau and we all disembarked. I waved to the German couple as they drove off down the road and then set off myself in the same direction towards Altdorf. The ride was spectacular if rather flat, the road clinging to the edge of the rock that plunged directly into the deep water of the lake. Occasionally the road would enter a dark, wet tunnel only to reappear at a point where it was physically possible to build a road in the open air. Many of the short tunnels had 'windows' cut into the rock so the view towards the other side of the lake could still be seen. They framed the view perfectly and the tunnel became a gallery of live landscape paintings. Just as it had done so back in France when I descended towards the Meuse, the weather added to the drama of the unfolding spectacle in front of and beside me and once again, I really didn't mind the dark clouds and intermittent rain to which I was being subjected.

At Brunnen, a small shore side resort I noticed the very first sign for the St. Gotthard Pass which simply stated 'Gotthard' and pointed up the valley. Although Brunnen itself was far from quiet, I could sense that I was entering a much more remote corner that remained off the track beaten by many who only make it as far as Lucerne. The people around me were prepared to sweat for their enjoyment; the walkers in stout walking books and carrying hikers' sticks, the cyclists wrapped up against the elements with tents and provisions and the bikers in thick, black leathers, carrying large boxes of supplies on their rear seats. This was no place for idle passengers. As if to emphasise that this was not a place for those who were contented with a walk in a park on a sunny day, a few kilometres out of Brunnen a large electronic sign listed the varying routes over the mountains; all were listed as offen or open but all that could change at a flick of a switch back at a control centre out of harm's way.

At Flüelen, I ran out of lake and the road was funnelled into the valley that would eventually lead me to the St. Gotthard Pass. That would be for tomorrow of course; my destination was Altdorf about three kilometres away from this south-eastern corner of Lake Lucerne.

Perhaps it was always on the cards that Altdorf would not be the place I would be staying on the night of August 3rd. The fact that I had failed miserably to book myself into the camp-site after my telephone conversation the previous day (or at least I presumed that I hadn't), the fact that I had explained to a South African traveller back at the camp-site in Lucerne that one of the delights of what I was doing was that I was never sure where I would be sleeping at the end of each day, and perhaps the fact that I cycled straight past the town without even noticing it. I was beginning to get the hint. The area around the town was surprisingly industrial. When you think of Switzerland, you tend not to think of factories, quarries and chimneys belching out smoke but you had them all here in the land that was cordoned off on three sides by the lake at one end and the mountains on each side. It didn't make it any easier to find that the road upon which I was cycling was also under-going some heavy-duty rebuilding and rerouting. I kept looking out for the signs, either for Altdorf or cycle route 3, but they all escaped me. I eventually paused to do some heavy-duty work of my own, inspecting the map and scratching my head. I had completely missed Altdorf and was already about one kilometre further along the valley. I knew little of what lay between Altdorf and Andermatt so I did the only sensible thing I could do in the circumstances which was to turn around and find the centre of Altdorf. At previous moments on the trip I had thrown caution to the wind and carried on regardless, but this environment didn't lend itself to being reckless.

This time I was having more luck and I found the centre of town and the tourist office which was located just down the road from a large statue of William Tell. He was striking a pose with a bow flung over his shoulders and what I presumed was his nervous offspring looking up to him thinking 'if you miss, that's the end of our father-son relationship'. The statue was placed just in front of a garishly-painted tower with an Alpine vista behind Wilhelm and his son-come-target. I wondered why, with all the beautiful scenery surrounding the town they hadn't found a spot to place the statue so that a real vista would be the backdrop. And where was the apple?

The helpful girl in the tourist office was a mine of information. I asked about camp-sites both in Altdorf and beyond and she confirmed that yes, there was one in the town and that it wasn't far away. This was presumably the one I had telephoned from Lucerne. Intriguingly however and contrary to what I thought, there was actually a camp-site in Andermatt. She produced a leaflet and from the picture on the front cover it ticked every box that your better-than-average Alpine camp-site should tick; stunning location, green meadow, not a caravan in sight, just a few tents dotted here and there and most importantly, no sodding hedges! I could sense a change of plan beginning to crystallise in my head. I enquired about the weather for the next couple of days and, after a few taps on her keyboard, Andermatt's answer to Michael Fish printed off the forecast. The following day would be clear and sunny, the day after that, stormy and wet. It seemed as though a window of opportunity had presented itself to me and that I would be daft not to take advantage of it. It was still only mid-afternoon; the cycle to Andermatt was about thirty kilometres. That would be a couple of hours on the flat but I knew I would be climbing substantially as well. Altdorf was at 456 metres, Andermatt at 1,437 metres. A kilometre of climbing. Could I do that it what remained of the afternoon? The incentive of course would be to be within a stone's throw of the St. Gotthard Pass – at 2,107 metres – the following day when the weather, according to the prediction, would be good.

I thanked my helper and went to sit on the plinth just below the Tells to weigh up the situation.

I came to the conclusion that it was a no-brainer; I simply had to do it. Imagine my disappointment if I were to cycle to the highest point of my trip and not to be able to take in a view that recorded what I had already achieved but also what was still to come simply because of a few clouds. I started pedalling.

Initially the route continued to be fairly flat but after around 10 kilometres the first climb kicked in. The weather at that moment wasn't on my side even though I hoped it would be twenty-four hours later. The views were increasingly breath-taking and any time not spent marvelling upon the work of nature was spent marvelling upon the engineering feats of the Swiss civil engineers who had managed to cram into an ever-thinning valley not just the road upon which I was cycling but an even-more-spectacular four-lane motorway and a two-track railway line. The routes criss-crossed each other like three pieces of spaghetti winding their respective ways up the valley, higher and higher.

After 500 metres of climbing the motorway plunged inside the mountain and disappeared. Shortly afterwards, the railway did the same thing leaving the road to continue its journey alone all the way to Andermatt. It wasn't long before I could see ahead of me the switch-back roads that formed the final barrier between me and my camping idyll but I knew that in that relatively short horizontal distance, I still needed to climb 400 metres into the sky. This was going to be the most significant challenge so far on the trip. The road ahead of me made the Vosges – my only previous experience of climbing with Reggie – look like mere pimples. When they did so, the switch-backs started gently, just one or two at a time but soon I was looking up at what seemed like a vertical wall of road flicking first left, then right, then left, then right over and over again in a mountainside of tortuous turns. I could see some parts of the road were hidden in galleries to presumably protect them from whatever the mountain had to throw down upon them. Please be kind, I thought. To make life even tougher, I wasn't alone on this road; the world, his wife, their kids and their caravan had chosen to take the scenic road as well. Goods vehicles were also fighting their way to the top as were the bikers leaning from one side to another on their machines making the most of the opportunity to test themselves and their bikes to the limit. I seemed to be the only cyclist but I assumed that all the others were cycling at the same slow speed as me and that I was holding my own. The weather, needless to say, hadn't improved and it was now raining hard. Whatever was beyond the Gotthard Pass, it surely couldn't meet this level of challenge. I paused briefly in a lay-by to take in the view of the portion of the climb that I had so far conquered as well as to steel myself for the remaining few kilometres. A couple of leather-clad bikers had done the same thing and they looked at me with a mixture of curiosity and pity.

Finally, the road began to straighten, level off and lead into the hanging valley at the edge of which Andermatt was sitting. I wanted a fanfare but didn't get one. All I received were the bewildered looks of the kids in the back of the cars that zoomed past me but I was smiling nevertheless; I had set myself a challenge and in just over three hours I had done it. Well done to me! And of course to Reggie as well.

Andermatt was spread out over what seemed like quite a large area; I don't suppose there is much pressure for space in a place like that. Initially, I wondered if I had indeed found the town with the picturesque camp-site that I had admired so much in the leaflet back in Altdorf as all I could see were large car parks and what-appeared to be empty industrial land. I persevered however and after a few minutes found the centre of the town, although no mention of a camp-site just yet. It had all the charm of your typical out-of-season ski resort; far too much concrete which was clearly designed to support pretty snow in the winter months but which in summer just looked plain ugly. The beauty of the place was its location however and what lay in the final stretch of my climb the following day. I cycled all the way through Andermatt and along Gotthardstrasse until I got to a point where the town was no longer the town but the view along the valley seemed familiar. On my right was a large building housing a cable car and the associated strings of metal hung over the road before darting up the mountain side at a steep angle just to my left. Just before me in the road was a sign indicating the direction to Camping Gotthard-Andermatt, the place I was looking for. It pointed to a shed just next to the cable car building. Not quite the idyll I had imagined back in Altdorf but I now realised why the view was familiar; it was the same one that I had seen on the front of the leaflet earlier. The car park of the cable car installation was dotted with camper vans and caravans (they weren't shown in the brochure!) and the washing facilities were round the back of the cable car building. The enterprising owner had clearly seen a way to sweat his assets when the snow had gone. My home for the evening was on the other side of the road and at least it was green, away from the man-made horrors of the shed, cable car and motor homes and had a cracking view.

I pitched the tent next to another cyclist who had a smarter bike (sorry Reggie) and a much bigger tent. How did he manage to pack that on the bike? I thought. The afternoon exertions had unsurprisingly made me a little hungry so I made my way back into the centre of Andermatt along the Gotthardstrasse and found a likely place to quell my hunger; the Hotel Schweizerhof. For once, I didn't seem to have any reluctance in entering a restaurant alone. I was now an adventurer striking out on his own and this is what adventurers just had to do. The restaurant specialised in Italian food (that influence was increasingly part of life as I approached Italian-speaking Switzerland) and I ordered the biggest pile of pasta they would serve, all washed down with half a bottle of house red. There was reason behind my partial temperance; I was, after all, not at the top quite yet.

To round off the evening I went to a bar just across the road and ordered a beer. The decor inside was verging on the seedy; lots of mirrors and dark reds and there was a collection of locals sat around the bar itself leering at every woman who had the courage to enter the building. I too took up position at one end of the bar, sipped my beer and relaxed. I got out my phone in order to post a message back to the blog and noticed that I had a missed call from my parents back in the UK. I was a little concerned that there was news that I needed to hear (why else were they calling?) so I went outside to find a good signal and called back, anxiously waiting for them to answer but hoping that the message, whatever it was, wouldn't take too long as the cost of the call would no doubt be exorbitant. My mother answered and it quickly became apparent that there was no emergency news to pass on; she had simply rung to wish me luck for the big climb ahead of me the following day. I recounted my efforts of the afternoon and how I suspected that the efforts required for the final stretch between Andermatt and the St. Gotthard's Pass itself may actually be relatively easy in comparison. Little did I know at the time that the challenges of Wednesday 4th August would be just as taxing as they had been on Tuesday 3rd although in a completely different and unforeseen way.

Cycling Day 16:

Wednesday 4th August: Andermatt to Bellinzona

6 hours 0 minutes in the saddle, 96 kilometres

There are views, there are great views and there are views beyond description. The one upon which I was feasting my eyes on the morning of the 4th August was one of the latter but I'll have a go anyway. The valley ahead of me was V-shaped. In the far distance it was cut off abruptly by a second valley and beyond that towered the snow-capped peaks of the high Alps. The valley sides in Andermatt were still green with grass and vegetation but as my eye travelled along the valley, the flora retreated and the browns and greys of bare rock became predominant. The sky was a rare blue with only a few high clouds in the east and these were far from the threatening dark clouds of the previous few days. But this view was just as much about what I couldn't see as what I could; it was also what it represented and how it made me feel when I woke and stood by the tent that bright and clear summer morning. This, I thought, was going to be the high point of my Eurovelo 5 trip both physically and emotionally. It was the point at which no one could turn around and mock me for stopping my journey should I decide to do so. I had already cycled well over 1,500 kilometres to that point and I had achieved something quite special, something of which I was justifiably proud.

In fact there were other things that I wasn't able to see in that view apart from my emotions. I wasn't able to see the St. Gotthard Pass itself. My view down the valley was looking towards the south west, not the south. Once I arrived in Hospental, a village some three kilometres from Andermatt, I would turn to the south and head up and along the valley for another eight kilometres before arriving at the pass. Not forgetting of course the small matter of climbing 700 metres, most of which was to be done between Hospental and my destination.

I was coaxed out of my valley gazing by a long zipping sound. It was being made by my neighbour and fellow cyclist on the camp-site who was just about to appear from his palatial tent. I assumed it would be a youthful traveller; his bike was modern, as was his tent; some adventurous, impetuous gap-year student who was escaping the rat race even before he was part of it. The zipping continued and eventually an entire segment of his tunnel-like tent was removed from the inside. The gap revealed a bearded man in his sixties, puffing on a cigar. Not quite what I had been expecting. We exchanged nods and I offered a 'morgan' to which he replied 'good morning' with a slight German accent. Perhaps he had been creeping around in the night and had found the small Union Jack sticker that was part of Reggie's frame. Or more likely, perhaps my morning greeting was just too English. He clearly hadn't left all his camping gear in a hotel somewhere as I had in Luxembourg and was busy putting it all to good use, boiling water in a pan for some coffee and opening up plastic containers in which were stored the cereals and milk that would eventually constitute a hearty breakfast. I was impressed even though he was putting my camping efforts to shame. I asked him (stupidly as on reflection there weren't many options) where he was going and he said he was heading for the pass just like me. His name was Claus Zimmermann and he was a teacher from southern Germany who had escaped the clutches of his wife for a few days and had journeyed into the Alps. It wasn't the first time he had cycled up to the pass and he sketched out the route for me verbally. I asked if he knew whether there was anywhere to camp at the top and he said there wasn't unless I wanted to risk a cold night of wild camping. The next camp-site was in a place called Bellinzona some 60 kilometres down the valley on the other side in the Italian-speaking Swiss canton of Ticino. That seemed the most likely place to head for but I put aside thoughts of finding somewhere to sleep to mentally prepare myself for the last push to the top. I packed away my chattels and said good-bye to Claus although I suspected we would be seeing each other again at some point between Andermatt and the pass.

My own breakfast was taken back at the shed which was not just the reception to the camp-site but also a make-shift transport café for any passing traveller. You couldn't fault the owner's sense for smelling out a commercial opportunity. Once fuelled up with croissants and a black coffee, I set off down the long, flat road leading to Hospental. I didn't notice whether Claus was ahead of me or not as I trundled along the easy-to-pedal route which was trying to lure me into a false sense of security. It wasn't succeeding however as I was more than acutely aware of the trials that were awaiting me once I turned left and headed south.

Leaving Hospental the road was much quieter than it had been on the previous evening as I had cut backwards and forwards up the cliff to Andermatt. What's more, the road was almost free of switchbacks. It clung to the right-hand side of the valley some fifty or so metres above the stream that was heading in the other direction to me and Reggie, curving gently around the mountains passing slowly from one line of contour to the next. I stopped occasionally not so much to catch my breath as simply to take in the view back down the valley that I was unable to appreciate while cycling. Invariably when I did stop, Claus would overtake me and then after a few minutes of cycling again I would catch up with him, exchange nods and make my way into the distance. It wasn't so much a story of the hare and the tortoise, more a tale of the tortoise and the even slower tortoise. I'm sure that at one point when I stopped to look back I could see Claus puffing on his cigar.

About half-way up the valley from Hospental, the road split and I paused. Forking off to the left was the modern road. The road to my right was the old road to the top that I had read so much about prior to my trip. Its key feature was that it was cobbled.

As I mentioned when I was back in Lucerne, the St. Gotthard Pass (named, incidentally after the patron saint of passes himself) was first breached in the 13th century but it wasn't until the late 18th century that the first horse-drawn vehicle was able to get to the top (and, one imagines and hopes, down the other side). About a hundred years later, efforts were made to get things through the mountain rather than over it and in 1872 the first railway tunnel was started. When opened to traffic in 1882, trains were able to travel from Göschenen in the north to Airolo in the south but it had come at a cost; for 15 kilometres of tunnel, 277 lives had been lost. At least that very same tunnel is still in use so the workers didn't die in vain and it transports five million people and twenty-five million tonnes of freight from one side to the other each year. In 1980 a road tunnel was opened which at the time was the longest road tunnel in the world (it has since been surpassed by the Chinese and the Norwegians). It has a reputation for very long queues at either end and in 2001 was closed for two months after an accident involving two trucks in which eleven people were killed. Efforts to conquer the mountain haven't let up in recent years. In 2002 construction started on the Gotthard Base Tunnel. With a length of 57 km, trains should start passing through it at the end of 2016 and it will become the world's longest tunnel, subject to those pesky Chinese and Norwegians beating them at their own game of course.

Some 600 metres above the level of construction of the base tunnel is where I paused to make my decision; new road or old. The new road offered a smooth passage to the top albeit at a slightly steeper incline. It was now mid morning and quite a few (faster, leaner and more Lycra-clad) cyclists had started to catch up with me and Claus (wherever he now was). They were all bearing left and up along the new road which in itself encouraged me to take the older, gentler road. However, that 'gentler' road was cobbled. I got off Reggie to inspect them carefully; compared with the brutes back in Lille, these were mere kittens, with flat tops and very small gaps between each one. I would take the cobble challenge of the old road and enjoy the peace and tranquillity of what was, in effect, a cycle track by any other description. Off I set only bumping very slightly as Reggie made his way over the stones. The road wiggled from side to side a little bit more than it had been doing up to that point but the ride was a delight, well away from the petrol heads who saw the main road as an excuse to speed up, apply their brakes sharply and slow down at every turn before hitting the accelerator once more. The only slight disturbance was from, ironically, a gleaming German car that was being driven repeatedly up and down the cobbles. It was presumably for an advertising campaign, being snapped by some unseen photographer hiding in the hills, or perhaps being filmed for a high-octane television car show. No doubt Claus and myself have since been air-brushed from the scene.

Eventually the road started to flatten out and the two roads, old and new, merged back into one. Ahead I could see a craggy outcrop of rock. Next to it a few cars had been parked and several people were sitting on the rocks overlooking some small ponds. I must, I thought, be there. If nothing else, there was no more land above the rocks in front of me which surely indicated that I had reached the pass. Indeed I had. Just past the rocks, the land opened out into a large, flat mountain-top expanse with two small lakes to my left and a much larger lake to my right. At the end of the lake was a collection of buildings and what looked like a white pyramid. A sizeable and full car park filled the area between the water and the buildings and tall plumes of wispy smoke were emanating from what looked like a couple of shipping containers on the left of the scene. First impressions were mixed.

This was an iconic moment on the trip. It had only taken me about one and a half hours to cover the 13 kilometres from Andermatt. I was so pleased with my decision to cut the trip from Altdorf to the pass into two leaving myself with what had been a relatively easy climb to the summit that morning. Trying to ignore the people, cars and activity around me, I placed Reggie next to the sign that informed everyone that this was indeed San Gottardo and that we were at 2,091 metres above sea level. I took his photo lest anyone later be suspicious that I had just given up the cycling back in Lucerne. The sign was covered with stickers from the four corners of Europe if not the World attesting to the fact that this cycling racing team or that classic car touring club had made it to the top. One sticker consisting of a line drawing of a dove stated simply that 'World peace is possible'. That's always good to know. Having shamelessly forgotten to pack my "Reggie and Andrew do the Eurovelo 5" sticker, I wasn't able to add my own words of wisdom to the collection.

It seemed a world away from the classy tourist trap of Lucerne up there at the Saint Gotthard Pass. It was more in line with the disappointing array of entertainment that you can find at Land's End or Stonehenge back in the UK. There was a museum which, if it had been free I would have wandered around. Unfortunately the first exhibit, which I could see just beyond the entrance desk consisting of some waxwork figures of the first people to cross the Alps complete with animal skins, didn't shout 'come in and pay a small fortune to spend half an hour with us in here'. I gave it a miss. Anyway, who needed a bunch of inanimate cave dwellers when there was enough amusement to be had outside watching their modem day equivalents? I sat on a bench next to one of the smaller lakes just opposite a horrendously loud Italian-speaking woman. She was, between sentences noshing on a bratwurst sausage that she had purchased from the stall at the back of one of the painted shipping containers I had noticed on arrival. It had been carefully placed just in front of a praying Virgin Mary. Nice touch. The sensory impact of the sausage stall didn't stop at the visual; it was also possible to smell the wood burning barbecue (which in fairness was not actually too unpleasant) as well as listen to an eclectic mix of elevator music blaring from some speakers. Beyond the sausage stall there was a souvenir hut specialising in stuffed St. Bernard dogs of every possible size. Surely they had got the wrong pass. That said, there probably isn't much of a market for stuffed St. Gotthards. To the left of all this action and downwind from the sausage stall was a cheese stand. I'm not sure whether the guy looking after it was trying to sell the stuff or was simply attempting to get it smoked on the cheap. On the far right was a collection of buildings; one housed the museum and a cafeteria, the other a hotel and restaurant but now having seen the place, I no more wanted to sleep up there than I wanted to spend a night in a pit of snakes. The large white pyramid housed some kind of temporary exhibition. It had been erected just next to an equally temporary wooden staircase leading up to a rock on top of which was a stuffed mule and what I assumed to be St. Gotthard himself. Let's hope they hadn't stuffed him too. Yet again, you really couldn't make it up.

I retreated from the hullaballoo back to the quieter parts of the St. Gotthard Pass and sat for a good rest by one of the lakes, silently watching the lifeless but calming water. I posted a valedictory message to my blog followers and then continued to sit on the grass contemplating the journey that lay ahead. I wasn't even half-way to Brindisi yet and still had a lot of cycling to come so I couldn't sit around forever on top of that big hill in Switzerland. But at least, I thought, the afternoon's ride to Bellinzona was downhill all the way. I would be able to switch off, take in the scenery and let gravity do all the hard work.

Just as there had been on the way up the mountain, on the way down there were also two possible routes; a faster one that spent much of its time hidden in galleries cut into the rock and in tunnels, and a cobbled one which must be one of the most recognisable of all Alpine switchback routes. In the first few kilometres alone there were more than twenty tortuous bends that would test even the most heat resistant of ceramic brakes on a car to their limit. As a result, all but the most boyish of boy racers had decided to take the fast road instead. Those that hadn't invariably ended up making a frustratingly slow journey down to the bottom on the switchbacks as they got stuck behind locals in small vans and the odd cyclist.

Claus Zimmerman had told me not to take the old cobbled road when I had bumped into him next to the sausage shipping container at the top, but on seeing the spectacular road from above, I ignored his advice and continued regardless. It was slow going; the cobbles didn't allow a bike to travel quickly downhill but the views were amazing and I paused frequently to close my jaw which had dropped many times.

After about ten minutes on the cobbles I heard a hard, loud click. I looked around at the bike but I couldn't see anything wrong... so I continued. But something was badly amiss. Reggie felt out of sorts; he had suddenly become floppy to cycle upon. I stopped again, got off the bike and investigated. One of the spokes on the rear wheel had broken. Damn! This was serious. I could change a punctured inner tube, perhaps even repair a snapped chain, but repairing a spoke at 2,000 metres was in the premier league of mechanical abilities. I wasn't. Worse than just the spoke, the entire back wheel had taken on a very large wobble. Near the top of a mountain, without the necessary technical skills or indeed equipment to help myself, I was in big trouble. But stopping wasn't an option so I tentatively continued to cycle along the switchback roads. Most were still cobbled so goodness knows what new damage I was inflicting on poor Reggie. Far below me in the valley I could see the small town of Airolo; I could only pray that there was a bike repair shop in town. At times I got off and pushed, on better quality stretches I dared to ride, conscious of the time; it was already mid afternoon. Eventually I arrived in Airolo.

It didn't look like the kind of place that would have a bike shop. Lots of restaurants and bars, but very few places of practical use unless you were either hungry or thirsty. In my very best Italian as I was now in Ticino, I stopped to ask for some advice from a passing local;

'Ho un problemo con la mia bicicletta. Posso mi dire si c'é un negozio per reparare ?'

He must have been impressed with my linguistic skills as he replied in a torrent of Italian of which I caught the most important bit which, roughly translated was along the lines of 'go down there mate, there are lots of.... bars and restaurants'.

Perhaps he had mistaken my urgent requirement after all.

Language issues aside, I did follow his suggestion but in my mind were images of having to take the bike on a train to Milan to get it repaired. In such circumstances, would I be sufficiently committed to the Eurovelo 5 cause to return to Airolo and continue my route from there? My mind was not made up. Needless to say, there was no bike shop to be found. After such an emotional peak just a few hours earlier, I was now beginning to plumb the depths of an emotional trough.

I could see a large train station at the bottom of the street which was so uselessly lined with the bars and restaurants. I pushed Reggie towards it and started to think about the next train south. Suddenly I noticed a sign saying, in English 'Rent a Bike'. It was a long shot but perhaps they could help me out. I wandered over to the building which was immediately next to one of the station platforms. The door was open and to my left was an Aladdin's Cave housing probably around 200 almost identical yellow bikes lined up in neat rows ready for hire. To my right was a half-opened door. I knocked and it opened slightly wider allowing me to see what was inside; it was a fully equipped bike repair workshop. My gob was smacked. I couldn't really believe what I had managed to find. Only one problem; there didn't seem to be anyone around. I wandered outside and then a couple of railway workers pointed behind me; someone had appeared. It turned out to be the guy who worked there. We agreed on French as a language of communication and he quickly informed me that it wasn't an easy problem to fix. I told him I would pay and his fears seemed to subdue somewhat. I stripped Reggie of his baggage and my new friend set to work. He was clearly a chap who knew his bikes and within seconds he had the wheel dismantled and was removing spokes from another wheel that he had in the workshop. Fascinating but at the same time terrifying to watch; was he going to stop and say 'sorry mate it's buggered' (which would surprise me not least because I didn't think he could speak English)? Fortunately, he didn't but continued to work diligently without ever once removing the cigar which was lodged firmly between his lips. Then came the 'bouquet final' when he started to balance the wheel. With the precision of a piano tuner making tiny adjustments to his instrument, this guy delicately tweaked the necessary spokes to give me a perfectly balanced wheel. Before I could blink, he had the wheel back on Reggie, tyre pumped up and was even checking the brakes; back and front! He said 40€ and I didn't argue. I sincerely hope that the money went straight into his pocket and not through the accounts of the Swiss National Railways. My bike was fixed and I was in with an excellent chance of making it to Bellinzona by the end of the day. I thanked him excessively, placed the panniers back onto Reggie's racks and set off once again down the valley.

Despite the best efforts of the strong wind trying to keep me pinned back towards the mountains, I made it to Bellinzona by late afternoon. The camp-site, Camping Bosco di Molinazzo couldn't have been easier to find as it was just next to the cycle route 3 a couple of kilometres outside town. It was a long strip of a place and the busy free camping area was on the very end of the site. I squeezed my erected tent in-between other cyclists and bikers before making my way back to the small campsite shop-bar where I had earlier seen a sign indicating that pizzas were on offer. And who should I bump into? Claus Zimmerman of course. I told him of my misfortune and then good fortune that afternoon and promised that I would always follow his advice in future; if given the choice, stick to the road with the best quality surface. He smiled and suggested we had a beer. I didn't dare contradict him.

Rest Day 3:
Thursday 5th August: Bellinzona

Bellinzona had never been part of the plan. My tentative route map (the one with lots of question marks) had suggested that I would stay in Airolo the night after having climbed to the Gotthard Pass and then the day after I would stop overnight in a place called Cadenazzo before heading south to spend my first night in Italy on the shores of Lake Como. I had clearly been very cautious with distances in the mountainous areas of my trip but as a result of coming all the way to Bellinzona on the 4th August, I was now a day ahead of schedule. Cadenazzo was only about five kilometres further south than Bellinzona and my next cycle should take me all the way to Como just over the border. But that wasn't going to be today.

During the night there had been an almighty storm. It was a pity I had only heard it rather than seen it as it must have been quite a show. With more flashes of light than your average celebrity wedding it had certainly been something to rival the fireworks back in Basel a few days earlier. The downside was that when I dared push back the flap of my tent, all I could see was rain. The occasional rumble of thunder and lack of wind indicated that we were probably looking at a long, wet day. However, the positive vibes generated by the events of the previous day – the cycle over the pass under gloriously blue skies and then the miraculous repairing of Reggie – were still oozing around my body. I knew I had made good progress so far, I was in an unexpected location which had a sizeable entry in my guide book so there must be something of interest to see here, it was raining and, more practically, I needed to wash my clothes. It all added up to having my third rest day of the trip. The free time would also allow me to spend a few hours planning the route in Italy more carefully than I had managed to do back in U.K..

It was quite some time before I emerged from the tent to start doing all these things however. I was more than happy to just lay back, listen to the pitter-patter of rain on my man-made fibre roof. Until, that was, there was a pitter-patter of rain on my man-made fibre sleeping bag. Damn! I had sprung a leak or rather the tent had. On investigation it wasn't so much as a leak, it was simply where the inner tent had been in contact with the outer tent at a point directly above me. This was actually most places in the tent as 'roomy' had not been a word used to describe my little mobile home back at the camping shop. It was a very snug fit to say the least. The contact between the inner and outer layers had probably been down to my erection technique rather than anything else. I made a mental note to try harder next time. If nothing else, it did at least encourage me to get up and in that respect it was bit like a Chinese water alarm clock.

First job was the washing. As anyone who has ever used a public washing machine, whether it be in a laundrette like the one I had used in Strasbourg or on a camp-site like the one in Bellinzona, there doesn't seem to be an industry standard way of paying for them to get your clothes clean. Coins directly into the machine? Tokens into the machine? Coins into a box on the wall? Tokens into the box? Coins in an electronic console with numbers connecting to a numbered machine? And where do the tokens come from? A coin-operated machine? Or from the reception? What happens if the reception is shut? How many tokens should I buy for the dyer? Or is it coin operated? I could go on. The system adopted by the powers that be at Camping Bosco di Molinazzo was, however new to me. After standing in front of the washer – a Zug Adora L, circa 1985 - and the more modern dryer – a Blomberg DV – for quite a few minutes trying to figure out exactly what to do (it reminded me of a task on The Crystal Maze; I half expected Richard O'Brien to walk into the room, blow his whistle and then leave, locking the door behind him), I eventually worked out that the method of control was a token-operated box fixed to the wall above each machine. By inserting a token, the electric current would be activated at which point I could operate the washer and the dryer both of which had no slot for money or tokens. I wasn't sure what would happen if the length of the washing cycle was longer than the amount of time purchased at the electricity meter but I would confront that problem only if it arose. Fortunately it didn't and I spent an idle hour or so lingering at the entrance to the washing room smiling politely at people who had arrived to do the same thing as me only to find that I had beaten them too it. They should have invested in a tent that leaks.

Not that the view from the wash block was very inspiring; just a row of caravans with large awnings attached to one side. They had battened down the hatches for this storm and I could see some of the depressed residents peering solemnly through the clouded PVC windows that were protecting them from the rain. One group of campers had erected a small picket fence around a patch of ground immediately in front of their awning. In the middle of this make-shift garden was a large table against which plastic chairs were now leaning to prevent them from collecting water. There was room for a good ten or so people around the table and they liked to entertain in style; as I had pushed Reggie past them on the previous evening they had clearly invited the neighbours round and were dining al fresco complete with china plates, heavy-duty cutlery and even (you probably won't believe this bit) a candelabra in the middle of the table. I hoped I wouldn't get an invite not least because I had inadvertently forgotten to pack my dinner jacket. How stupid of me.

I continued to watch the rain fall, smiling to myself when I realised that the climatic conditions inside the washing machine were probably considerably more arid than those prevailing in Ticino that morning in August.

Task one completed, I moved on to more stimulating activities and decided to explore the town of Bellinzona itself. I debated whether to cycle or not and eventually decided not to do so. Reggie deserved a rest just as much as I did and I simply fancied a day being a normal tourist rather than a cyclo-tourist so I locked him to the perimeter fence of the camp-site and set off into town.

Bellinzona is the capital of Ticino although I have to say I'd never heard of it until the previous day. Even when I had, I thought it was just a stopping off point en route down the valley. Well, thanks to Napoleon, it is more than just that. One of the first things I noticed after the twenty minute walk into the town centre was a small plaque outside the police station thanking the diminutive Frenchman for making the town the administrative centre for this region. The main attractions apart from the well-maintained and attractive streets and squares were Bellinzona's three castles; Castelgrande, Castello di Montebello and Castello di Sasso Corbaro. I chose to explore the first one, the Castelgrande which was centrally located and towered over the other buildings around it. As any castle worthy of the name, it had had a tortuous history of ownership and development over the centuries. Construction began in the 13th century (interestingly around the same time as people started to make it over the mountains just to the north; I assume there was a connection) but this castle hadn't been preserved in aspic for the last hundred years to cater for the conservative needs of the mass tourism market; it had been modernised! Between 1984 and 1991 an architect called Aurelio Galfetti carried out extensive restorations and he had gone a bit further than simply patching up what was already there. He managed to insert a lift shaft deep into the rock beneath the castle. It was accessed by walking through a concrete tunnel which narrowed just above head height to form a tall but thin vertical space. Once you had taken the lift to the top, there were modern fortifications which fitted seamlessly with the more ancient architecture surrounding them. The modifications were both clever and effective.

The highest points of Castelgrande were to be found at the top of the White Tower and Black Tower. I chose the Black Tower and was rewarded with a 360 degree view of the town, the other two castles and the valley heading north and south. The other castles incidentally were built to try and form a barrier across the valley. The string of fortifications ultimately became redundant when the Swiss won the town of Bellinzona under the Treaty of Arona in 1803. It reminded me of the ultimate futility of the Maginot Line on the eastern border of France that I had seen a couple of weeks previously. All three castles were as dark and foreboding as the weather.

I wandered around the rest of the town at half-speed. I had been feeling lethargic all day; nothing to do with the efforts of the previous two days just the fact that when I had looked out of my tent that morning and seen the soggy sight outside, I had mentally switched off and had done everything very, very slowly. I have to say it was a thoroughly relaxing technique to adopt. I paused at a café which was situated half-way between the town centre and the camp-site for a couple of beers and watched the rain slowly begin to fade away. By the time I reached the gates of the camp-site, it had actually stopped although it had left everything, including Reggie and the tent dripping wet in its wake.

I hadn't been able to access the Internet since Lucerne but I did manage to do so that evening via the Wi-Fi at Camping Bosco di Molinazzo. When I logged onto my blog, I noted with a smile that the bar chart telling me how many visitors I had had over the last couple of weeks had peaked at the same time as I had crossed the Alps and quite a number of people had posted kind congratulatory comments. Before planning my next move south, I sat in the camp-site reception replying to those people who had gone out of their way to offer me encouragement.

I wasn't really sure whether I had yet passed the half-way point on my trip but crossing over into Italy at some point the following day would certainly feel like I was doing so. I had notched up just under 1,600 kilometres in two and a half weeks; the estimate was for a total of between 3,000 and 3,500 over five weeks so I must have been there or there abouts. Clearly the previous week had been affected by the weather; not very summery, but the high point, both literally and metaphorically at the Gotthard Pass had been achieved under blue skies and at times sweltering conditions. That one day had made up for the sandwich of washed-out days which had sat around it. I spent a few moments reflecting on the changes I had seen so far from leaving the UK to arriving at the southern tip of Switzerland. Southern England had been the hors d'oeuvres, a taste of things to come. Northern France had been familiar, almost predictable as I knew it so well. Luxembourg had been interesting and laid back; the kind of place in which you would like to live if you could afford to do so. Eastern France had been more industrial and linguistically diverse than I had imagined with some real gems that I had been able to discover. German-speaking Switzerland had been dramatic and physically beautiful but without the quaint prettiness you find in the French-speaking areas around Lake Geneva. Each country had thrown up its own surprises and I was sure that Italy would do the same thing in the weeks to come. I had lots of people to meet over the border and to adopt Donald Rumsfeld's eloquent but much derided line, I would be meeting the known knowns (Basil and his wife Liz in Puglia), the known unknowns (Simone in Pavia, Marcello in Rome and Massimo in Benevento), perhaps the unknown knowns and almost certainly the unknown unknowns. I just hoped it wouldn't rain as much.

Cycling Day 17:

Friday 6th August: Bellinzona to Como

4 hours 27 minutes in the saddle, 75 kilometres

The free-camping corner of Camping Bosco di Molinazzo had already been busy when I had arrived on the Wednesday evening; by the time I was preparing to leave on Friday morning, the management had certainly packed in the punters. It resembled the grounds of a pan-European music festival with cars, motorbikes and bicycles from all over the continent and tents of all shapes, sizes and colours. My own tent had originally been pitched with a nice band of personal tent space around it. That personal space was now being invaded by guy strings, car tyres (still attached to the cars I hasten to add) and washing lines from my European neighbours who had moved in the previous evening. I had a distinct feeling that as soon as I packed the tent away and rode off into the distance, the patch of ground would be pounced upon by space-hungry campers in a desperate search for more land. I was beginning to see the attraction in the picket fence strategy after all.

The canton of Ticino is split into two geographically unequal parts. The larger, northern part is called Sopraceneri, the smaller southern part Sottoceneri. I would be cycling from one area to the other and in the process passing over the Monte Ceneri range of mountains. That said, compared to my efforts earlier in the week, the 350 metre climb that I would have to take on was hardly in the big league of cycling achievements.

It wasn't difficult to join up with the Route 3 on leaving the camp-site as, if you remember, Camping Bosco di Molinazzo was handily placed on the route itself. After a short ride around Bellinzona and its southern suburbs I was soon cycling in the middle of the wide, flat plain of land heading west along the banks of the River Ticino itself. However, before the river emptied out into Lake Locarno, I needed to take a few right-angled turns around the edges of the farmers' fields that would eventually take me to the southern edge of the plain at Cadenazzo where I would start my modest climb towards the Passo Monte Ceneri.

If it hadn't been sign-posted as the Passo Monte Ceneri, I would probably have not noticed the fact that I had cycled through it. It didn't have any distinctive mountain pass features; there was no point at which I could look back and see one valley and look forward to see another. It was just a long straight road with mountains on either side. There weren't even any made-made clues such as food being sold from the back of a large shipping container, a waxwork museum or even any miniature St. Bernard dogs on sale. Clearly someone was missing a trick!

The remainder of the morning's journey was a gentle, at times off-road route which was predominantly downhill. As I neared Lugano, I noticed that the route 3 wanted to keep me away from the town centre, just as it had done in Bellinzona. I was beginning to see that this was a common feature of long-distance cycle routes. Are you a cycle path planner? Do you understand that not every cyclist loathes urban areas? They are places of life, food, drink, information and accommodation. Why do you have such an aversion to them? Yes, they are invariably full of traffic and pollution but is there not room for some kind of compromise? Especially in a place as pretty and as bicycle-friendly as Lugano. I knew this for certain as when I deviated from the route 3 and headed down into the perfectly positioned waterfront area, I couldn't help but smile at the posters which informed me that 'Il bike sharing arriva a Lugano!'.

Lugano was relaxed, friendly and intimate. As soon as we arrived in the pedestrianised area I got off and pushed Reggie through the streets towards the lakeside. All the buildings were pristine and painted in pale creams, pale pinks and not-so-pale terracotta. Red flowers adorned many of the balconies and a small group of men were playing giant chess in the square under the shade of a tree. It was undoubtedly a very elegant place. I leaned Reggie against the ornate railings overlooking the lake and took a seat on an equally elaborate bench a few metres away. I could have sat there and admired the view all afternoon. On the other side of the lake I could see a deeply wooded forest rising steeply out of the water only interrupted by the occasional small settlement near the shoreline. This was all such a contrast from the towns and villages I had passed through so far en route from England and for the very first time I felt as though I had made it as far as southern Europe.

When I did eventually move, rather than making efforts to rejoin the route 3, I stayed close to the lake and followed the road south towards Melide where a bridge would allow me to cross the lake to Bissone. I noticed on my map a strange quirk of political geography; the town of Campione d'Italia on the opposite shore. It's a very small enclave of Italy which is less than one kilometre from the rest of the country if you chose to scramble up the barren hill behind the town. I wondered why the politicians hadn't come to an agreement to transfer just a thin strip of Switzerland to Italy so that this small community could join up with the rest of the country. But then again, it's probably been making a fortune for many years by being a famous little enclave so I could see perhaps why the bureaucrats and mandarins in Bern and Rome were leaving well alone and maintaining the status quo.

The early afternoon ride to Chiasso was just as gentle as the morning's ride had been from the Passo Monte Ceneri to Lugano. I arrived in the border town at around 2pm and was intent on sticking to the route 3 signs all the way to the end, wherever that may be. I was hoping for some valedictory signage congratulating me on having followed the route (on and off) from Basel to Chiasso. Unfortunately the signs stopped, without fuss or ceremony outside the train station. They didn't even direct me as far as the border crossing.

When I did find the border post some five hundred or so metres down the road from the station there was an equal lack of fuss and ceremony. The one solitary border guard nodded at me as I cycled under the overhanging roof of the building he appeared to be guarding. Arriverderci Svizzera I thought, Buongiorno Italia! And cycled up the hill towards the centre of Como.

There was no sudden change at the border; the transition between Switzerland and Italy had really started as soon as I had cycled over the Gotthard Pass two days earlier. I had enjoyed Ticino, especially on a linguistic level; it had been nice, after several days of having to try and cope with German to be in an area where I could at least have a go with the language, for better and, admittedly sometimes for worse. I was able to string sentences together in Italian; my communication in German had been very much at the frustrating word level and I had frequently resorted to using English or sometimes French.

Prior to my trip, people had warned me about cycling in Italy. They had told me that not only were the roads dreadful but also that the drivers were fast and erratic. But was this true? Were my online advisors simply repeating well-worn clichés about the Italians and their habits that didn't hold up to scrutiny? According to the European Commission, in 2009 Britain was the safest place in Europe to be a pedestrian, cyclist or driver with 'only' 39 people per 1 million inhabitants being killed on the roads. This compares with 45 in Switzerland, 66 in France, 71 in Italy, but surprisingly 89 in Belgium and 95 in Luxembourg. If I had to guess, I would never have put the Belgians and Luxembourgers up there with the 'hot-headed' Italians but the statistics would have me believe otherwise. The overall European figure in 2009 was 70 deaths per million inhabitants so the Italians were only slightly above the continental average. It has to be said, however that this mean figure is skewed somewhat by the truly dreadful figures emanating from places like Poland (120), Greece (129) and Romania (130). Those are the places to avoid next summer on your holidays but if you've already booked yourself two weeks in the Greek sun, you might want to phone the travel agent and make sure it's an all inclusive deal which keeps you confined inside your luxury hotel complex. You will still have to risk the coach trip to and from the airport however. Good luck. Anyway, whatever I was about to experience cycling in Italy, I had already safely cycled through two countries which were statistically much more dangerous albeit only for a couple of days.

Statistics aside, I was determined to be open-minded about the Italians. It is very difficult to prevent preconceptions from becoming misconceptions so I would be no more or less careful than I had been in the previous countries in which I had cycled and would treat both the drivers and their roads with the respect that they deserved or perhaps didn't deserve.

On arrival in the centre of Como I took inspiration from my guide book once more for a place to stay. L'Albergo Posta was recommended; 'good budget rooms in a great central location on Piazza Volta'. This was only a couple of minutes walk from where I was sitting at the time so I finished my end-of-cycle beer and wandered along the street to locate the hotel. Without much fuss I had a bed for the night for a reasonable 60 €, much less than I was expecting to pay in this classy lakeside resort. The room was basic but it had all I needed. Unfortunately it wouldn't be possible for Reggie to join me in the room as he had done in Strasbourg so I secured him to a lamppost immediately outside the entrance to the hotel. My request for him to do so wasn't completely wasted however; later that evening the proprietor said that I could put him in the restaurant on the ground floor overnight. I told Reggie not to drip on the polished tiles or eat the breakfast bread rolls. He didn't do either.

Anxious about my state of mind – engaging in spoken conversation with Reggie seemed to be taking the personification of my bike a little too far - I went out for a stroll around town to soak up the early Friday evening atmosphere. It was gratifying to see that places exist outside the United Kingdom where young people have other things on their mind apart from an obsession with getting blind drunk at the start of the weekend. La passeggiata, the Italian art of taking a walk in the evening, had started; young couples, old couples, middle-aged couples, families, single men with bikes... OK, it didn't quite fit the image but Reggie was my company for that warm August evening. Despite my earlier efforts, he just wasn't very chatty. Most partners would probably protest if they were chained up outside a restaurant while their other half went inside for a meal but strange though it may seem, Reggie didn't say a word when I was forced to do this to him outside the McDonalds restaurant in Via Caio Plinio II.

You are probably now aghast at the thought that I had even entertained the idea of eating in a McDonald's restaurant. In my defence, I did have my reasons and in fairness, I had successfully avoided all ultra-fast food restaurants for the previous three weeks so I wasn't doing too badly thank-you. My principal reason for doing so now was to access the Internet. The Posta hotel didn't have Wi-Fi and as most travellers know, a reliable place to access the Internet for free is your local McDonalds restaurant. What I had forgotten was the legislation that has been introduced by certain European countries as a result of terrorist activity over recent years. It had been a problem for me when I was travelling around Europe by train a few years prior to my cycle along the Eurovelo 5. Spain and Italy had both been problematic with Internet Cafés requiring identity checks before you were able to get online. In the Wi-Fi world that had exploded since my last great European odyssey, Italy had remained implacably opposed to a free-for-all in the wireless Internet world and the practical consequence for me as I sat in the McDonalds in Como trying to access their Wi-Fi was that I needed to do so via an Italian mobile phone number which obviously, I didn't have.

I hadn't worked this out however until I was sitting at a bench in the window of the McDonald's keeping a beady eye upon Reggie on the other side of the road with a Big Mac and fries on a tray before me. It was mildly annoying as I needed to get in contact with Simone, my online contact who was planning to come and meet me in Como the following morning and escort me to his home town of Pavia just south of Milan. I resorted to posting an open message to him on the blog encouraging him to reply by posting a comment which would then automatically get emailed to me via the mobile phone network. Later that evening he contacted me via text message and we arranged to meet outside Como station the following morning at 9am.

My fast-food feast finished, Reggie and I rejoined the passeggiata which was continuing at its slow pace around and about town. The facade of the duomo looked fabulous in the setting sun but by the time I had gradually made my way back to the lakeside jetties the sun had disappeared over the horizon. I sat for a good while eating an ice-cream and watching the wooden piers bob up and down on the water. The sky was just as cloudless as it had been all day and I dared to wonder if all the bad weather was now behind me.

Cycling Day 18:

Saturday 7th August: Como to Pavia

5 hours 16 minutes in the saddle, 96 kilometres

Deciding to go online and write a blog about my preparations and subsequently the trip itself had been one of the best decisions I had made since first dreaming up the idea of completing a long-distance cycling challenge. It was always written to myself which was fortuitous as in the first few months I was the only one who actually read it. Gradually however, as blog posts accumulated I began to build up a bank of facts, figures, maps, opinions, statistics, links, contacts, truths, untruths etc... which themselves started to be picked up by people searching online for facts, figures, maps et al about a cycle journey from London to Rome and beyond.

Simone had first contacted me in June 2010, about six weeks prior to my departure;

My name's Simone and with some friends I work in a cycle co-op in Pavia. I'm also a bike enthusiast, for all kind of pedal powered vehicles. I saw your blog and I was immediately fascinated by your task. Looking at your map, I saw you will probably pass through Pavia. I don't know if you'll stop here, but if you need some kind of accommodation, help, or even some riding friends for some miles, feel free to contact me.

Best regards and good luck.

Simone

This was someone who had never met me, had never spoken to me, knew precious little about me but clearly had some kind of faith in me to make it as far as northern Italy and was willing to trust that I was a fit and proper person to be accommodated in his house. It was all genuinely touching. I suppose that I decided to put my trust in him simply because he had done the same for me and it turned out to be well-placed.

I arrived at the train station in Como well before our arranged meeting time of 9am. I had no idea how I would recognise Simone but logic dictated that he would have a bike with him so I would be unlikely to meet the wrong person outside what was a very quiet station entrance. I sat on some steps and waited.

At around ten to nine a figure appeared at the other end of the station building. He had a bike with him so I assumed (correctly) that it was Simone and we exchanged greetings in Italian and English. I already knew from our exchange of emails prior to my departure from the UK that he spoke excellent English so from that point onwards our conversations were mainly in my mother tongue rather than his. He was in his early thirties and sported an impressionist painter's beard and moustache which gave him an air of cycling dignity. Simone was a man who knew his stuff when it came to cycling and bicycles and he immediately reminded me of Iain back in Deal. He had brought with him a spartanly-adorned fixed wheel bike with bullhorn handlebars and just a single front wheel brake. He had named his bike Alan, kind of. Reggie had be named Reggie for reasons of consonance; Reggie Ridgeback, Ridgeback being his brand (his family!) name. The provenance of Alan as a name for Simone's bike was a little more thoughtful. Alan was the name of a factory near Padua which was the first to start mass producing aluminium frames back in the 1970s (it went on to be the first place to start mass producing carbon-fibre ones in the 1980s) and the word 'Alan' comes from the first two letters of the words 'Alluminio Anodizzato' (or 'anodised aluminium'). There are no doubt lots of Alans being pedalled around Italy and indeed the World but for the purposes of this story, there was only one and it was being ridden by Simone.

Simone sketched out the route that we would be taking which basically involved going into the centre of Milan for a coffee and then continuing south along a canal until we arrived in Pavia later in the afternoon. As the crow flies it would be 40 kilometres from Como to Milan and then another 30 kilometres from Milan to Pavia. If we were to follow a canal for the second part of the journey, 30 kilometres was probably a good estimate of the distance. However I suspected the first part would be significantly longer than 40 kilometres as we would need to weave a careful path through the extended suburbs north of Milan.

It was useful to have a guide on that first full day of cycling in Italy as I tried to readjust my senses to new styles of road signs, road markings and general cycling conditions. There was no map reading for me to do although I occasionally glanced down at my home-made handlebar platform which supported the map to see where we were but more out of curiosity that necessity. Wherever we could we tried to cycle side by side on the road in order to have a conversation. This was something that Alain, my cycling companion from Boulogne had encouraged me to do in northern France but whereas he was dismissive of the frustrations of the passing motorists ('we are allowed to do this in France!'), Simone took a more pragmatic and probably safer approach by returning to cycle in single file when we were in an area of busy traffic. Increasingly this was the case as we approached the centre of Milan.

It was difficult to gather accurate first impressions of the Italian motorists and the conditions of the roads. Neither were particularly good but would I not have had the same thoughts if I were cycling in the suburbs of most European cities where the drivers tend to be more aggressive than on open country roads and where the road surfaces take a constant battering from the volume of traffic? I would need to bank a few more days worth of experiences before I was able to say with any certainly if the Italians and their roads lived up to the poor reputations about which I had been warned. Of the two, I was probably more preoccupied by the quality of the road surface bearing in mind the broken spoke incident of a few days earlier, my eyes spending more time than they would have normally done trying to pre-empt any large bumps and holes in the road so as not to jolt the back wheel more than I had to. Some of the streets in the heart of the city were cobbled which didn't help my nerves especially as they were more in the style of Lille rather than the Gotthard Pass, but Simone, Alan, Reggie and I survived the experience completing the first half of the journey by pushing our bikes through the magnificently opulent Galleria Vittorio Emanuele II and into the Piazza Duomo where we sat for a rest on the steps in front of the cathedral.

I quite like Milan. I've been there on numerous occasions in the past and have spent many aimless hours wandering around its streets. It is often said that the city likes to think of itself as a country apart from Italy and you can kind of see why. The people are brash, confident and stylish, the buildings imposing, imperial and classy. It's a place that looks north towards the industrial and financial might of the Germans and French rather than south towards the rest of Italy and Africa beyond. On a trip to Naples a few years ago, I found myself in the square outside the train station; it was a scene from another continent with chaos, smells, and colours that were distinctly non-European and a world away from Milan. How Rome, both the city and government it accommodates manages to hold a country of such diversity together is perhaps the miracle of modern-day Italy.

Simone was good company and I immediately felt comfortable having him as a cycling buddy. We sat munching his sandwiches and idling away the time as life in the large square passed before us. The sky was still a deep blue (had I finally said good-bye to the dreary weather of Switzerland?) and the four sides of the piazza were looking immaculate under the bright spotlight of the sun. We chatted about my journey so far and what was yet to come. Simone explained his plans for opening up a co-operative bicycle business with some friends next to the train station in his home city of Pavia but the project was coming up against the bureaucratic tangle of local government. He would find out later in the summer if his plans had the financial support of a charitable foundation. For me the cycling thing was just an excuse for a different kind of holiday but for him it was much more and I dearly wanted his venture to succeed. I discovered later in the year that unfortunately, it hadn't – the money was not made available – and as a result Pavia has lost one of its greatest cycling champions. Simone later moved to Venice to complete his studies in Oriental languages which is slightly ironic as Venice is one of the least bike-friendly places you can imagine (it is banned!). The World needs more cyclists like Simone but Venice probably doesn't.

Before we headed for the Naviglio di Pavia which was to be our guiding line of water in the afternoon, we detoured slightly to explore the Castello Sforzesco which was about a kilometre to the north west of the Piazza del Duomo. The architecture of this sprawling complex and the adjoining Parco Sempione is in stark contrast to the buildings which surround them both. The castle itself is named after the mercenary leader Francesco Sforza although its origins predate him by around a hundred years having been the home of the Visconti family from the mid 14th century. Sforza married into the Visconti family, became the Duke of Milan and moved in. Over the centuries the Castello has housed successive rulers of Milan; the French, then the Spanish, then the Austrians, Napoleon for a while and then the Austrians once again, or rather it seems to have housed their troops being, for much of its existence a barracks. The twentieth century has seen it become the home of cultural and artistic endeavours although it didn't escape Allied bombs during the war and suffered serious damaged as a result. Clearly they had had the builders in since as when Simone and I cycled through the entrance it was looking good.

Once our cultural diversion was over, we got back to the serious business of cycling to Pavia along the canal. It took us from the southern suburbs of Milan, south to Binasco at which point it kinked slightly to ensure that we arrived in Pavia and were not sent off towards the Italian Riviera. We had Napoleon to thank once more for the canal; not only had he sorted out the administration of Bellinzona further north in Ticino, but he had clearly stuck around in the Castello Sforzesco for long enough to ensure that there was a canal linking Pavia and Milan. Whatever you think of the man, you can't deny he got things done. Perhaps that's why the British exiled him to Saint Helena.

As we approached Pavia, I noticed a large church a couple of kilometres east of the canal. Set in the middle of otherwise flat countryside, it seemed a little out of place. Simone explained that it was the Certosa di Pavia and that it had been built by the Viscontis as a mausoleum. The word certosa refers to a Carthusian monastery. Carthusian monks are not great talkers, at least not to each other. The bulk of their communication is with God himself and they spend much of their time in their cells where they pray, work, take meals and sleep. They only leave their room when required to attend mass. Now I don't want to stretch this analogy too much but there is a parallel with the long-distance cyclist in there somewhere. As a lone cyclist, you have to be happy with your own company and the conversations that you have (and believe me there are many) are with a person that only exists in your mind. In my case it wasn't God but there was on on-going conversation with someone taking place along the Eurovelo 5. Usually the 'someone' was myself but often it would be with a relative or friend. Sometimes it would be with an anonymous person who simply acted as a sounding board for my thoughts. I'm not sure whether God responds very often to the Carthusians, but the great thing about having conversations with yourself is that you are able to regulate the answer. Perhaps the day when you are no longer able to do so is the day to stop cycling and make a few more real friends.

The certosa behind us, it wasn't long before we were jolting up and down on the cobbles of Simone's home town of Pavia. Pavia, according to my guide book, was 'a comfortable provincial town with an illustrious history' although it did go on to say that this claim to fame lent heavily upon the Certosa di Pavia that we had just cycled past. It was teeming with crumbling buildings, some, unfortunately more so than others. One tower of the duomo collapsed in 1989 killing four people who were unfortunate enough to be stood under it at the time so when we parked our bikes in the main square of the town to celebrate our arrival with a beer, I couldn't help but glance towards the buildings that surrounded us to give them a quick once over. It would have been so disappointing to have been silenced by a brick falling from on high, let along be flattened by a collapsing tower.

Fortunately, we survived the experience and cycled a couple of kilometres out of town to Simone's flat where I was introduced to Elettra, his girlfriend. She was just as charming and welcoming as her boyfriend had been all day but the next bit I found difficult to comprehend. Not only were Simone and Elettra willing to take a day out of their schedule (which, admittedly wasn't too packed with activities as they were both unemployed), but they were willing to move out of their one roomed flat for the night so that I could have the place to myself. As you can imagine, I protested (although not to the point where I thought they might actually change their minds and send me off to a local hotel), but they were having none of it. Co-incidentally they had student friends who lived in the centre of town but who were away for the summer and were going to spend the night in their flat. It was another case of serendipity in action along the Eurovelo 5, but I have to say that I'm not sure I would move out of my own flat back in the UK to let a complete stranger take up residency for the night. Perhaps I need to revaluate my own generosity.

Once showered, Simone and I set off once more to explore a little more of the town. This time we headed south to cross the River Ticino. Hang on, didn't I leave the Ticino after it had cut through Bellinzona and emptied out into Lake Maggiore a few days ago? Apparently not. The River Ticino had continued to flow from the other end of Lake Locarno and taken the easy (and more picturesque?) option of sweeping through the Lombardy countryside west of Milan and then south to Pavia. Could that have been an alternative route? I wondered. We crossed the Ticino over a rebuilt bridge, the original having been fatally damaged by a few Allied bombs but you wouldn't have noticed unless someone had told you and in my case, Simone did. On one end of the bridge was something that I hadn't seen since Dover; a reference to the Via Francigena. Remember that? The pilgrimage route from Canterbury to Rome. Here was a sign being loud and proud about its existence and I would continue to see them, off and on, over the length of my route all the way to the Italian capital. I wouldn't be following them but it was a reassuring thumbs up that I was heading in the right direction and taking an efficient straight-line(ish) cycling route.

Simone and Elettra's hospitality seemed to have no boundaries. For a young unemployed couple who lived in a modest flat in northern Italy they were certainly pushing out the boat for me and it was about to be pushed just a little bit further at Ristorante Giulio. I would have been happy with something simple back at the flat but eating out at least gave me the opportunity of repaying the hospitality of my hosts so I was more than delighted when a visit to a local pizzeria was suggested. We drove the short distance towards the restaurant which was situated just outside central Pavia. It was a popular place with a terrace packed out by hungry Italians and their families tucking into their Saturday evening meal. We opted to sit inside where the air was cooler but the atmosphere just as frenetic and it was only then that I noticed something distinctive about this Italian restaurant that set it apart from most; I appeared to be the only foreigner in the place. Surrounding me was a cloud of Italian chatter; Italian families, Italian conversation, Italian arguments and the unmistakable smell of good, simple Italian food. The atmosphere of the establishment was intoxicating in itself although we didn't let that hold us back on ordering some quality Italian wine. I ordered the speciality, a pizza and a few minutes later was presented with a circular disc of goodness that was so large I couldn't see the plate upon which it sat. For all I knew, I could have been eating off the table itself.

The conversation flowed as continuously as the River Ticino. Wiping the last smudge of ice-cream from my lips, we asked for the bill (well, Simone did) and I reached for my euros to pay for all three of us. It would be a small price for having been provided with a cycling guide, not just a bed but a whole flat, a tour of the town, evening entertainment and a lift home to boot. But they wouldn't allow me to pay. I tried, but failed to convince them that it really would have been a pleasure, a small token of appreciation but they just wouldn't listen. When it came to making the payment, I couldn't of course battle with Simone's Italian in his discussion with the waiter. I had lost the fight and didn't pay a penny for what I had eaten and drunk. It was almost embarrassing how welcoming they had been but it was completely in character with my experiences of the rest of the day and crowned what had been an amazing introduction to the Italian portion of my trip along the Eurovelo 5. Grazie mille!

Cycling Day 19:

Sunday 8th August: Pavia to Salsomaggiore Terme

6 hours 30 minutes in the saddle, 137 kilometres

Wake up in a hotel room there is not a great deal to do apart from get up, shower and get dressed. Wake up in someone's flat when the occupants themselves are absent and there are a whole host of things to do to keep you from having a shower and getting dressed. Bookshelves to explore, DVD and CD collections to peruse, coffee table magazines to leaf through... I spent an intriguing few minutes that morning just wandering around the ground-floor flat having a look at how the Italians live. It was fascinating.

Once my inspection had finished and I was showered and dressed, I made the most of the opportunity of having a large flat surface – the tiled floor of the flat – to spread out my maps which, when pieced together, gave me an overview of the next week's cycling from Pavia to Rome. As I had been reminded of on the previous day, for this portion of my trip I would be following more or less the route of the Via Francigena and my first obstacle would be the Apennine range of mountains which lay between the flat plain of the Po Valley and the west coast of Italy. The plan was to cross these mountains via the Passo della Cisa. This would require me to head east from Pavia before taking a sharp right turn just before Parma and climb to over 1,000 metres over the pass. From there, I would freewheel down towards La Spezia on the coast before cycling south to Pisa. I envisaged a day off in Pisa where I could also take in the much-recommended town of Lucca before continuing towards Siena and finally to Rome itself. My main concern was camping. Would I be able to do it as easily as I had done in France and Switzerland where most small towns seemed to have at the very least a council-run camping municipal. I had never camped in Italy before and wasn't sure to what extent the Italians were big campers. My guide book mentioned a few but they just didn't seem to be anywhere near as ubiquitous as they had been further north. To help me, I had downloaded an 'app' for my phone back in the UK which claimed to list all Italian campsites but I knew from Simone for example that there was a camp-site in Pavia and it wasn't mentioned on the app (or indeed in my guide book). This was, however an encouraging sign that perhaps there were more places to camp than I imagined. Piecing together all the information I could gather, I marked the maps with lots of red triangles to help guide my passage over the weeks to come.

Barely was the ink on my map dry when I heard the mechanism of the lock being turned and Simone and Elettra returned home. I refrained from welcoming them and asking them to come in; this was, after all, their flat to begin with although there were a few moments of uneasy transition as I shifted from being resident to guest.

Unless you are really into full 'English' breakfasts, it's difficult not to admire the continentals for their morning eating habits. In Britain, if you opt out of the morning fry up, most people tuck into a minimal, dare I say puritan breakfast consisting of some allegedly-healthy cereal with low-fat milk, toast with cholesterol-busting margarine, perhaps a piece of fruit and tea or coffee with an artificial sweetener. Or is that just me? Our European cousins have no such reservations about filling up on a calorie-packed morning feast to rival even the best lunches or evening meals. I remember once in The Netherlands being shocked at seeing a lump of Gouda cheese being cut up for breakfast and served with ham. The Germans tuck into slices of sausage while the French invest in breads, pastries and full-fat coffees like they were going out of fashion. Simone and Elettra were no exception to the continental rule that breakfast is indeed the most important meal of the day and it wasn't long before their kitchen table was piled high with bread, fruit, honey, jam, apple juice, biscuits, cereals, full-fat milk, sugar, coffee and of course, cheese. Not just any cheese but local Stracchino direct from the cows of Lombardy. I didn't get the impression that this was anything special either. Apart from the fresh bread, everything else on the table had been sourced from different locations within the kitchen and pieced together like an intricate jigsaw. And as far as I could see, there were no bits missing.

Weighed down with a full stomach, I bid farewell to Elettra but not to Simone; I had taken him up on his offer to accompany me at least some of the way from Pavia to my destination, Castell'Arquato. This was a restored medieval town just over the regional border in Emilia-Romagna about 30 kilometres from Parma and importantly, according to my phone app, it had a camp-site. It wouldn't be a long ride so I would have plenty of time to take in the delights of the town on arrival. At least that was the plan.

The morning's cycle was a flat one following the course of the River Po to Piacenza and on arrival we made our way into the centre of the town along the deserted Sunday morning streets. Although our exertions had been minimal, we did need a top up of food so we sat under a parasol outside the first café that appeared to be open. Unfortunately it wasn't even though the evidence in front of us – people sat outside being served food and coffee by a waiter – suggested otherwise. Simone was just as baffled as me, but it's never a good idea to argue with someone who could potentially be serving you food and drink only moments after having had their illogical argument pulled to pieces so we moved on and into the very centre of town.

It's said that Italy is home to two-thirds of the World's antiquities and it's easy to believe that statistic when you come to a relatively unknown place like Piacenza. In most other countries, this would be in the top ten tourist destinations in the land with its renaissance palazzos, its medieval churches and arcaded piazzas. Here in Italy, it is just another living, breathing, beautiful town with buildings that continue to have a functional status way below that which their historic grandeur would dictate; shoe shops, dentists, insurance offices, language schools and mini supermarkets all housed under splendour more befitting of higher causes. We eventually found a café that was not only open but willing to serve us some food and drink near the train station. I thought Simone would use the proximity of a direct line back to Pavia to make his excuses and return home from this point but he chose to continue to accompany me as I headed south along the SP6 towards Castell'Arquato.

His turning point did eventually come when we arrived at a non-descript fork in the road just before the small town of Carpaneto Piacentino. I thanked him for his assistance, guidance and hospitality; he had made my first couple of days cycling in Italy a real pleasure and I sincerely hoped that one day we would have the chance to repeat our experience, perhaps even back in the UK although he might have to get used to an empty morning stomach if he did.

Simone turned around and cycled north and I continued south towards Carpaneto and past a curiously bent chimney on my left. I was bemused as to how it could possibly stay upright and chuckled to myself as I cycled. I could not have been happier; the cycling was going well, good weather seemed to have finally become a regular fixture of each day, I didn't have far to travel to my interesting destination and the camp-site that I knew for certain existed. To cap it all I had a comical chimney to entertain me. Life and cycling was good!

Clearly it couldn't last but I was a little surprised how quickly my little bubble of nirvana collapsed around me. Barely five minutes after having said my good-byes to Simone I heard a horrendous sound of metal being ripped from Reggie's back wheel and then mangled around the other remaining wheel supports. It had happened again; another spoke had broken. I jumped off to inspect the damage, carefully plucking each of the remaining spokes to see if any of them had been affected. It appeared that they hadn't which was a minor cause for celebration but it still left me with a repair job to tackle at some point over the next 24 hours. I wrapped the offending spoke around one of its neighbours (I couldn't remove it as it was still attached to the rim of the wheel), lifted Reggie off the ground and spun the wheel to assess how big was the wobble. Fortunately, it didn't seem to have one which was another reason for low-level rejoicing. Following my Alpine spoke incident the previous week, one of my online technical advisors Jim Rawnsley had reassured me that touring bikes tended to have lots of spokes and one breaking was not the end of the world or rather the wheel. Iain Harper, my host in Deal and another Internet follower recommended that if it should happen again I would be well-advised to loosen the back brake so that any wobble wouldn't lead to further damage being inflicted on the wheel by misaligned brake blocks. I had no detectable wobble so this didn't seem an appropriate course of action just yet but I would keep it in mind. I feared that if I couldn't easily find a place to repair my bike in Castell'Arquato I may well be calling upon their advice again to try and locate a suitable establishment. Other online commentators incidentally were of less practical use; Basil, my host in Puglia was more interested in the family links of Claus Zimmerman, my cigar-smoking Alpine cycling companion asking whether or not he was the brother of Robert Zimmerman, otherwise known as Bob Dylan. I think Basil may have been on the local red wine as he was reading of my misfortune in the Alps.

But back to the Po Valley. I continued my route gingerly towards Castell'Arquato glancing down every few seconds to see if the wheel was beginning to distort but it wasn't and I took considerable solace from this visual evidence of lack of serious damage. Slowly my confidence began to build and it was with considerable relief that I approached my destination where at least I would have a little time to consider my longer term options. I could see the medieval town on the hill to my right and it did look as beautiful as the guide book had promised. Hopefully its beauty would be a visual massage for my troubled state of mind later in the day once I had settled into the camp-site.

I was at what appeared to be the main crossroads in the town. Turn right for the old quarter, straight on for Lugagnano, turn left for Salsomaggiore Terme, but no sign to indicate a camp-site. Opposite me I could see a car park and I reasoned that there might be a map of the town somewhere there so I cycled over to the small collection of huts that served as home to a snack bar and some toilets and I was in luck; there was a detailed town plan! But no indication as to where the camp-site was located. I dug out my phone and opened the app to check the address; Via Castellana. I found the road on the map and cycled off to find it keeping my eyes open for anything loosely resembling a tent. After about a kilometre I decided to turn back; I must have missed the sign, surely. There was nothing so I returned to the car park, shed and map and sat on a bench immediately opposite a fibre-glass friesian cow (with not just udders but also horns!) who looked at me nonchalantly through weary eyes. I stared back at him with an equally dejected expression on my face. To confirm what I feared, I drafted a question in my mind and asked a passing local (the shopping bags were once again the giveaway);

'C'è un campeggio qui vicino ?' but the answer was as negative as I imagined it would be so I sat back on the bench and, if I had allowed myself to do so, could have cried.

My situation mirrored that of the high and low of the day when my first spoke had broken in the Alps, but at least then it wasn't combined with the uncertainly as to where I would be staying that evening. It was 5pm, I had a broken bike and no camp-site at which to stay. Ever the optimist, I tried to think positive; my bike was rideable, there was another red triangle on my map indicating that there would be a camp-site in Salsomaggiore Terme and it wouldn't be dark for quite some time yet. I sent an SOS message to the blog asking my Italian-speaking followers to carry out a little bit of research on my behalf to see where the nearest repair shop was, forced myself to smile (if only to piss off the plastic hermaphrodite cow) gently lowered myself onto Reggie and made haste for my new destination. It was disappointing not to have had the opportunity to spend any time in Castell'Arquato, but needs must and I needed a camp-site.

The climb out of the valley bottom in the early evening sun rewarded me with the most beautiful views that I had seen since leaving the Alps. Rolling, dark green hills with idyllic farmhouses dotted in and amongst the vineyards. This was very good therapy and with my wheel continuing its efforts not to wobble, my mood quickly lifted. I picked my way across the countryside, along deserted lanes and through Salsominore (which seemed logical) before arriving in the spa town of Salsomaggiore Terme itself. I paused at a small shop to buy some water and as I was coming out I asked a gentleman who was wandering down the street a similar question to the one that I had asked forlornly back in Castell'Arquato but this time I didn't want to give the impression of doubt so I assumed that I was correct in my assumption that a camp-site did exist;

'Dov'è il campeggio?' It did the trick and I was soon having a surprisingly detailed chit-chat, in Italian with my new Italian friend.

'Di dove sei?' he enquired.

'Sono da Inghilterra e vado a Puglia' I replied.

'Quanti chilometri avete in bici ?'

'Più di duemila'

He did more of the speaking than me and I kept interrupting him with lots of vital expressions such as 'non ho capito' and 'Può ripetere?' but I certainly felt as though my Italian had had a good shake down before he waved me on my way towards the small town of Bagni di Tabiano. It didn't matter that it was another three kilometres further east and up a hill; I was about to find somewhere to pitch my tent and that made me a happy man once more.

I was sufficiently delighted on arrival at the bizarrely-named Camping Arizona that it was of no consequence that the place I had found ticked most of my 'camp-site from hell' boxes; square pitches with hedges, lots of caravans and screaming children around every corner. I erected my little tent between the gable end of an innapropriately-named 'mobile' home and the overflow pitch of a family whose geneological tree would have given even the most patient of researchers cause to tear out their hair. That said, they were kind enough to lend me their mallett which assisted me in forcing my pegs into the hard, dry ground and they all decamped to the camp-site restaurant after a while to leave me, Reggie, my baguette, some Philadelphia full fat cheese, a tube of Pringles, a packet of biscuits and a bottle of Montepulciano to while away the evening.

Once more, my journey had been rescued from the jaws of disaster. I would worry about the repairs to Reggie in the morning before hopefully heading for the hills and the Passo della Cisa in the afternoon. That was the plan, but I did wonder in the haze of my Italian red wine what event would befall me the following day and consign it to the dustbin of cycling history.

Cycling Day 20:

Monday 9th August: Salsomaggiore Terme to Berceto

5 hours 20 minutes in the saddle, 100 kilometres

By the time I woke the following morning, my Internet hounds had done their work. Sally, an ex-colleague and Italian teacher in the UK and Simone, now back home in Pavia had both sent the names and addresses of two bike shops in Salsomaggiore Terme. The town was only three kilometres away so that seemed a reasonable plan for the morning. I was, however, concerned that it was Monday and if Italy was anything like France (and in many respects it is), a Monday was not a great day to do anything which involved expecting a small, specialised shop to be open. As I checked out of the camp-site, I discussed my concerns with the owner. He was a fluent English speaker who must have come top of the customer relation class (we'll meet some of his fellow students who didn't quite make the grade a little later) and he was gushing in his advice as to how I should solve my spoke problem, recommending that I shouldn't go back to Salsomaggiore Terme but instead head for a place called Fidenza. Signor Arizona (OK, perhaps not his real name but the title of the camp-site had to have come from somewhere) was sceptical as to whether the two places in Salsomaggiore were going to be open – he tried to call them but it was far too early for anyone to have been there – and anyway, it was a bit of a hilly, up and down route to take with my delicate wheel (although the same journey in the other direction the previous evening had not dealt it a fatal blow). It would be much better, he suggested, to cycle 8 kilometres on the flat to Fidenza. What's more, his son, Arizona Jnr. knew of a bike shop that would have me pedalling out of town with a full set of spokes quicker than you can say Speedy 2000 which was fortuitous as that was the name of the shop.

The other advantage of heading for Fidenza rather than Salsomaggiore Terme was that it was en route to Parma, my town of last resort should Fidenza not come up with the goods and let's face it, there are worse diversions to take than that to the home of Italian ham and hard cheese. I just hoped that the latter would not be quoted back to me later in the day if all my repair efforts came to nothing. As if I didn't have a sufficient number of good reasons to head in the direction of Parma, Simone had now also supplied me with the names of quite a few bike shops in the city so all in all, I was very hopeful that at some point soon I would be sorted and heading for the mountains. I thanked the Arizonas for their assistance and set off along the gently sloping road towards Fidenza.

It wasn't long before I arrived and using the map that had been drawn for me by Arizona Jnr. I was soon approaching what looked like a bike shop. It sat below a modern four-floor apartment block in the suburbs of the town but lacked the brash signage usually associated with such establishments. There was just one very tasteful circular sign with the name Speedy 2000 curving around an energetic italic cyclist. I had certainly found the right place but it did seem a bit quiet, and where was the door? As I was looking quizzically at the shop window, a man in a dark pink polo shirt whizzed past me on a bike and shouted something which was clearly supportive. Perhaps they didn't get many cyclists riding four-panniered bikes coming through Fidenza; this non-descript suburb was, after all, a bit off the tourist trail. I instinctively called him back with a shout of 'Signor, mi scusi!'.

For the fourth time in as many days I preceded to explain to an Italian stranger that I had a problem with my bike and that I needed to find a repair shop that was open. Speedy 2000 didn't look as though it was. The gentleman ushered me around to the side of the building where we discovered that the shop did, after all have an entrance but it only confirmed my suspicions; 'Chiuso' it said on a sign. My new acquaintance was not a man to be beaten and he clearly saw in my predicament a challenge for that Monday morning. He introduced himself as Angelo. I'm not making his name up this time; he really was called Angelo although I never managed to confirm if his surname was Gabriele. Angelo was in his late fifties, had a lazy right eye and a significant number of teeth missing which made him speak with a slight lisp. He had a pair of spectacles on his nose and a pair of sunglasses hanging from his neck. Quite a character, but one I was glad to have bumped into as he knew of not one but two other cycling shops in Fidenza. He lead and I followed. On arrival at the first shop he seemed to be known by the small group of men who were gathered in the entrance and an incomprehensible high-speed chit-chat ensued. At one point one of the guys came over to inspect Reggie from close quarters. I acknowledged his approach with a simple 'buongiorno' but he ignored me and returned to the debating chamber just a few metres away. After a few moments, this cycling College of Cardinals dispersed and Angelo came over to deliver the verdict;

'Non è possibile qui perché non hanno gli strumenti corretti per il lavoro'. They didn't have the appropriate tools.

But Angelo was not beaten and we made haste to the second shop. As we cycled across town, I couldn't help but notice what a bike-obsessed place Fidenza was, much more so than any of the other Italian towns I had so far visited en route. The pedestrianised main street was chock-a-block with bikes of every shape, size and design. I was beginning to understand why Angelo had offered me such a welcoming shout when he had first seen me peering into Speedy 2000's window; this was clearly a città della bicicletta!

On arrival at Fidenza's third and what I feared to be final bike shop, I couldn't help but notice that it was called Pelegrini. Surely it was a positive omen that told me this was going to be the place where Reggie would receive satisfaction, especially as he had been escorted here by an angel. It would have made a nice story if that had been the case but the disgruntled mechanic shooed us away after a few cursory comments about already having enough work to do, that he was the only person working and that the shop was closing for the holidays the following day.

I felt for poor Angelo. He had tried his utmost to help me out and for reasons completely out of his control, had failed to do so. He cycled with me to the edge of town to point me in the direction of Parma. It didn't really matter that we had failed to find anywhere to repair poor old Reggie; what did matter was that I left the place thinking nothing but positive thoughts about Angelo and the town of Fidenza. So, if you ever happen to be in the area, do me favour; pause your journey, go to the main square, order a drink and toast Angelo. And should you have any problems whatsoever, don't be surprised if you see a guy with a dodgy eye and funny teeth offering to help you too.

Angelo's last piece of advice was to look for the bike shop in Parma called Del Sante. This was interesting as it had also been recommended by Simone in the list of places he had sent me. But before I could do any further investigating, I had to cycle the 20 kilometres to Parma along the dead straight Via Emilia. The first few kilometres were fine, but as Parma loomed in the distance, the traffic began to build and I inadvertently turned onto the dual carriageway by-pass along with all the lorries full of ham and cheese. Had I been a Dutchman and had it been breakfast time, I would have been in seventh heaven, but I wasn't so made every effort to escape the noise, filth and pollution of the trucks as soon as I could. It was at some point on this dual carriageway that I passed the 2,000 kilometre point of my journey. I would have liked to have stopped to take a photo, as I had done when I had reached the 1,000 kilometre point in eastern France but I feared that by doing so I might get flattened by a passing juggernaut full of cheese so I continued cycling.

I was on the lookout for Via San Giuseppe as that was where I would find Del Sante but on the main street into the centre of the city I noticed a bike shop so I stopped. There was an old chap sitting outside on a plastic chair. I could see immediately he was one of the under achievers from the Emilia-Romagna customer relations course where Signor Arizona had excelled. Before I had barely opened my mouth to utter the words 'ho un problemo' he informed me they didn't do repairs. This argument was undermined somewhat by what I could see behind him through an open door; a fully-equipped workshop. I sensed he was a man who didn't enter into arguments so I moved on but I couldn't stop myself from smiling broadly and tossing a cheerful 'grazie mille' in his direction. He didn't respond.

Undeterred I continued down the same street and there was another, similar shop. Again, customer relations were not a high priority and I was brushed off by a guy who said he was far too busy. To his credit however he did give me some simple directions to help me find Del Sante and within minutes I had done so.

Del Sante was clearly a much more professional outfit than either of the other bike shops I had so far encountered in Parma. It consisted of a large showroom at the back of which was a long counter behind which three corporately-overalled staff were standing. Behind them was an immense stockroom. I approached one of the men and was told, yes, no problem. I sighed with relief, as did Reggie in his own bike way by letting a little bit of air from his tyres. We were ushered into the workshop where a young guy was working on a very old bike. He was being watched by another man who was as old as the mechanic was young. I nodded at both men, relieved Reggie of his panniers and found a crate upon which to sit. It was a bit like being at the hairdressers but without the fashion magazines to browse. I tried to make conversation with the old chap but he said he didn't understand me (although he did, curiously manage to answer my one question; the old bike wasn't his). Was he the big chief Del Sante himself? I wondered. After a while he left and the young mechanic picked up Reggie and we started to talk. His name was Alessandro and we 'chatted' to the best of my abilities while he worked. Not only did Reggie soon have a new spoke but also new brake pads back and front and some pumped up tyres to boot. An excellent job had been done and it was 28€ well-spent. I probably sounded excessively grateful as I thanked Alessandro but I don't think he quite realised what a struggle it had been to find him, his workshop and his skills.

Parma had never been part of the plan and if it had been later in the day I would have probably just stayed for the night, even if it meant a cheap hotel. However, it was only just lunchtime and I reckoned I was still in with an excellent chance of making it to the Passo della Cisa. My discredited phone app had told me there was a camp-site at a place called Berceto, just a few kilometres from the pass, so I crossed my fingers and set off for the mountains.

Ironically, my detour to Parma had actually helped me more than just a little. If I had left Salsomaggiore Terme that morning with the intention of making it to the Passo della Cisa, I would have spent most of the previous few hours climbing up and down the valleys that lay between Camping Arizona and the road to the pass itself. By being forced to come back onto the Po Delta, and cycle south-east towards Parma, I was now able to join the road to the pass at the point which it started without having to hurdle a series of small mountains. That said, it did take me a while to find the correct road and the lack of road signs in areas outside the towns and cities was not helping me. At one particular T-junction I had to stop, park Reggie in the middle of a (deserted) road and toss a coin as to which way I should cycle. The only sign present was the one painted to the tarmac ordering me to 'stop' before turning but there was no clue as to what I would find if I decided to go left or right. Straight on was not an option (although it was the direction in which I needed to travel as I could see the mountains in the distance) unless I wanted to take Reggie off road and through a farmer's field. The tossed coin sent me right and after a while I was able to ask a father and his son, both of whom spoke impeccable English, as to where I should be heading. They pointed me in the appropriate direction and eventually I started seeing signs for the Passo della Cisa.

The next problem I had was trying to work out how much progress I was making towards my destination. Although I knew it was about 40 kilometres from Parma to the pass, the twists and turns of the road must have added another 10 kilometres to this figure. In France, every settlement whether it be the largest of cities or the smallest of hamlets proudly identifies itself with a sign when you arrive and when you leave, the same sign appears but with a red diagonal line across its face to indicate you have indeed escaped. It all seemed a bit more hit and miss here in Italy. I entered village after village as I climbed further into the mountains looking for any small clue that might indicate where I actually was but on most occasions, the places remained completely anonymous. I suppose I could have stopped and asked someone if I had really wanted to know but it was only out of curiosity (there was only one road so I knew I was heading in the right direction) and anyway, the villagers that I saw were mainly old men playing cards on the terraces of the local bars and old ladies knitting outside their front doors. They gave the distinct impression of not wanting to be distracted from their respective activities.

However, as if to compensate for the lack of information given by its neighbouring towns and villages, the small town of Calestano went positively (and literally) over the top by announcing itself to all comers by attaching its name to an excessively large motorway-style gantry above the road, not just on arrival but on departure as well. I wondered how they ever managed to get planning permission but on reflection, this being Italy, they probably never asked. Calestano clearly had aspirations and I wasn't that surprised when I arrived in the middle of the town to find a large field where a stage had been built around which several hundred white plastic chairs had been arranged. There were no posters to indicate an upcoming event (the signage budget had been spent elsewhere) but clearly something big and exciting was about to descend upon the town. Perhaps it was the annual awards night for Italy's most spectacular motorway gantry sign. Calestano was certainly in with more than just a fighting chance.

It was about another two hours before I cycled into Berceto and I did so nervously as I needed the camp-site to exist. It was too late in the afternoon to contemplate cycling down the other side of the Apennines and I hadn't seen any hotels advertised en route as I approached the town. I arrived at a small car park overlooking the red-tiled buildings of Berceto and wondered where the camp-site might be. Usually such places are fairly distinctive; there always seems to be someone who likes vividly-coloured tents which tends to help. But not apparently in Berceto. I was on the verge of becoming anxious when I turned around and spotted a green upside-down V. Could this be what I was looking for? Next to it was written 'Pianelli' which matched the name provided by my phone app. That was a very positive sign but there was no indication just how far away the camp-site might be. Would it be like one of those signs for McDonalds dotted around the French countryside which promises a tasty fast food snack '3 minutes à gauche' but which also forgets to inform you that you need to be travelling in a fighter jet to get there in the time stated. In fairness, there was no time stated, but a number of kilometres would have been nice.

I followed the sign and to my delight, after only a few minutes I found Camping i Pianelli. Now, who needs an expensive film set in New Zealand when you could come to make your film about Hobbits at Camping i Pianelli, just outside Berceto? I half expected Bilbo Baggins to pop his head round the corner of the reception or for Gandalf to summon me to his cottage. Set into a steep hillside over-looking a gorgeous valley, all you would have needed to do would be replace the mobile homes with a few wooden ones and grow grass on the roofs. Hey presto! An instant Hobbit village.

It was a very pleasant young woman rather than Frodo who dealt with me at the reception. I was quickly getting the impression that this camp-site had been worth the effort and not insignificant amount of stress involved in wondering whether it existed in the first place and then actually finding it. It was pretty, quiet, well-maintained and even had an area set aside for campers with small tents which I only had to share with one other camper, an Italian called Guido. He was also on a bike and, like me, was heading for the coast the following day. He had a rainbow flag that he attached to a bush with the word 'pace' or 'peace' in white letters on the front. I'm not sure what particular point he was trying to make but it certainly summed up that idyllic evening high in the Apennine mountains. It seemed the perfect place to raise a toast to my small, Italian A Team; my camp-site advisor Signor Arizona, my guardian angel Angelo and my mechanic Alessandro all of whom had played their part in making this another memorable day on my way to Brindisi.

Cycling Day 21:

Tuesday 10th August: Berceto to Pisa (via the Passo Della Cisa)

7 hours 4 minutes in the saddle, 151 kilometres

The altitude profile from the UK to Brindisi was like lop-sided M with the first upright – the Alps - being taller than the second – the Apennines. Once I had passed over the Passo della Cisa, I would not reach such heights again on my journey south. That said, the trailing right-hand side of the letter M would be very jagged to say the least as I first descended to the coast and then went up and down the hills that cover the length of the Italian Peninsula.

That was to come however and from what I could gather from my map, the cycle from Berceto to Pisa would require little, if any effort. That said, it was still some 10 kilometres up and along a windy route to the pass so I wouldn't be able to sit back and let gravity take over at least for the first hour or so of cycling. It was difficult not to think about my experiences climbing from Andermatt to the Gotthard Pass a few days earlier; the high of achieving my first great climb followed by the anguish and stress of the broken spoke not far into my descent towards Airolo. I was praying that the road surface on the way down to La Spezia would be as forgiving as it had been on the way up to Berceto and that I wouldn't encounter any cobbles.

Fuelled by a large piece of focaccia bread from the Hobbit's mini-market at Camping Pianelli, I set off at roughly the same time as my peace-loving fellow cyclist Guido. We hadn't chatted much the previous evening as his level of English made my level of Italian appear advanced, which of course it wasn't and there is only so much conversation you can stretch around the basic questions of life such as 'Come ti chiami?' (what's your name?), 'Di dove sei?' (where are you from?), 'Dove vai andare domani?' (where are you going tomorrow?) and 'Perché pace?' (why peace?). The final question resulted in a long and convoluted answer to which I nodded but couldn't really comprehend. If I had wanted to elongate our discussions it would have been back to the more mundane questions and answers of school-boy Italian but I didn't really want to know if he had any brothers or sisters or indeed a pet. Asking him to describe his bedroom may have been interpreted in all kinds of strange ways. There is a message there for us language teachers. So when Guido and I did meet from time to time along the road up to the pass, discussion was limited to the odd 'va bene?'. I seemed to be travelling slightly more quickly than him (it must have been the absence of a large flag in my panniers), and arrived first at what I thought was the pass. There was a large sign labelling the place as 'Passo Cisa', similar to the one against which Reggie had been photographed at the Gotthard Pass and it too was covered in the stickers of passing travellers. But whereas the Swiss had gone down the commercial route, the Italians had kept to simplicity; there was nothing more than a fabulous view along and down the deeply-wooded valley.

Guido cycled past but didn't stop. Strange, I thought that you would come all the way up a mountain and not pause for a few moments at the top to contemplate the meaning of it all. He must, I reflected, have been here before. My own contemplation over, I too cycled on and around the corner... to the Passo della Cisa, part two. I could now see that Guido had indeed stopped for a breather. I can't have been the first person to cycle, walk or drive to the pass and not realise that there was more to it than the modern brown sign with the stickers. And how could I possibly imagine that any country would miss an opportunity to fleece the passing traveller of a few of his savings; to my right was a stone hut sporting the sign 'Souvenir Passo Cisa'. A little old lady was sitting outside reading her newspaper under a parasol; in front of her on a table was a spread of random pilgrimage-themed objects for sale (although no St Bernard dogs) and in a large pot to one side, a collection of walking sticks. I was thankful however that there were no shipping containers blocking the view, no hoards of loud tourists and not even a museum. There was a church which had been built at the top of a long flight of steps and of course, another, much older and more stylish sign informing everyone who had made it past the first one that this was also the Passo della Cisa and that we were at 1,041 metres above sea level.

My second period of contemplation completed, I eased Reggie over the brow of the hill and he slowly began to gather momentum down the road towards La Spezia and the coast. There wasn't a cobble in sight.

The cycle from the Passo della Cisa to La Spezia was everything that the ride from the Gotthard Pass to Airolo should have been; three hours on a downward path and no broken spokes. The view wasn't as good as its Alpine cousin but I saw more of it simply because I was not preoccupied by a wobbly back wheel. One thing that was missing however was the Mediterranean; I had imagined that it would appear in the far distance as soon as I cycled through the mountain pass but it was obscured by more mountains and then as I approached the coast at La Spezia, the large container port at the very heart of the town blocked my view of almost everything. It wasn't until I was fifty metres from the sea that I actually saw the Mediterranean for the first time and although it wasn't in the most stunning setting it was a delight to sit under a row of palm trees and celebrate my achievement of crossing the European continent from the English Channel to the Mediterranean Sea with a cheese panini from the snack bar that was conveniently placed nearby.

Cycling day 21 was turning out to be a bit too easy, certainly compared to the days I had experienced post Gotthard Pass; the weather was perfect, the cycling easy, Reggie was in good shape (as was I) and I was making excellent progress en route to Pisa. The plan for the afternoon was to cycle as close to the sea as I possibly could (without getting wet) in the direction of the leaning tower and then to choose one of the many camp-sites that were located along the coast where I would pitch my tent for two days. It was my intention to take the next day as a 'rest day' and to spend it exploring Pisa and nearby Lucca and then head south to Siena the day after.

The coast between La Spezia and Pisa was one long gradual arc, or at least most of it was. In order to get to the start of the curve at Massa, I needed to navigate my way across or through or over or around a wooded headland. The easiest option would have been to take the main road and completely by-pass the area but my map hinted that there may be a way around the coast and with tantalisingly interestingly-named places such as Muggiano, Lerici, Frascherino and Montemarcello to tempt me, I was willing to give it a try. I cycled out of La Spezia with the ships and shipping containers to my right. It was strange to see such a place in such a central location. Usually container ports are 'hidden' (to the extent that that is possible to do that) in out-of-town locations; here it was the main attraction if you are into that kind of thing, but I can't say that I was so I doubled my efforts to escape the town and find the road that would lead me on my route around the coast. I was left scratching my head at various junctions as I tried to make my way from one windy road to the next but as I put clear distance between myself and La Spezia, I wasn't disappointed with what I found.

Lerici was the main attraction, a town that was everything you expected from an Italian seaside resort; smart, sophisticated with a hint of exclusivity. Most of the hotels had their own private bathing area and cars were banned for all but residents of the town. I doubled checked the sign; bicycles, whether you were resident or not were fine. The people frequenting the place were equally smart and sophisticated but also beautiful. I half expected there to be signs banning not just cars but banning the ugly. These spartanly clad bellos and bellas were sunning themselves on the pristine beaches and at the very end of the town jutting vertically upwards out of a large flotilla of yachts and sailing boats was a handily-placed castello for when your average well-heeled Italian decided that he or she had achieved their desired shade of mahogany and needed a cultural diversion.

There was only one thing missing; foreigners. The Italians were keeping this little corner of their land secret or so it appeared. All the cars in the car park on the edge of town from where non-residents were obliged to walk were Italian and all the chatter was Italian. And let's face it they also all looked Italian (who else can do beauty and style so consistently well?). I didn't as I took in the scene from my vantage point behind the railing above the circular four-star Hotel del Lido. If the expression existed in Italian, they would surely have put up a sign saying 'no riff raff'. Or uglies.

On leaving Lerici I was in for a bit of a long boring ride by the sea. Not that I saw much of it. The Mediterranean was once more hidden, this time behind the strip of parking lots, bars, restaurants, and private beaches that were on my right. On my left as I headed south were either three-star hotels (none were one, two or four) or private villas hidden behind metal gates. And it went on for about thirty dead-flat kilometres. Just as they had been in more exclusive Lerici, all but a very few of the cars I passed (and there were thousands all parked up, with barely a gap) were Italian. This answered the question I had been asking myself for some time while cycling through excessively quiet towns and villages since arriving in Italy; they had all come to the coast to cool off.

Eventually I arrived at Viareggio just ten kilometres or so from my destination of Pisa. I've never been to Venice Beach in California, but this was how I expected it to be. There was clearly a history to tell; elegant buildings that were crumbling and attractions that still had charm but lacked a sense of excitement. I quite liked the place although after so much monotony in the afternoon, even a drab high street back in England might have resembled the Las Vegas strip.

If I was being lulled into a trance by the long, straight road south, the dual carriageway upon which I found myself in the late afternoon between Viareggio and Pisa was enough to snap me out of my hypnotic state. I say dual carriageway but the only thing that told me for certain that I hadn't got my green (autostrada) and my blue (other roads) mixed up and had ended up on the motorway (easy to do as the colours indicate the opposite kind of road if you are accustomed to driving in the UK) was that I could see the motorway just yards away to my left and surely not even the Italians would have built two motorways next to each other. The dual carriageway eventually slimmed down to a single one and this in turn became an urban artery leading into the centre of my destination, Pisa.

The day of cycling from the Passo della Cisa to Pisa had been the longest so far along the Eurovelo 5, beating by just one kilometre the 150 kilometres I had cycled from Charleville-Mézières to Luxembourg some two weeks previously. My average speed of 21.3 kilometres per hour matched exactly that achieved on the flat canal cycle from Colmar to Basel which to date had been my record and with over 2,200 kilometres cycled, I was now into the final third of the journey from Berkshire to Brindisi.

I found Camping Torre Pendente by simply following some signs from the main road. It was situated less than a kilometre away from the famous tower with the same name although that particular attraction remained concealed behind the modern clutter on the western side of Pisa. I would leave paying it a visit until the following morning. For the time being, I was happy enough settling into what would be my home for the next two days. It was certainly one of the best-equipped sites that I had so far used on my journey and had an area set aside for small tents, which, I am sure you are now more than aware is my mark of camp-site distinction. In fact it had two such areas and I chose the one which had netting strung up above the pitches. I had once seen this method of creating shade being used to great effect in the centre of Madrid and it does make you wonder why such a simple idea hasn't caught on more generally elsewhere in excessively sunny places. If you happen to be in the netting industry, it could become a valuable stream of income for your company once the Wimbledon rush has vanished in late summer. Just a thought. And if you happen to be in the washing machine industry and are looking for innovative ways to improve your product, take a leaf out of the Camping Torre Pendente wash room and start making machines which add their own powder. What a simple yet brilliant idea which doesn't appear to have caught on either! I know it wouldn't be great news for the likes of Unilever and other powder manufacturers but whoever is running Camping Torre Pendente clearly has an imaginative streak that could serve the wider world of business well. A less innovative idea although one that was unique to this camp-site in Pisa was its tannoy system which kept we campers up-to-date with the goings on around the bar and swimming pool area. There was a jazz band playing at 9.15 for example which although I didn't go along to watch, provided the background music for my rudimentary evening meal of bread and cheese.

My only regret was that the brains behind this camping operation had never seen fit to invent a method of eradicating mosquitoes. I would have no doubt been unhappy about a low-flying plane crop-spraying the place but perhaps some inaudible low or high-frequency hum could have been broadcast via the tannoy system which would have seen the little bastards off and have prevented them from dining on me within minutes of me finishing my own evening meal. The mosquitoes were about to replace the weather as my main cycling gripe.

Angelo, the angel of Fidenza

Another day, another mountain pass

No riff-raff in Lerici on the Italian Riviera

A day off in Lucca, dodging the mosquitoes

Reggie's dashboard; the solar charger was worse than useless

Sunset over Lake Bolsena

After battling the wind en route to Rome, a felled tree near the Vatican

Marcello, my host in the Italian capital

Imperial Rome

Southern Italy; wide valleys & blue skies

Ian & Mia, summer workers at the organic farm stay in Sora

Massimo, my host in Benevento, Aitza & Paolo

A nod to the future in the barren landscape of
Campania

One of the Laghi di Monticchio;
the most peaceful evening of the trip

Matera; World Heritage site but postman hell

Liz & Basil, two welcoming faces in Cisternino

The lighthouse at the very end of the Eurovelo 5
in Brindisi.

A final evening passeggiata

Rest Day 4:

Wednesday 11th August 2010: Pisa and Lucca

"Greg, do you wanna go up this thing?" shouted a loud American as I stood in the Campo dei Miracoli well before 9 o'clock on my first day of rest in Italy. Greg was, of course being invited to climb the tower by what looked like his mother although I was a little concerned that if the rather rotund Greg and his equally-corpulent carer were both to climb to the top, the monument would have to be renamed the Ever-so-slightly-more-leaning Tower of Pisa. My camera was poised.

Even at that early hour, the area around the tower and neighbouring Duomo, Baptistry and Camposanto was heaving with tourists. I dreaded to think what it would be like later in the day. The congestion would have been eased somewhat if we tower-gazers had been allowed to use the grass but there were signs; 'vietato calpestare il prato ' usefully translated into English; 'do not walk on the grass'. Strictly speaking, this did leave open the option of simply sitting on the edge, or indeed rolling towards a quieter spot in the middle but I wasn't going to risk it, especially as there was an on-the-spot fine of a bizarrely precise €25.82 . The empty acres of grass did, however, give the campo an air of tranquillity, albeit a false one and it was possible to admire the buildings without the masses of tourists spoiling the view.

The history of the over 800-year-old tower is well-documented – I'll leave you to research the detail – but what most guide books won't yet tell you is that the work to remove some of the tilt and restore the stonework of the building is now at an end. The ever-greater angle of tilt had been reversed by 48cm by 2008 but it was only in February 2011 (some six months after my visit) that the final pieces of scaffolding were removed from the upper layers of the tower, by trained mountaineers. According to a recent BBC report 'lasers, chisels and syringes' were used in the clean-up job which puts real meaning into the expression 'face-lift'. Such has been the success of the operation to straighten (slightly) the tower, it no longer holds the title of the World's Wonkiest Building. This has now been handed to the leaning church tower in Suurhusen near Emden in the north-western corner of Germany. I wonder if they let you walk on the grass there.

Back in Pisa, I sat for a time on a step overlooking the tower wondering if Greg and his mum were yet at the top. It didn't appear to be moving but I had made sure that I was not in the line of collapse of the tower just in case. As I did so, I watched people in front of cameras striking frozen poses arms outstretched, the palms of their hands almost vertical and their bodies angled in such a way as to give the impression they were preventing a heavy weight from falling, adjusting themselves slightly according to the photographer's instructions. They reminded me of dancers waiting for the music to start in a particularly frenetic disco routine. I was tempted to play some from my phone to see if they would spring into action. Do you think their family and friends back home were ever fooled by their visual trickery?

If truth were to be told (and so far in this book, in the main, it has), I felt a bit of a scruff. I was wearing the white t-shirt that I had bought back in Strasbourg; it was one of the few things that hadn't been through the wash cycle in the self-soaping washing machine the previous evening but was by far the coolest (in the temperature sense) thing I had to wear. It was stained and dirty which made me look more like one of the syringe-wielding restorers of the tower rather than another tourist. Only my guide book and lack of chisel gave any clues that I was here for pleasure, not work. I made a mental note to pop into the Pisa or Lucca branch of H&M to refresh my wardrobe, if indeed they existed.

The queue to climb the tower was already a long one so I decided that my time would be better spent heading to the station from where I would catch the next train to the town of Lucca about 20 kilometres north-east of Pisa. After a slow journey on a rickety old train which trundled through San Giuliano Terme, Rigoli, Ripafratta and Montuolo I arrived at Lucca itself. As far as I could see, no-one got on or off the train at the stations at which we stopped. Italian State Railways or Ferrovie dello Stato as they are known locally have clearly not cottoned on to the fact that all out-of-the-way places in Italy in August are actually empty as everyone has headed to the beach in their car. At least the futile pauses the train made en route to Lucca added to the sedate pace of my day so far. I really wanted to avoid the risk of this day ever moving into top gear.

Lucca had been recommended to me by countless people and it was an undeniable gem of a place to visit. My guide book told me it was '…a delightful place in which to wander randomly' and ever the one to follow instructions, I spent most of the time doing just that, getting repeatedly lost in the maze of long, narrow, windy streets. At first glance, it is a fortress of a place hidden behind four kilometres of thick protective walls but once inside, with cars banished from much of the central area, I found an intimate town which although busy, didn't seem to have attracted the loud and proud tourists that were still trying to hold up the tower back in Pisa. The bike had not been banished however – the signs making this very clear; 'eccetto bicicletti' ('except bicycles') – which had led to a roaring trade being done by bike hire shops. I was, however, happy to stay on two legs for the day. My saddle sores were still non-existent and I put that down to the good 'airing' my inner thighs and lower buttocks had received on my days off. So far, these had been taken roughly every five days or so and the ratio of five days in the saddle to one day off it seemed to be keeping discomfort at bay.

I wandered first through the Piazza Napoleone (he gets everywhere!), gratefully using the trees that ran along one side of the square to protect me from the sun that continued to shine. I really had said good-bye to the bad weather and looked forward to a couple of weeks of uninterrupted blue skies all the way to Brindisi. From there I headed to the heart of the town and the main square where I found the church of San Michele in Foro beside a large market square whose traders had, unfortunately packed up and gone. Lucca is famed for its towers – at the start of the 14th century there were over a hundred of the things – but now only a few remain and the one attached to San Michele in Foro was the tallest remaining example. Most of these towers were built as campaniles, or clock towers and they are undeniably elegant, especially when viewed from afar which is what I was able to do from the top of the protective walls. The most striking of the remaining towers, certainly from my vantage point on the eastern side of town, was the one which had what appeared to be a large bush growing out of the top. Below the bush I could see lots of people mingling around so unless this was the annual meeting of the Lucca Tower Appreciation Society who had arranged a private viewing, it was open to the public. I decided to investigate.

You would think that an object built of red brick, 44 metres tall and with a tree planted on the top would be easy to find but it was quite some time before I was able to locate the entrance to the tower in the small maze of medieval street over which it, well, towered. It was called the Torre Guinigi and was built by the prestigious merchant family after which it is named. If they had built it only to serve as a clock tower, you can't help but imagine the delight on your average Italian merchant's face the day the pocket watch was invented. No longer would they have to invest colossal sums in equally colossal edifices just to work out what time to have lunch.

I queued for my ticket, paid and started to climb the tower. I couldn't quite get out of my mind the story of the tower back in Pavia which had collapsed in the early 1980s killing the four unfortunates who happened to be standing below it at the time. In addition, most of the Torre Guinigi was hollow and the staircase wrapped around the square interior wall. Just as it is almost impossible to hear the Nutcracker Suite and not think about eating a well-known chocolate bar, it was equally challenging walking up the stairs of the Torre Guinigi without casting your mind back to the scenes in Hitchcock's Vertigo where James Stewart tries in vain to chase after Kim Novak before she falls to her death from the top. (Or does she?) But I'd paid my money so I continued up the tower. Eventually, the staircase stopped and I entered a large room. Above me and the rest of the tower climbers were those who had already made it to the top and who were now admiring the view from the platform. Unfortunately, there was only one ladder that enabled both those climbing and those descending to move from the room to the platform or from platform back to the room below so I, along with all the others had to be patient and wait out turn. Eventually I arrived at the front of the queue, climbed the short ladder and escaped onto the open air of the platform.

To say it was a busy spot would be a slight understatement. It was packed. Most of the platform was taken up by the large beds into which the trees had been planted. There were signs asking people not to walk on these beds but it was almost impossible not to do so if you wanted to move around the edge of the tower and happened to encounter someone heading in the opposite direction, so narrow was the path. The beds themselves contained hard-as-iron baked earth. Goodness knows how the trees managed to survive when all their nutrition had to come out of that. I could only suppose that there was some unseen mechanism below our feet that permitted them to be fed and watered. The view was, as you might very well expect, a spectacular one, dominated by the red roofs of the buildings below but feminised somewhat by the pale yellows and pinks of the walls of the buildings upon which they were sitting. In the distance, beyond the fortified walls were the gentle green hills of Tuscany. It was undeniably pretty, especially if you were able to block out the noise of the families who were outstaying their welcome at the top of the tower. I can only assume that this was the case as suddenly the speaker that was firmly concreted into one of the tree beds sprung into life, first in Italian and then in English. I didn't quite catch the Italian but I certainly understood the much shorter English translation;

'Get off now!' it squawked.

This was rather an alarming message to hear. Logic would suggest that the much longer Italian version went along the lines of 'Would you please not walk in the beds at the top of the tower and use the path instead, even though this request makes no sense whatsoever as the earth in the beds has baked solid and the paths were designed for size zero models' and that the English of the person at the bottom of the tower who was sitting in front of a CCTV screen and a microphone was somewhat limited. But I wasn't going to let logic dictate events. It might just mean that the tower is about to crumble and that those of us on top needed to get our back sides off the thing pretty damn quickly! I headed nervously for the ladder but at the bottom was a long line of people intent on heading in the other direction. Do they not know that unwritten rule about letting those who are on the train get off before you get on? After much foot-tapping, I eventually got my turn on the ladder and made a hasty descent back down to ground level where my heart rate slowly returned to its normal speed. Once back on the street, I glanced up to the trees protruding from the top. The tower was still standing.

I finished my wanderings later that afternoon in the oval-shaped Piazza Anfiteatro where I sat cradling a beer and reading up on the history of what surrounded me. Every so often, I was required to place the glass or my book, sometimes both, on the table in front of me and slap my leg or arm rather sharply. I had not turned to self flagellation, I was merely trying to eradicate the mosquitoes who had graduated from mildly annoying to being a major source of grief.

If you look at a map, Pisa sits in a lowland area with lots of blue lines indicating both natural and man-made waterways. The tower is or rather was sinking into the swamp upon which Pisa is built. I hoped this meant that as soon as I escaped the big puddle the following day, I would also escape the damned mosquitoes as they were making life very, very uncomfortable. If I were to have counted, I would have had a number of bites that rivalled the number of kilometres that I had pedalled on some of my most impressive days in the saddle. I posted a plea to my web followers asking for ideas as to how to beat the little bastards and Puglian Basil suggested Avon body milk but as far as I was aware, the Avon Lady didn't do house, or even tent calls in Italy.

What is the purpose of the mosquito? That's a question that must have been posed countless times down the centuries. It is a creature that is universally despised. There is a respectable organisation called the American Mosquito Control Association or AMCA whose primary purpose is to provide '...leadership, information and education leading to the enhancement of public health and quality of life through the suppression of mosquitoes.' Where do I join? I hate to bring this down to a battle of the sexes, but when it comes to mosquitoes, it's the females who are the bad guys, or rather the bad girls. According to the AMCA 'Female mosquitoes' mouthparts form a long piercing-sucking proboscis. Males differ from females by having feathery antennae and mouthparts not suitable for piercing skin.' The association goes on to explain that 'Mosquitoes can be an annoying, serious problem in man's domain. They interfere with work and spoil hours of leisure time. Their attacks on farm animals can cause loss of weight and decreased milk production... mosquitoes are capable of transmitting diseases such as malaria, yellow fever, dengue, filariasis and encephalitis to humans and animals.' If the species does have a solid argument that would hold up in front of the toughest of Old Bailey judges while being cross examined by Michael Mansfield, why hasn't evolution kicked in and made we humans immune to their 'charms'? The little flying monsters do have a few supporters who point out that they are a vital link in the food chain and that they are an important source of nutrition for bats who eat up to 500 of them per hour. That only begs the question as to whether or not we would miss the bats if they too were to disappear. Discuss.

Back at Camping Torre Pendente I invested in four citron candles but they had little, if any impact. I had two of the four candles balanced on my knees as I sat cross-legged on the ground like a yoga student. When I looked at the map and specifically the location of Siena, it didn't appear to have the same geography as Pisa so I was hopeful that when I left town the mosquitoes would disappear as quickly as they had appeared on previous evening. Siena would be my destination the following day although I might have greater things than mozzies to worry about. One of the two annual 'Siena Palio' was due to start on the 13th August. The following day was the 12th. Did that mean that the camp-site in Siena would be crowded out by people eager to see some of the four-day spectacle that involves horses been ridden around Campo at full pelt? You may remember the scene from the James Bond film Quantum of Solace where Daniel Craig appears from a manhole cover only narrowly missing the approaching horses. I was about to cycle into that. Mind you, if you are a horsey type, would you be camping I wondered? The campers and the horse crowd seem two very different social groups. However, if you are a horse lover then you may well choose to stay well away; the race itself doesn't seem in with any chance whatsoever of getting a seal of approval from the RSPCA anytime soon.

As I was mulling over what the next 24 hours may bring and trying to rival the bat population in its hourly mosquito kill rate, the camp-site tannoy burst into life and the night's entertainment was announced. It would be a magician and, according to the English version of the announcement he '...will be performing on the swimming pool'. That's not magic I thought, that's a miracle.

Cycling Day 22:
Thursday 12th August 2010: Pisa to Siena
5 hours 57 minutes in the saddle, 117 kilometres

All of my rest days were eagerly anticipated but even more so were the days immediately following when I was able to get back onto Reggie and start pedalling again. It really was a case of absence making the heart grow fonder. The spoke incidents were beginning to be forgotten and I felt as though I was playing the role of a touring cyclist quite well. The routine tasks of each day – dismantling the tent, packing up, finding my way out of town, route planning and execution, ensuring I was eating and drinking enough to sustain the long days of cycling, finding somewhere to sleep, unpacking and erecting the tent – were becoming second nature.

For my cycle from Pisa to Siena, I called upon the services of the Michelin man to do my route planning for me. The French tyre company and travel advisor has an option on its route-finding website for cyclists and when I plugged in my departure and destination points using the desktop computer opposite the reception at Camping Torre Pendente it calculated a route of 106km that would take around 7 ½ hours. I had done similar distances in around 6 hours on previous days so I wasn't too concerned by the rather long day suggested. The proposed route would take me via Montopoli in Val d'Arno, south towards Castelfiorentino and Monteriggioni before arriving in Siena. All three of these interim towns sounded as though they warranted exploration. It was just a pity that I didn't really have the time for three lunches.

Pisa wasn't the easiest of towns from which to escape. You'd have thought that the prospect of leaving behind all those mosquitoes would have encouraged me to find the appropriate road as soon as I could but I couldn't. I eventually concluded that the signs were simply wrong (I would have more evidence by the end of the day to back up my argument that only a fool believes 100% in what the Italian signs would like you believe) and used the idiot-proof tactic of guiding myself out of town and in the required direction with the help of that great celestial sign, the sun. It wasn't making things up and I was soon heading east towards Montopoli in Val d'Arno along the SS67.

The classification of the different roads upon which I was cycling was a little confusing to say the least. Obviously I kept well clear of the A roads, A being for autostrada or motorway but those roads that I was able to use were either SS - strada statali, SR - strada regionale, SP - strada provinciali or SC - strada comunali. Each of the names derives from the layer of government which owns and looks after them, the state, the region, the province or the municipality respectively. So far so good, but many roads seemed to have more than one classification and I can only surmise that this is because they never got around to changing the signs following the not infrequent change of ownership from the state to the region or the province. Where changes in signage had taken place, many regions kept the old number of the road and just changed the acronym that precedes it but they appear to have neglected to change all the signs. Result; confusion for me and Reggie as demonstrated that morning on leaving Pisa.

Montopoli in Val d'Arno announced itself, in four languages, as a '10th Century medieval town'. I wasn't sure it was up there on the list of must-see Tuscan destinations but it ticked many of the boxes you would have expected and I sat for a while on the steps of the local tourist office, opposite an idyllic-looking hotel called the Quattro Gigli or Four Lilies. I was a little bit envious of the people who arrived and departed through its ornate entrance. Their budgets were clearly a step up from my own. How nice it might be to do this long cycle and to stay in that kind of homely luxury every evening. A woman arrived to open up the tourist office behind me and tossed a merry buongiorno in my direction in the process snapping me out of my morning reverie. I filled my water bottles using the water fountain outside the office and cycled out of town.

I spent the rest of the morning following a shallow valley full of heavy-hanging sunflowers nearing their point of exhaustion. They were drooping under the weight of all the ripe seeds amassed in their heads and the fields in front of me were beginning to turn from bright yellow into golden brown. I was continuing to navigate partly by the sun and partly by the map. The roads were almost deserted and the iconic Tuscan scenery was just starting to kick in.

I arrived in Castelfiorentino at precisely midday; I could hear a clock striking twelve in the older part of town as I cycled through the more modern suburbs. It was a very different kind of place to Montopoli in Val d'Arno where I had paused earlier in the morning to sit and daydream. I cycled along the pedestrianised high street and stopped to have lunch outside a quiet café where I was the only customer, until that is I was joined by a large American chap who explained (without being asked to do so) that he had a holiday home in the town. He was accompanied by his equally over-size dog and informed me that he had just deposited his family in a more exciting corner of the town. He had retreated to this quiet spot to read the paper but ended up chatting to me instead. He was curious about my journey and just a little bit sceptical as to whether I would ever finish it. Under normal circumstances I would have weighed in with counter arguments as to why I was confident that I would indeed complete my journey but the calm location and midday sun beating down on the terrace encouraged me to let him do most of the talking. Moving his mouth was probably the only exercise his body ever got so by keeping quiet I was probably doing him a favour. I was just glad that I had met him here at the 2,300km point rather than somewhere in northern France where potentially he could have made me turn around and head for home.

I left town on the SS429 which then became (intermittently of course) the SR429. This connected to the SR2 which would take me all the way to Siena. I had about 50km to cycle that afternoon and I reckoned that if I were to arrive at my destination in good time then I would at least be able to explore the town before the horses took over the following day. But it was at times difficult to judge if I was indeed making good progress and I put the constant head-scratching down to those pesky Italian signs. This time it wasn't the reference numbers of the roads that were at issue, it was the distances that they indicated. The first time Siena was signposted on my stretch of the SR2, the sign told me that it was 18.5km away. Great, that's probably about an hour of cycling. A few kilometres further down the road the distance to Siena jumped to 24kms. I doubled checked my direction but yes, I was cycling with the sun slightly behind my right shoulder which indicated that I was heading in a south-easterly direction. I continued but after only a few minutes, another sign said Siena was now 19km away. That was a very quick 6km! At Castellina Scalo my faith in the distances sign-posted hit rock bottom when I spotted a fourth sign indicating that Siena was 25km away on the SR2. I gave up looking and just pedalled.

Perhaps the words of the fat American back in Castelfiorentino were beginning to have an effect on me after all as when I arrived at the camp-site in Siena, a gloom of depression took hold. I'd found the site fairly quickly upon arrival as it was well-signposted (after the water-walking magician the previous evening, a second miracle in under 24 hours!), located a couple of kilometres out of town on the other side of the valley to the historic centre, but I started scratching my mosquito bites as soon as I stopped pedalling. I realised that as I had cycled, the little bastards had continued to munch their way through me but clearly my mind had been focussed on the business of cycling and I had merrily ignored them. Now that I had stopped for the evening, all my hands wanted to do was scratch the bits of my body that had been attacked, and believe me, there were parts of me that you wouldn't think were accessible to a mosquito but which clearly were. Things were about to get worse. I sat on the bank of sun-bleached grass just above the small plateau where I had pitched the tent only to realise that the mosquito air force had called in ground troops to join them in battle; there were ants everywhere! I stood up and brushed the soldiers from my lower body and legs, zipped up the tent to try and keep it hermetically sealed from the land and air onslaught and escaped to the camp-site bar. Just as the weather had cast a shadow over my journey in eastern France and Switzerland, it looked as though Mother Nature, in the form of the mosquitoes and the ants still had it in for me as cycled south in Italy. When I was at school my geography teachers taught me that hostile environments were in far off places, not in the sodding European Union. And as the American had pointed out, it was still another 300km or so to Rome, and getting on for 1,000km to Brindisi. My journey was far from over. As I sat in the bar waiting for my beer to be poured I even started to shiver. Was it Malaria? I wondered. It really wouldn't have surprised me if that had been the case.

Another thing that had been questioned by the American (I was seriously wishing I'd gone without lunch) was how I was going to return to the UK following my arrival in Brindisi (on the off chance that I made it there at all of course). This was a subject that I had purposefully avoided planning in any kind of detail in the months leading up to my departure; it would have been like measuring the FA Cup in order to buy a display cabinet even before you'd played a match. There were various options, some more fanciful than others and they included flying back (the most likely as I needed to be back at work on the 1st September), catching the train (it would take a couple of days and would involve a lot of logistical faffing around) or even 'ferry hopping' (which would have necessitated winning the lottery, giving up work and extending my trip by another couple of weeks at least; it would be fun however mixing a bit of short distance 'cruising' across the Mediterranean with some more cycling, notably from Barcelona to Santander in northern Spain before a final ferry home to Portsmouth). Turning around and cycling home was never a contender. So, assuming that I would be flying home from Brindisi, at what point should I make an effort to buy a ticket? More worryingly, would there be any tickets to buy? Puglia is one of those up and coming places served by the popular budget airlines. It was a possibility that all the seats might already be sold leaving me to 'plane hop' home, at great expense via Rome, Milan, and Paris or Brussels. If that were to be the case, it terms of cost, it would be worth my while revisiting the ferry option. I did the best thing in the circumstances and decided to continue ignoring this whole aspect of my trip until I was much further south.

I made another key decision as I sat in the bar which was to think positive. I was, after all, in Siena '...the perfect antidote to Florence, a unified, modern city at ease with its medieval aspect, ambience and traditions' extolled my guide book. My one visit to Florence on a previous Italian holiday hadn't encouraged me to sign up for the fan club so Siena sounded more than promising. But it was now too late in the afternoon to make a meaningful visit to the other side of the valley so I contented myself with continuing to read about this 'antidote' of a place when not wondering what the antidote to my scores of bites might also be.

When I returned to the area where I had earlier pitched the tent, I was somewhat alarmed to discover that there appeared to have been a murder. A long red and white tape had been stretched between two trees to segregate my small plot of land from my newly-arrived neighbours. There was, however, no sign of a body, at least not a dead one. I looked up to see that my fellow campers on the plateau that evening were a very innocent-looking group of elderly Dutch cyclists. The tape had been put in place so as to ensure they had enough space for their numerous tents, tables, chairs and, of course bicycles. In fact, the amount of equipment they seemed to have brought with them was far in excess of what they needed so I asked one of them if I could borrow a chair for the evening. The grey-haired lady obliged and we started chatting. They were all on a Tuscan cycling holiday but one where all the equipment was being carried in a van to their next destination every day. What a civilised way to do things I thought. Note to self: when next planning a long-distance cycling trip, employ someone to act as chauffeur for my baggage. But if I could afford that, I'd probably be staying at the Quattro Gigli.

Comfortably positioned on my requisitioned chair with a clear 'no man's land' of air between me and the ants below, I looked across the valley to where I could see the rooftops of the old part of Siena. The most striking building was the 97m tall Torre del Mangia. The tower sits at one end of Il Campo, which was to be the location for the following day's entertainment and excitement. My arrival in Siena on the eve of the start of the build up to one of the two annual Palios might, I thought, be yet another bit of serendipity along the Eurovelo 5. If, that is, the mosquitoes and ants didn't finish me off first.

Cycling Day 23:

Friday 13th August 2010: Siena to Bolsena

6 hours 23 minutes in the saddle, 122 kilometres

It was my worst night of 'sleep' yet. Did I ever get any? I doubt it. As soon as it became light outside, I escaped the tent in order to scratch more freely. A shaking tent may have given my fellow campers the wrong impression. Not that they would have seen me as they were all still sleeping comfortably in their own tents and caravans. What was their secret? Why was I being targeted by the mosquitoes in a way others were not?

A 2007 report from New York University provides some clues claiming that certain human characteristics may attract mosquitoes. Amongst the 'top candidates' are pregnancy, body temperature, alcohol and 'odorant markers based on blood type'. Well, at least I wasn't pregnant. According to The Institute of Pest Control Technology in Japan, my O blood type puts me in the most susceptible group, but I couldn't do much about that. Alcohol, however, was a factor I could have regulated. According to the Americans, drinking even very small quantities of beer can increase your 'mosquito appeal' substantially. Oh dear... I was consuming significant amounts of this aphrodisiac every evening after my cycling exertions of the day. But I remained ignorant of the research and its findings as I travelled further south and further into the mosquito zone and as a result was left to concentrate on cure rather than prevention.

The combined medical wisdom of my back-up team (my Internet followers) suggested antihistamine tablets to quell the urge to scratch and a product called Autan which came in an aerosol can and at a price – I bought two at an eye-watering, arm-scratching €9.80 each – but as any military historian will tell you, warfare comes at a hefty financial cost, and this was a battle I needed to win. Once purchased, I swallowed two of the tablets and sprayed the insect repellent liberally over the bare parts of my body (and a few of those that weren't). I was armed and ready for battle.

Friday 13th was not unlucky for the flag sellers of Siena. Almost every man, woman and child walking through the gates of the city had one in their hand. The flags were brightly-coloured with flamboyant designs and were also hung from most of the buildings that lined the warren of street leading towards the Piazza del Campo where, in three days time, the Palio horse race would actually take place. Each flag represented one of the seventeen contrade, or districts of the city that are eligible to 'compete' (they actually draw lots) for a place in the final. Only ten are able to do so (probably health and safety) and when the contest takes place on the final day, the jockeys race bare-back around the piazza three times, the first to finish being crowned champion. It was like the Grand National, FA Cup Final and a mass pub brawl rolled into one, or it would be once the action started for proper later that evening when the first of the trial races would be held.

I cycled along one of the long, narrow streets within the historic centre, trying to fathom my way towards the Campo only to be stopped and reprimanded by a policeman for being on a bike. It didn't seem to matter that small delivery vans were whizzing erratically up and down the very same street as if it were the pit lane at Monza. Not wishing (or able) to cause an international incident, I didn't respond to the official but dismounted and pushed Reggie further into the heart of the city. In all fairness, cycling became increasingly impossible as I neared the main arena as the volume of people on the street increased exponentially although this didn't seem to deter the guys in their three-wheeled Piaggio vans. And it wasn't even 9 o'clock in the morning. Heaven knows what it would have been like later in the day or, God forbid, the following Monday.

It would have been nice to venture into the square itself but circumstances were working against me. As I arrived on the Via Banchi di Sotto which curved around the northern end of the Piazza del Campo like a hook about to snare its pray, I was able to peer through the short tunnels that funnelled spectators to their positions around the 'square'. Some were closed to the general public and heavies stood at the far end ensuring that only the elite were able to pass through. Others were simply blocked by the wooden grandstands that had been erected to support the masses. It was clear that unless I could find a parking place for Reggie and secure him to something firmly attached to the ground – this was a thief's paradise – I would have to delay seeing Siena's main attraction, the Campo, until a future visit. I wasn't too disappointed as after all, towns and cities are much more than the buildings and open spaces that appear on a map. They are just as much places to soak up atmosphere, to listen to the noises and to smell the smells of occasions like this. Although any future visit may well be more informative about the history and culture of Siena, it would be hard to beat experiencing the slice of life that I had managed to cut into on this hot August morning.

I pushed and then cycled Reggie along the spaghetti-like lanes which took me away from all the action and once more through a gate of the city, this time to the south where I paused to ponder the view and the horizon beyond. The plan was to continue along the road I had used to bring me to Siena, the SR2, all the way to the Lago di Bolsena. This circular body of water was situated more or less exactly half-way between Siena and Rome, a journey of more than two-hundred kilometres. As I stared at the increasingly Tuscan landscape before me, I could sense the excitement building in my stomach; if everything went to plan, I would be in the Italian capital by Saturday evening and in anyone's book, that would be one heck of an achievement. But first, I needed some breakfast and some black coffee to keep me awake after my restless night in the tent.

I found it after twenty-five kilometres in a beautiful out-of-the-way town called Buonconvento. It wasn't actually very 'out-of-the-way' as it lay on the main road to Rome but it certainly felt that way after all the hullaballoo of Siena. The main street in the centre of the village was traffic-free and I took up position outside one of the few bars to watch the world go by while sipping my way through two small, black, but immensely effective cups of Caffè Boasi coffee, the contents of which must surely be on the list of prohibited substances in many countries. As ever, there was a small squadron of mosquitoes having dog fights around me but as I watched, they seemed to be keeping their distance. The Autan appeared to be working. Some of them did dare to land on my exposed flesh but suddenly bounced off like a ping-pong ball being fired at concrete. I felt like a James Bond villain looking smugly down upon my beaten foe, thinking I had won the war but secretly knowing that I had merely won one small battle. Why is there never a purring white cat to stroke when you need one?

It was turning into quite a muggy day. It was very hot but as I made progress along the SR2, the blueness of the sky faded to a cloudy white. Navigating my way from town to town was easy – there was only one main road - and the cycling far from challenging as the hard work had been completed by those who had built the road. It swept gently around hills rather than over them and the engineers had seen fit to build embankments and one longish tunnel where they thought the incline might have been a bit too arduous for the average car or lorry to endure. It was the kind of road that I would normally have shunned, being as it was a major link from the north of Tuscany to Rome, but it was so quiet that it would have been silly not to take advantage of its smoothness and speed.

As I approached the tunnel, there was a faint rumble of thunder in the distance. This was a predictable extrapolation from the gradually greying skies I had noticed earlier. When I exited on the other side of the hill, it had started to rain but not to such a great extent that it would make cycling difficult or indeed dangerous so I continued to the wonderfully-named San Quirico d'Orcia where I climbed the hill away from the SR2 and took shelter from the light raindrops under the awning of the Ristorante da Ciacco in the very centre of the town.

I'm not the greatest fan of rain, as you probably recall from my descriptions of the dreary days of the wet stuff back in Switzerland. If you cast your mind back a little further however to when I was descending into the valley of the Meuse in France, you'll remember that I love a good thunder storm and if that had been Act 1 of the Wagnerian opera, Act 2 was about to be unleashed. Cue music! Suddenly there was a crash of thunder the likes of which you only expect to hear when Charlton Heston enters shot in a beard and the Red Sea parts before him. It was quickly followed by similarly deafening cracks and bangs. The wind picked up and with it went some of the tables and chairs next to where I was sitting. A rush of waitresses ushered us all inside the restaurant while leaving the upturned tables to their own fate. Reggie, laden-down with the chattels of camping seemed OK for the moment and he didn't budge from his position leaning against the exterior wall of the café but I was poised to rescue him from the dark forces of nature should it be required. Inside the establishment, the proprietors were doing good business as everyone was captive for a good half an hour or so waiting for the elements to abate. I munched my way through two foccacia panini and knocked back several cups of coffee before having the time to browse the local newspaper that had been discarded by a previous customer.

It was boredom rather than the rain letting up which eventually coaxed me back out onto the small square in front of the restaurant. The violent aspects of the storm had ventured further down the valley and we were left with heavy drizzle which, compared to what had come before, seemed quite tame. I donned my raincoat and went to explore. In the opposite corner of the square to the restaurant was the Horti Leonini, an ornate formal garden from which visitors were banned. Any exploration needed to be done from behind a low gate next to the square. Of more interest to me was a sign in another corner of the piazza. It identified the town as being on the route of the Via Francigena, 1,795km from Canterbury and only 203km from Rome. I reached for my notebook and it was indeed one of the few places listed by Archbishop Sigeric on his description of the route. My own journey from Canterbury had been somewhat longer than his because I was taking a more easterly route, but it was nice to think that I had paused for rest in a place that the great man himself had stopped at just over a thousand years previously.

It was nearly 2pm before I decided that the rain probably wasn't going to stop completely. I hadn't yet made it to the half-way point between Siena and Bolsena so I needed to crack on with the cycling. Battening down all my hatches, I returned to the main road and continued pedalling along the SR2. The landscape was dominated by Monti Amiata which rose 1,700 metres out of the ground to my right and was to remain there for much of the afternoon glaring down upon my damp journey. Eventually the rain did stop; the speed of the storm was much quicker than that of a man on a bike although I did wonder if it would take a rest itself further down the valley. Casting my eyes away from the mountain and down from the skies, the undulating hills before me were far less threatening. What I could see were the postcard views that everyone associates with this part of Italy. Isolated farmhouses sat on top of rounded hills with long lines of poplar trees linking them to the winding roads that curved in and amongst the fields that surrounded them. The land was predominantly arable and the crops had, on the main, been recently harvested giving the landscape a scruffy, cropped haircut kind of look. Some fields had already been ploughed in preparation for new seed being planted, others hadn't so the colours were a patchwork of browns, dark yellows and gold.

I had expected the area to be filled with quaint villas converted into luxury retreats for rich German businessmen and British celebs but the dwellings I saw were clearly still in use as farmhouses with old tractors sitting on the driveways, not swanky brand new Aston Martins. Or was that the impression they wanted to give to keep the paparazzi at arms length?

The higher I climbed the more remote the area became. There were a few rumbles of thunder in the sky but I thought nothing of it; it was just the storm ahead making its way to Rome. Not far from Abbadia San Salvatore the road reached its highest point and, just as it had done earlier in the day, entered a tunnel but at 900m, it was substantially longer than its little brother further north. Cycling in tunnels can be fun (and illegal – remember Chatham?) but also just a little bit scary. I paused to switch on my red flashing light to make sure that cars approaching from the rear could see me and headed into the dark. Not one vehicle overtook me throughout the near one kilometre length but the noise of oncoming vehicles was multiplied by the echo generated by the tunnel walls and my heart raced a little faster as each one whooshed past me heading north. Who needs simulated theme park experiences when you can get them for free in a place like that?

Only half glad to leave the tunnel, I reappeared into Tuscany where I was met with a wall of water. The storm which I had assumed was outpacing me had decided instead to ambush me on the other side of the hill through which I had just travelled.

Throughout the now downward journey towards the border with Lazio the storm continued. Thunder, flashes of sheet and forked lightening. This was one serious storm. I wasn't sure what the advice was to do when cycling in a storm but as there were no settlements at which to pause I simply had to continue. Would my rubber tyres be sufficient protection against a bolt of lightning that happened to direct itself towards me and Reggie? I didn't like to think about it.

The appropriately-named town of Acquapendente – it means 'hanging water' in reference to local waterfalls - came to my rescue but whereas San Quirico d'Orcia and earlier in the day Buonconvento had oozed Tuscan charm, Acquapendente didn't yet appear to have filled in the application form for a bit of European Union makeover cash and it wasn't the greatest welcome to the Lazio region of Italy. Or was I guilty of once again writing off a jewel of European civilisation just because of a bit of water? Its saving grace was that it was only 10km from the shores of the Lago di Bolsena so I could afford to sit out the storm and not be too worried about not yet making it to my final destination. I did so on a wooden platform which served as a covered terrace for a bar in the town's main square.

I finally moved from my wet position on the decking when it appeared that the very edge of the storm was passing overhead. To my left was blue sky, to my right was a dark rain-bearing cloud heading south. Maintaining the earlier logic of a storm moving quicker than your average cyclist, I jumped back on Reggie and followed the edge of the cloud. If only I had waited another few minutes. All I managed to do was prove that a cyclist can indeed cycle at the same speed that a cloud travels and all the way from Acquapendente to the shore of the lake, I was rained upon, the annoyingly reluctant blue sky just managing to stay what appeared from the ground to be only a few metres behind me in the sky.

Not only were the heavens punishing me that afternoon; so was the hellish road surface which since entering Lazio had seriously deteriorated. A section worthy of some kind of international award for its appalling state of repair was the bit of 'road' between Acquapendente and Bolsena. Truly, amazingly, mind-bogglingly appalling. How any elected representative in the Lazio region of Italy can drive along that surface and not think 'Mmm... We must make a provision in next year's budget to improve that road' is beyond me. But clearly not beyond them.

I needed some form of therapy to ease my furrowed brow and it was to arrive in the form of the town of Bolsena and a large glass of Moretti mosquito aphrodisiac for only €2.50.

As I descended (and dripped and dodged the holes in the road) towards the shores of the lake and then cycled clockwise around the water towards Bolsena, I passed countless signs inviting me to stay for the night at their particular camp-site. My heart wasn't in camping however. After the previous sleepless night in the tent, the soaking I had received and now the battering I had endured from the road, I needed at least a modicum of comfort that night and I realised that this would probably be most likely found in the town itself.

First impressions of Bolsena were very positive. It was a small town about half a kilometre from the lake itself, popular with Italians and had some form of historical merit courtesy of the small castle on the hill behind the central square. It immediately reminded me of Lerici, the exclusive coastal town I had cycled through earlier in the week. It just didn't have the 'exclusive' tag which suited me fine. I asked at the tourist office for a budget hotel recommendation and they sent me off to the Pensione Italia which was only a few minutes' walk from the main square. My guidebook backed up this advice describing it as 'the cheapest hotel' in town.

I arrived to find a hidden diamond of a hotel. There were no frills, but it was located in the kind of building for which boutique hotels worldwide would pay top dollar. I eased the large wooden doors on street level open and pushed Reggie down the immaculate bare stone corridor that lead to the stairwell where he would be spending the night. The pensione was on the second floor and after the short climb I was greeted in Italian by a delightful middle-aged lady. I noticed a reference to the Via Francigena on the wall and she asked if I were a pilgrim to which I replied 'si e non' to cover all bases. I really didn't want to be thrown out onto the street at this early stage of negotiation simply because of my lack of religious conviction but neither did I want to tender a bare-faced lie. She proceeded to guide me to a windowless, but equally spotless room. A skylight provided some natural light. The price would be €35 (I would gladly have paid more) and once the door closed behind her, I collapsed onto the bed and dozed.

An hour or so later I realised that I probably needed to eat so I dragged myself off the bed, shaved, showered, managed to find some cleanish, dryish clothes and went off to drink my €2.50 Moretti in the main square. The storm had now passed and there was a beautiful deep blue sky as I climbed the stairs towards the ramparts overlooking the town. The view was stunning as I gazed across the town, beyond the lake and towards the eastern horizon where the large orange sun was just about to vanish.

I was no longer in Tuscany but just as there is a Peking Palace in Reading and dozens of Aberdeen Steakhouses in London, I saw nothing wrong in eating that evening at Il Toscano. Just as they had done in the Pizza Hut in Luxembourg, my fellow diners kept my imagination active and amused. In front of me were three old ladies accompanied by a younger woman who I assumed was one of their carers. They were not speaking to each other at all. They had clearly said everything that needed to be said in the previous eighty years and had run out of conversation. The carer occasionally tried to encourage a bit of discussion but got short shrift. I couldn't hear what they said when the odd word did appear but they could have been three old ladies of any nationality in any restaurant worldwide. They were all wearing pearls so had clearly done well in the marriage stakes dismissing their husbands to spend their inherited pensions on nights out like this. Good luck to them.

At another table a middle-aged couple were taking part in some sort of sponsored silence. She was rather large and inelegantly smoking a 'fag' in a way that she thought was the height of fashion but wasn't. He had a Bluetooth device in his ear and at one point got very excited when someone called him. He engaged in an animated conversation the like of which he had never had with his wife. If anyone were to have walk in without seeing the device in his ear they would have no doubt come to the conclusion that she was deaf and that he was on day release from a secure institution.

The background noise to the evening's events was being provided by the extended French family behind me. They had every generation present, the oldest of whom required the menu translating into old French francs before he considered ordering. One of the party thought it was appropriate to use the words 'putain' and 'con' in polite society (look them up in a dictionary). They were probably at a campsite down the road with a caravan, awning and picket fence to mark out their territory. Did I encounter them back in Bellinzona? I wondered. The rest of the campsite must have been enjoying a quiet night in their absence.

Later arrivals were a former rock star, his third wife and a daughter from the second. A lead singer with Italy's foremost heavy metal group in the 1970s, he spent all his money on women and alcohol. He wasted the rest. Sorry, old joke. The daughter was mildly embarrassed by her father and kept looking round to see if anyone recognised him. She secretly hoped that someone would but the only ones who were in with a chance of doing so were the three old ladies. Unfortunately by that time in the evening they had disappeared to slide up their stair lifts to bed.

The uncouth Frenchman (and this bit I'm not making up) was now talking about, err... sodomy. It was time to eat my cheese and make a move back to the Pensione Italia.

Cycling Day 24:

Saturday 14th August 2010: Bolsena to Rome

7 hours 17 minutes in the saddle, 135 kilometres

Barring any last minutes hitches (and after recent events, I wasn't counting them out just yet), it was destined to be a momentous day; I was going to complete the London to Rome part of my trip. Most cyclists I had heard of or read about when researching the trip had done that journey (or Rome to London). Few had gone further and chosen to complete their journey at the official end of the Eurovelo 5 in Brindisi. In fairness, I would imagine most cyclists making the journey from the British capital to its Italian counterpart would never have heard of the Eurovelo 5. As I have said previously, it is a route that exists as a largely unwritten chapter in the annals of cycling history and anyway, Rome is as good a place as any to decide to stop pedalling and put your feet up. Which is kind of what I was planning on doing anyway, albeit for a short period. My next day of rest would be taken in Rome and I would be staying with a local resident called Marcello. More about him later.

Apologies but I'm going to say it anyway. All roads lead to Rome, and my central Italian road of choice, the SS2 certainly did. However, wary of the fact the SS2 was quite a major road, my plan was to branch off it at some point after the town of Viterbo to skirt along the western shore of the Lago di Bracciano and then take a more westerly route into Rome than would have been the case if I had stuck to the main road. I was hoping that the roads I had chosen would also be a little quieter. I had wanted to use a bicycle-friendly route that an online follower called Tim had alerted me to some weeks prior to my arrival in Italy. He had written;

'I don't know if you have picked this out already, but there seems to be a traffic-free cycle route in Rome from the A90 / GRA ring road in the north at Castel Giubileo into the heart of the city. From what I can gather it runs right down the western bank of the tiber. If so it'd be a great way of cutting right into the city from the north, without dodging so many APE trucklets and Vespe!'

Indeed it would. What Tim had found was the Tiber Cycleroute but unfortunately when Marcello, my host in Rome heard that it was my plan to make use of it, he broke the bad news that one of the bridges along the route had been closed for many months and that if I chose to cycle that way, a long detour would be required. So the roads it would be.

After escaping the windowless cell at the Pensione Italia, the first thing to strike me as I made my way back to the main square in Bolsena was the greyness of the sky. I studied it for a few moments and decided that the dark bank of cloud that I could see in the far distance was heading in the same direction as Reggie and me. This didn't bode well for a rain-free day. The saving grace (or so I thought at the time) was the brisk wind which I hoped would mean that any inclement weather wouldn't stick around for long. For once, making sure I was on the correct road out of town was easy as there were only two choices. What's more there was a well-placed sign at the end of the piazza; turn right and head back to Siena, turn left and cycle the (alleged) 113km to Rome. I turned left and right on cue, it started to rain. Great timing!

The morning's ride was a rather unglamorous one, especially as I neared the suburbs of Viterbo. There were no longer great vistas to keep my mind occupied so instead I concentrated excessively upon the strange squeaks, rattles and vibrations that Reggie had developed. I put all of these down to the drenching that we had both received on the previous day; the rainwater had clearly washed away much of the lubrication which he needed for his various bits of metal to glide past each other with only a smooth, satisfying hum being emitted. I paused to re-oil the chain from a small bottle that I was carrying with me but this just wasn't doing it for poor Reggie. He needed a full-scale massage courtesy of some muscled mechanic with a pot of grease rather than a squirt from a dainty plastic container. I had a plan. If I got off just before a road-side garage and started to examine Reggie quizzically, I would no doubt attract the attention of the mechanics and their grease. They would come over and satisfy Reggie with the kind of lubrication that, if he were human, would lead to them being charged for lewd conduct in public.

Much to my surprise, my strategy came up trumps at the first attempt. I stopped at a small service station where I could see several overalled chaps filling cars with petrol and working on another which had been hoist up into the air. Within seconds of me crouching down to fiddle with Reggie's chain, over walked a mechanic with some heavier duty oil who proceeded to give him the once over. We exchanged a few pleasantries, I tested Reggie by cycling him around the forecourt in a big circle and much to my delight, the squeaks had gone. Brilliant! I then gestured to a hose that was strewn along the ground and my new friend nodded before walking over to turn on the tap. I was able to wash away all the gunk that the roads of Lazio had thrown up at Reggie and which had become lodged in inaccessible areas under his mudguards. With a broad smile I waved good-bye on a squeak, rattle and vibration-free bike.

By mid-afternoon the weather conditions had switched from being fairly passive rain showers and light breezes to aggressive constant drizzle and fierce wind. It had also become relatively cold. It was a battle as I lowered my head and body, stared down at the tarmac (or what was left of it after the cars and lorries had given it a good seeing to) and pedalled hard. It was no fun whatsoever and what should have been an easy-going triumphal march towards Rome quickly developed into a chronic war of attrition. Frustration was starting to set in and at one point I had what can only be described as a tantrum as a stream of four-letter abuse was broadcast across the Italian countryside but directed at no-one in particular, just the situation of being there, at that time and in those conditions.

Respite came in the form of Bracciano where I sat on an empty stage that had been set up at the foot of the walls of the medieval castle which overlooked not only the town but also the adjoining lake of the same name. The fortress above me provided an effective wind shield and the temperature seemed to have climbed just a little. It had also stopped raining and the sky was much brighter. The pause gave me time to check my messages and Marcello had been in contact with instructions as to how we could rendez-vous. Having met and been entertained by Simone in Pavia the previous weekend, I wasn't in the least bit apprehensive about meeting Marcello. From what he had told me about himself, he was, like Simone, a cycling enthusiast and was used to welcoming cyclists passing through Rome into his home. I had found him, or rather he had found me via the Warmshowers website, the same place where I had first had contact with Alain who had guided me through northern France. Marcello had been following my progress via the satellite tracker that was strapped to Reggie and within an hour of entering the province of Lazio en route to Bolsena the previous day, he had sent a welcoming message. I estimated that I would arrive in the capital at around 6pm following a late afternoon cycle of 40kms, so that was the time we arranged to meet in the Piazza del Popolo or the Square of the People. I just hoped that wouldn't be too many of them around at 6 o'clock as it might make finding Marcello quite a challenge.

A more immediate challenge however was awaiting me beyond the protective shadow of the castle in Bracciano. The wind had been gradually building all day long from the fresh breeze encountered on setting off from Bolsena to the strong gale on my final approach to Rome. Wind is the bane of a cyclist's life. The elements can throw much at you – as I had experienced on many occasions since leaving the UK – but nothing is quite as fearsome as a strong head wind. It can turn any cycle, even a downhill one, into a titanic struggle and the forty or so kilometres between Bracciano and Rome fell well within this category. Combined with the continuing poor quality of the roads and the increasing lack of patience shown by your average Roman motorist, I did wonder if someone, somewhere was trying to hint that I should simply stop my journey somewhere north of the capital and go home. Perhaps all roads didn't lead to Rome after all.

But of course I didn't turn back and eventually, with much strained calf muscles, I began to sense that I was approaching the ancient city. I say 'sense' because once again it was a puzzle trying to work out exactly where I was or how far I had to travel so erratic and scant were the signs that gave me the kind of information I was looking for. The first clues that I was nearing the end of the day's cycling were signs for the Vatican City which made sense as it occupied a position in the west of Rome. But whoever it was who was trying to keep me away from the Eternal City hadn't given up quite yet. As I cycled down a hill behind the Pope's pad, a tree had just been brought down by the wind and was blocking my path. Cars were beginning to do high-speed three-point turns in the road and it wasn't even possible to push Reggie around the side of the tree as even the pavement was blocked. When in Rome, do as the Roman's do so I tried to follow the zippy cars which had done u-turns in the road and I soon found myself at a junction on the other side of the felled tree. It was then that something strange happened. It was almost as if my mysterious adversary decided to throw in the towel. The wind disappeared and I was left alone to cycle beside the long, high walls of the Vatican City before bouncing up and down the cobbles on the road that lead to the colonnade marking the boundary between St.Peter's Square and Rome itself.

I had reached that momentous point which had not only kept me battling all day against the wind but which had also been in the back of my mind since leaving home in mid July. Before me was one of the great sights of western civilisation; St. Peter's Basilica. I had been here before so I knew what to expect but on that occasion I hadn't just cycled for 2,600km to get there. It was quite an emotional moment. I stood Reggie on one of the marble slabs that form a ring around the piazza, stepped back and took in the view. I had done something which many, including our old friend Archbishop Sigeric had done before me and which many would do after I had gone. But equally I had done someone that many more dream of doing but never actually realise. Although my journey was far from over, I could have ended it all there and I would still have achieved something that was far from unique but which on a personal level, was quite special. And very satisfying. Very, very satisfying. I had cycled all the way from London to Rome. Wow!

I would really have appreciated a small fanfare or at least a piece of white tape through which to cycle but the organising committee of the Andrew and Reggie Cycle to Rome long-distance cycling event had never got around to being formed never mind setting up such a welcome in St. Peter's Square. Not having anyone to hug, it didn't take long for me to bring myself back into the real world. And reality was telling me that I only had twenty minutes to make my way across Rome to the Piazza del Popolo to find Marcello.

Not only was I now one of the small (but no doubt significant) number of people to have cycled from London to Rome, I had come to the conclusion that I was also one of the even smaller group of people who had cycled to central Rome from the outskirts of Rome. It wasn't much of a cycling city or at least I hadn't seen much evidence of it being such a place up to that point. I hadn't passed any other cyclists, I hadn't seen any cycle routes or even any friendly blue signs indicating some special provision for cyclists and to top it all I had received some strange glances from the Romans I had so far encountered. 'Che cosa è che strana macchina?' they probably didn't say to each other as I cycled past. Clearly the cycling bug had yet to bite the Italian capital.

I pushed Reggie along the Via della Conciliazione which lead down from the Vatican to the Castel Sant'Angelo, crossed the Tiber and cycled along the long curve of the eastern bank of the river towards the Piazza del Popolo. On arrival, I was gratified to see that it wasn't yet living up to its name and despite it being 6pm on a Saturday evening, the passeggiata had yet to get into full swing. That said, it was a big square (well, more of an oval; the Italians were clearly a bit more inventive when it comes to the shapes of their principal open spaces – St. Peter's 'Square' is anything but) with quite a few people mingling around. This was very different to meeting Simone back at a deserted train station in Como. I would have to leave it to Marcello to come and find me so I sat down on a bench and waited to be discovered.

After only a few minutes of nervously waiting like a ransom delivery boy with a briefcase or in my case pannier filled with non-sequential used bills, I heard someone called my name;

'Andrew!' I turned to see a man in his late thirties with a shaved head, small beard and portly figure. He had a bike to his side and apart from the beard, he was the Italian version of me. However, whereas I was wearing Lycra, he was wearing a t-shirt of the Italian Red Cross.

'Welcome to Rome!' he said as I approached to shake his hand.

We exchanged greetings and Marcello quickly explained what we were going to do; we would cycle over to his flat where I could relax and shower and then we would eat. It was a simple but effective plan and just what I needed. Marcello's English was word perfect but strongly accented and very fast. I had to concentrate to fully understand but the more he spoke, the more I became accustomed to his way of speaking.

Marcello lived in a flat in the area of central Rome just to the east of the main train station with his girlfriend Margherita and their dog, Ambra. He was clearly one of the few experienced cyclists in Rome and set off at a startling pace as we first cut through the gardens of the Villa Borghese just next to the Piazza del Popolo, through crowded streets (I did suspect at times that I had lost him but he miraculously re-appeared at the next junction) and along the ancient walls of the city before arriving at his flat which was on the first floor of an apartment block, immediately opposite a raised urban transit route. If I hadn't have known otherwise, I would have thought I was in New York rather than the inner suburbs of Rome. But for all its ultra-urban features, the neighbourhood had character and life. Moving away from the main road there were local restaurants and corner shops where Marcello paused for supplies. He was on first-name terms with the owners; this was clearly more of a community than perhaps it first appeared.

Marcello and I chatted as he prepared chicken curry. Margherita was away for the weekend so I would not meet her before I left on Monday morning but the dog was friendly. He worked for the government tax authorities during the week and at the weekend donned the Italian Red Cross t-shirt and got on his bike to assist visitors to Rome, especially those who had medical issues during their visit. He had been welcoming travellers, mainly cyclists to his flat for several years and at Margherita's insistence, they had kept a visitors book. This made fascinating reading and I made sure that before I left I had added my own comments. The curry was as good as the conversation and it was all washed down with an enormous slice of melon. Poor Ambra had eaten earlier but it didn't prevent her from looking up at us mournfully from her position on the floor, just wishing she too could tuck in. Marcello and I chatted about what I could do in Rome the following day, Sunday as he would be back on his Red Cross bike so wouldn't be free to join me. I hoped I wouldn't succumb to the high temperatures that had been forecast and find him leaning over me offering help in his official Red Cross capacity.

Curry and melon demolished, I was struggling to keep my eyes open. It was back to being a non-cycling tourist the following day and what better place to be a tourist than in Rome. That said, to make the most of my day off, I needed a good night's sleep.

Rest Day 5:

Sunday 15th August 2010: Rome

As mentioned earlier, this wasn't my first time in Rome. In late 2002 I had been invited to spend New Year with a friend who herself had been offered the use of an empty flat in the Trastevere district of the city. Along with another friend we spent the week leading up to the end-of-year celebrations wandering around the city, ticking off the main sights and generally soaking up the atmosphere as well as the food and wine. The Trastevere area, just south of the Vatican on the west bank of the Tiber was full of character with narrow, cobbled streets leading up a hill that provided the perfect vantage point to watch the New Year's Eve fireworks exploding over every corner of the capital.

It was all very different from the graffitied streets behind the central station where Marcello had his flat. My host had left quite early to attend to his Red Cross duties which gave me a little time to sort out the practicalities of a long-distance cyclist, mainly the washing which, once completed I placed beneath the window of my room to dry. That wouldn't take very long at all as the sun was shining and the sky was a cloudless blue. Leaving Reggie to stand guard next to the clothes airer, I set off on foot to revisit the city, its attractions, its monuments and most temptingly, its coffee shops.

I was in no hurry whatsoever – I had, after all, seen most of the main attractions on my previous visit – and was prepared to follow my eyes as they sought out interesting nooks and crannies rather than the directions of a map or guide book. If I got lost from time to time, so much the better. The streets leading back up to the station were arranged in an orderly grid pattern which made navigating them easy but at street level, chaos had begun to take over with cars and bikes parked at obscure angles, wheely bins overflowing, thin terraces set up outside bars and restaurants, homeless men still snoozing under their blankets and potted trees standing sentry on either side of the entrances to some of the shops and cafés. Where the walls were not graffitied, posters had been stuck one on top of another, sometimes ten or even twenty posters deep to form a thick layer of advertising miscellany with none but the newest doing the job they had been stuck there to do in the first place. Some roads were tarmaced, others still cobbled but this had no impact upon the driving of local residents who seemed happy simply to judder a little more over the cobbles as they zipped up and down at the same speed, irrespective of the driving conditions. And amongst all this, the Romans were starting to escape their flats and fill the streets with life. This being a Sunday morning, I imagined that many would be on their way to morning mass although the table football games that had been set up outside a bar on the opposite side of the street to the church I passed appeared to be competing for business quite successfully.

My route to the station was guided somewhat by the ancient Aurelian walls of the city which ran parallel to the railway tracks although predated them by many, many centuries. I passed into the heart of the capital through the San Lorenzo gate which connected a little incongruously with the immense length of the twentieth century Roma Termini train station.

By late morning I had made it to the Trevi Fountain, almost entirely by accident as I wasn't following a map. Unfortunately, so had many other tourists who were busy tossing coins behind their backs and into the water. I was living proof of the superstition dictating that if you throw a coin into the fountain you will one day return to Rome being true as I remembered doing just that on my previous visit to the Eternal City. According to a BBC report in 2006, €3,000 per day is thrown into the fountain with the money being collected each night and given to a local charity which uses it to fund a free supermarket for the poor. Theft of the coins before they get anywhere near the needy is, however a constant problem which wasn't helped when in 2003 a judge declared them as 'discarded money' and as a result free for anyone to take, in the process exonerating the fountain cleaner stood before him in the dock who had been doing just that. Needless to say the law was changed as a result of the judge's unwise words and the shelves of the free supermarket remain well stocked to this day.

The most surprising thing about the Trevi Fountain is not the fountain itself, but rather the size of the square in which it is located. In order to get a decent picture of the thing you need to be using a camera with a very wide-angle lens which I wasn't so I contented myself with a snap of the tossers throwing away their money instead. I did of course join them before moving on, if only to leave open my options for future visits to Italy.

This was no bad thing as I still have a reason to return to Rome in the future. My next port of call was the Pantheon, one of the best (if not the best) preserved buildings of ancient Rome but just as it had been back in 2002, it was closed to the public. In 2010 it was because something was happening inside and there was a throng of people standing in and amongst the magnificent columns supporting the even-more spectacular pediment above. I couldn't get anywhere near so yet again had to admire its greatness from a distance. Few buildings can be so awe-inspiring. Not only has the architectural gem been standing in place for nearly 2,000 years (although originally erected in 27BC it was rebuilt by Hadrian in 125AD if you were wondering), the dome, which is in effect the roof to most of the building, has no visual supports. But the thing that intrigues me the most about the Pantheon is that it is made from concrete and the aforementioned dome is to this day the largest unreinforced solid concrete dome in the world. We tend to associate this mix of cement, stone, sand, lime and water with modern-day buildings, usually monstrous ones, but here it was being used to formidable effect by the ancient Romans. In a book called The Roman Pantheon: The Triumph of Concrete that I don't claim to have read, David Moore says that 'On the surface, at least, this structure appears to violate all modern building codes and should have fallen down hundreds of years ago.' He then, presumably goes on to explain why it hasn't. It's an astonishing thing next to which to sit and stare. I did just that. Again.

If you cast your mind back to my very first rest day back in Luxembourg, I raved about the local museum and how its well-presented, informative and above all interesting exhibits had allowed me to put the city into some kind of context when I later spent the rest of the day strolling up and down the streets of the capital. The history of Rome is a little more widely known than that of Luxembourg, but it did seem like a good idea to try and replicate the strategy by seeking out the Museum of Rome, if indeed it existed. So I looked it up in my guide book which confirmed that it did and that I would find it on the south side of the Piazza Navona. This long, thin square was only a few minutes' walk from the Pantheon so it wasn't many minutes before I was standing in front of the entrance to the Museo Nazionale Romano. I paid my €6,50 entrance fee, was searched and allowed to wander around. There were lots of busts and sculptures and it was all housed in a very impressive building with colourful and intricately-painted ceilings but there wasn't much of a 'story' being told. All the labels to the exhibits were in Italian which didn't help. Where were all the buttons that any self-respecting museum has in abundance? No wonder there were no children around testing them to the point of destruction. In fact, the lack of fellow visitors was about the only thing that the Museo Nazionale Romano had in common with its Luxembourg equivalent. After a respectable amount of time I made my way back to the entrance, smiled at the security guard who smiled back before returning to the important job of reading his newspaper, undisturbed.

What a lost opportunity! I thought to myself as I walked the length of the Piazza Navona, past the Egyptian obelisk at its centre and into the bright sunlight ahead of me. At which point I stopped; something was wrong. My guidebook had said that the Museo di Roma was at the southern end of the 'square' (this one was pencil thin) and here I was walking away from the

Museo Nazionale Romano, into the sun and hence towards the south. I double checked my guide book and my map. The Piazza Navona had been built upon and almost north-south axis. There was no mistaking that. Which meant that either the esteemed Rough Guide had cocked up or I had. It wasn't looking good for my map-reading credibility but at least there was no-one with me to witness my error.

I continued walking and eventually found myself at the other end of the Piazza Navona where I found the, err... Museo di Roma. Goodness knows what the other place had been. I decided to give the Roman authorities a second bite of the museum cherry to see if they could match the educational efforts of the Luxembourgers, paid my 8€ and went in. It was, however, another ornate palace of assorted memorabilia from the last 2,000 years of Roman life, mainly paintings which only made me wonder what I was doing inside when I could and should have been out there looking at the real buildings and views. There was one silver lining to my museum disappointment; the view through the window from the upper floor of the Museo di Roma. Surely one of the best views possible of the Piazza Navona. It was just a pity that I had forked out the better part of 15€ to appreciate it. Before I left, I took a few moments to leaf through the many pages of the visitors' book which were full of bland platitudes in the languages that I could understand and, I assumed, in the languages that I couldn't. I was however not the only person to be a little under-whelmed by the whole retelling of the history of Rome thing for on one of the pages someone had drawn an enormous cock. It wasn't of the feathered variety.

I don't know whether Ridley Scott ever came to Rome when preparing his Russell Crowe epic Gladiator – he certainly didn't film any of it here – but if he did, he clearly wasn't paying attention when he got to the Monumento Nazionale a Vittorio Emanuele II, which, despite only being completed in 1935 makes an infamously embarrassing appearance in the computer-generated skyline of his film which was set in around

200AD. Oops. Not many people have much positive to say about this over-sized, elevated colonnade that takes up an imposing position just next to the main archaeological site leading up to the Colosseum. I would imagine that Sir Ridley is one of them when he gets reminded about his little error. It has often been described as the typewriter or the wedding cake but it has one saving grace common to many aesthetically-challenged tall buildings around the world; when you look out from the top you not only have a great view but you have a great view without the Monumento Nazionale a Vittorio Emanuele II. And in recent years that view has got even better as a stylish glass lift has been attached to the back of the building allowing access to a roof-top terrace where the views are not just great, they are spectacular. My favourite by far was the view along the length of the Via dei Fori Imperiali towards the Colosseum, which incidentally, had been built by 200AD and Mr Scott did get right.

From my lofty position I could cast my eyes beyond the circular walls of the monumental temple to ancient blood and gore and see the hills that lay to the south-east of Rome. Beyond them were the final kilometres of my journey along the Eurovelo 5 to Brindisi. I had set off from home precisely four weeks prior to my arrival in Rome and I should, I thought, be able to make it to Brindisi by the following Sunday, two days ahead of schedule. The plan was to cycle to a place called Sora on the following day. This was a stopover that had been recommended by my final online contact, Massimo and I would be staying with some of his friends on a 'farm stay' although I wasn't yet sure if that would mean picking any fruit or digging up a field. On Tuesday I would hopefully make it as far as Benevento to meet and stay with Massimo himself. On Wednesday I would take one final day off before continuing on an increasingly easterly route to the Laghi di Monticchio where I would be able to camp overnight. On the Friday I would cycle to Matera, an historic jewel of southern Italy before finally making it as far as Cisternino where my good friend Basil, who had waved me good-bye in mid July from his flat in Berkshire would be waiting

243

with his wife Liz to welcome me and Reggie in style. From there it would only be a short morning's pedal towards Brindisi which would mark the completion of my long cycling odyssey. After a couple of days rest and relaxation in Puglia, I would fly back to the UK courtesy of a (hopefully cheap) flight from either Brindisi or Bari a little further north on the Adriatic coast. That said, I had yet to buy a ticket but I would attempt to do that in Benevento on my day off with Massimo.

As I glided down towards ground level in the glass lift, the birds-eye view of Rome gradually returned to that of one of the many cats that roamed wild amongst the ruins of the Roman Forum. I retraced my steps back towards the railway station, pausing briefly to inspect the departures board which told me I could be in Lecce in the very heel of Italy by just after 10pm that very evening. I momentarily considered it as an option before smiling and moving on.

Back at the flat, Marcello had already arrived home after his day spent tending to the needs of the tourists who hadn't made it to the end of the day in one piece. We chatted as I leafed through his visitors' book which was mercifully lacking in pictures of penises and as he stroked the amazingly placid Ambra who was slumped on the sofa to one side of him. One way in which I as a passing short-stay lodger could say thank-you to Marcello was to invite him out for something to eat at a local restaurant of his choice. Reflecting carefully upon my experiences back in Pavia where Simone had insisted upon paying for my meal, I made it clear from the outset that this particular meal would be at my expense and once that was agreed (Marcello didn't, quite rightly put up much of a fight!), we headed out to a place just around the corner. The establishment occupied a corner plot and from what I could see consisted of only one rather shoddily-built storey. It was surrounded by five-storey apartment blocks and I could only surmise that a similarly high building had once been positioned there but that it had since disappeared for a reason unbeknown to me. Marcello requested we sit outside so when we were lead into the building itself I was initially rather puzzled. However I began to understand on entering a second 'room' which had walls but no ceiling where we were able to eat our pizzas under the clear night of Rome.

The restaurant was called La Mucca Bischera and described itself as a griglieria-pizzeria. Had I had known at the time that the name of the restaurant translated into English as The Foolish Cow, a state of mind not that far removed from a mad cow, I may have developed an urge to go vegetarian, but I remained ignorant of the rather disconcerting name and enjoyed the evening nevertheless.

Cycling Day 25:

Monday 16th August 2010: Rome to Sora

8 hours 7 minutes in the saddle, 145 kilometres

The Romans, unlike the English, don't like to go out in the midday sun or even the morning sun which is one reason why Marcello was so keen to cycle to work early; it was much cooler at 7am than it would be only a couple of hours later. Not that I considered this to be an ungodly hour; back home in the UK I had been cultivating a reputation as an eccentric morning commuter happy to cycle to work at 6am (or earlier in the summer months) for several years. In this respect I probably was a mad Englishman, but I did see the logic of avoiding the midday heat and as the sun seemed to be an increasingly reliable fixture in the sky as I crept slowly south, I could foresee my morning departure times becoming earlier and earlier.

Marcello cycled with me for the first few minutes after leaving his flat until we reached a point where he was able to point in an easterly direction and say buon viaggio! We shook hands and I cycled head on into the rising sun. This would probably have made a fantastic picture from Marcello's perspective; a silhouetted lone cyclist pedalling off into the distance. From my perspective perched on Reggie, it was inconvenient to say the least as the traffic lights were all but impossible to decipher and the cars and trucks were anonymous and scary black boxes overtaking me at speed.

The cycle out of the Italian capital was in stark contrast to my entrance into Rome two days earlier. The latter had been through relatively affluent, well-maintained suburbs and the prevailing weather conditions had made the experience a predominantly 'northern' one. This Monday morning ride out of the capital was very 'southern'; the suburbs were much more expansive and run-down. Apart from the cars, the pace of life around me seemed to be in a lower gear and sultry climatic conditions were beginning to develop even at that very early hour of the day. I have no idea where the line between northern and southern Europe is drawn, but as I cycled through the urban clutter of south-east Rome, there was no mistaking that it had now been crossed.

Although the sun was making the visual aspect of my journey quite challenging with my eyes over-compensating as a result of the low sun edging its way vertically above the horizon, I knew that if I rode into the direction of the sunrise I couldn't really go wrong. So I was a little surprised when I realised that actually, I could and I had. The road was littered with signs of all shapes, sizes and functions; you name the service or product that you want and I guarantee that somewhere along my route that morning you would have found someone trying to persuade you purchase it from them. The preponderance of advertising signage was perhaps the business community's attempt to compensate for the lack of investment in signage by the government. After leaving Marcello near the centre of the city, I had to cycle nearly ten kilometres before finding even the smallest reference to the number of the road upon which I was cycling and when I did it told me that it was the SS49a. This was not great news for someone who thought he was on the SS6. I stopped to consult my map and realised that I had been a little too keen to cycle east rather than south and had ended up cycling along the wrong arterial spoke of the Rome road system. Logic dictated that I make a right turn across the now relatively sparsely-populated scrubland that was taking over from the concrete jungle of the capital in an attempt to hop to the next spoke in the wheel. The plan worked and after a short ride heading directly south rather than east, I hit the SS6 before my detour had become excessively inconvenient. To my delight, public funds had been devoted to informing passing travellers that they were indeed moving along the SS6; every kilometre a small blue sign told me so along with the number of kilometres I had cycled since leaving the centre of Rome.

The problem with setting off early was that after a couple of hours in the saddle, my mind and body would start to reprimand me for being so stupid in getting out of bed before they had had sufficient time to recover from the previous day's exertions. Although the previous day had only been spent wandering the streets of the capital, that was certainly the case as I cycled away from Rome. It was only just after 9 o'clock but I needed sustenance of some sort so when I found a small café-come-bakery at the side of the road in Cesareo, I stopped to refuel. The sign on the awning promised pasticceria e gastronomia. I wasn't too fussed about the gastronomia but the pasticceria, or pastries sounded good and they were. As I slurped my coffee and munched my way through two delicious sugared croissants, I struck up conversation with a charming Italian couple who were very inquisitive about what I was doing. Initially the interest was from the man but once I confirmed that I was English and not German, the woman's eyes lit up in a manner to rival the brightness of the neon bar sign above her head and she joined in the conversation too. The chat resembled many that I had taken part in since leaving home but whereas back in the UK and in northern France, there was always an element of scepticism implied if not expressed by my interlocutor (and probably by me) as to whether I would get anywhere near my destination point, I was increasingly finding that the scepticism had been replaced with genuine admiration for what I had done. These short exchanges were my equivalent of EPO, the infamous performance-enhancing drug as they gave me an immediate injection of motivation. As a result, by the time I left the terrace of the café in Cesareo, I was high not just on the espresso coffees and calorie-laden pastries I had consumed but also thanks to two strangers who just happened to take an interest in what I was doing. It was just a good job I wasn't German.

My short break also allowed me to look at the map in a little bit more detail and consider how exactly I was going to get to Sora, my destination and ponder over the arrangements that had been put in place allowing me to spend the night at the farm stay. The route was not too complicated and would take me through countryside and via the towns of Palestrina, Fiuggi, and Alatri. My map implied an up and down route as I would be trying to avoid the main road in the bottom of the valley. The plans that had been put into place by Massimo, my online contact who I would be meeting the following day in Benevento were a little clearer if only because they were so simple; I was to meet a man called Tomasso at 6pm at Sora train station. I knew nothing more about Tomasso or indeed the 'farm stay'. The whole thing had an air of mystery attached to it and I was half expecting Massimo to text me a coded sentence that I would have to utter upon suspecting that I was standing next to Tomasso at the station;

'The birds fly high in the sky in a Puglian summer' I would perhaps have to whisper.

'Welcome to Sora Mr Bond' he would reply.

It all works better if you read it again with an Eastern European accent and for the moment at least, assume that I have changed my surname.

If the strong coffees were working wonders in encouraging me to write the script of the next 007 movie, they were having an equal effect upon my ability to put some distance between me and the big city as soon I was in beautiful open countryside en route to Fiuggi. As I had suspected, the twisting route on my map equated to lots of ups and downs as the road clung to the side of the valley and repeatedly crossed the contours of the land. The general direction was upward, however the compensation was significant as when I glanced to my right, the wide panorama of the green valley opened up below me. I was amazed just how quickly this had happened. Here I was in deep countryside with mountains in the far distance on the other side of the plain, barely a car on the road and the only settlements that I could see were no bigger than a small village. Only a few hours previously I had been in the heart of one of Europe's largest cities dodging early-morning commuters and straining to make sense of the urban mess that surrounded me.

If only I were able to share my experiences with the outside world. Unfortunately my iPhone which had served me extremely well since leaving home in the UK had decided to stop connecting to the mobile phone network. In fairness, it was nothing to do with the smartphone and everything to do with the infrastructure into which it was trying to plug. It was almost as if the authorities had decided that south of Rome, people weren't too fussed about having access to quality network coverage. Perhaps they weren't. Even when I could clearly see that the phone was connecting to the network that allowed for calls to be made, more often than not the data side of things would not be functioning. This was a frustration that I came to live with but it made for often sporadic messages being posted on the website and pictures appearing long after they had been taken. All this, of course, had to be put in the larger context of my journey. I was cycling for the experience and sharing it with others was only one small part of what I had planned to do. It's also worth spending a few moments to reflect upon how far technology has come in only a few short years. Holiday photographs taken before the digital explosion of the 1990s remained hidden for many days if not weeks after they had been taken. Has this changed the way in which experiences such as long-distance cycling adventures are perceived? Does the escapism aspect diminish to the point of extinction if we are able to share thoughts, sights and sounds at the click of a few buttons or are we developing a vicarious escapism by embracing those who choose to be embraced thanks to new technology? Discuss. It's these kinds of things that you think about on quiet country roads on Italy.

Fiuggi was a nice find to the extent that it was ever 'found' located as it was on the road to Sora. I left the main road to go and explore a little and after a few minutes cycling I could see what appeared to be the centre of town built on a small hill to my right. I followed the signs directing me to the centro storico but before I was able to make any progress up the hill, the road insisted on taking me all the way round the other side of the town and then, when I finally did start climbing towards the rounded peak, the road wound round the hill in a manner that made you wonder if any gradient of road that couldn't be described as 'shallow' had been banned by the local council. I continued to pedal and the road continued to curve around the hill until eventually it flattened out completely and opened out onto a large piazza. To the right was the entrance to the strangely out-of-place Grand Hotel which had been painted pale pink and cream. Beyond the hotel was a viewing point looking towards the north and opposite the hotel were a couple of cafés. It was my intention to return to one of these for an ice-cream once I had explored the very top of the town which was still a few minutes' walk along and up a narrow cobbled lane.

Once I had done so, I found a second piazza, this time long and thin with medieval buildings on either side. It was all very well-kept and pretty with bursts of green courtesy of the bushes planted outside the doors of the houses and craft shops. But once again, it was almost deserted. I couldn't help but wonder how a large hotel like the one I had just seen could make any kind of living in a place which appeared to be so starved of visitors. I did question whether I had entered a private area closed off to passing travellers such as myself and Reggie, almost embarrassed to take any photographs lest I be invading anyone's privacy.

Back in the square next to the Grand Hotel, I sat on the terrace of the Martini Café. It was an elegant establishment so much so that I was a little wary of looking at the menu for fear of it being out of my price comfort zone. Reading from right to left – I'm British so used to that method of deciding what to eat - I wasn't too shocked so ordered some sandwiches (which came complete with the crusts removed) and a chocolate, strawberry and raspberry ice-cream cone. Those flavours were chosen mainly because I knew for certain what they were in English; had I been more adventurous I could have chosen from the dozens of other varieties on offer.

The hotel opposite had got no busier since my foray into the very storico centre indeed I noticed that most of the many shutters on its windows were closed. Was it actually open? I asked myself. To the right of the hotel complex was a theatre and a group of three people came out to practice their acting. I suppose because I could tell that they were acting and not just having an argument in the street the play can't have been that good. And then for the remaining half hour or so of my early afternoon break, I eavesdropped on a conversation that was taking place at a table just a few metres away in English. An Italian guy in his late 50s who gave the impression of being a local player was with two young, female Americans. They were clearly on some kind of extended stay in Italy, perhaps to study, perhaps to work – I couldn't quite decide – and had, via a family contact, been introduced to this aging Fiuggian Lothario. He couldn't wipe the smile off his face and the Americans, who had only just arrived in town were too polite not to smile back. He talked about his family, home and businesses and they cooed back. The denouement of that particular drama would have made good entertainment back at the theatre which did make me wonder if all three of them were just better actors than the threesome who had 'argued' before me earlier. Perhaps I just happened to be their first audience.

At around 3pm I finally dragged myself away from my anthropological studies in Fiuggi and back to the road to Sora from where I continued along and down the valley towards Frosinone. Unfortunately, shortly after Frosinone, some heavy investment had been ploughed into the road that I had imagined would guide me towards Sora, so much so that it had become a dual carriageway complete with central reservation. As a result of this major upgrade bicycles had been prohibited from using it. However, all the signs for Sora, now in abundance, were intent on directing me back towards this super-strada as it was known. It was as if Reggie had become a motorway magnet, constantly fighting against the 'attraction' of the very main road. It was a painstaking job picking out the smaller roads that took me in the same direction as the forbidden main road and it was with a sense of relief that I finally arrived at the start of a very long straight road that would lead me directly into the centre of Sora.

The three kilometres of the Viale San Domenenico had been built parallel to the railway line, or was it the other way around? The road had probably come first. Was it a Roman road? In these parts most roads must have some form of Roman origin but they generally not straight. Whatever its origins, I knew that if I followed the road and could see the railway sporadically a couple of hundred metres to my right, I would arrive at a point where the train station would be sign-posted. And it was. The station itself was at the end of a road perpendicular to the first. Just in front of the station was a fountain around which buses could turn in order to head back into town and there were a few cars dotted here and there. Nothing much seemed to be happening and I could see only a few people, most of whom were sat outside a small bar opposite the entrance to the station. I was expecting Tomasso to be on a bike – Massimo had told me he would be cycling down from the farm stay to meet me – but I saw no likely candidates. I checked my watch and it was about ten past six so if he had arrived bang on six, he would have still been hanging around. You have got to be at least a little bit tolerant when it comes to meeting a long distance cyclist; I thought I had done pretty well to make it to Sora almost on time. I cycled around for a few minutes, glancing into the darker corners of the area around the station and even pushing Reggie through the entrance of the station and onto the platform to see if anyone was waiting there. I could find barely a soul never mind one with a bike who was actively looking for me.

I shrugged my shoulders and went to sit outside the appropriately-named Arrivo bar where I ordered and was given a small beer. My fellow drinkers were a rough looking bunch of drunks and I could sense tension between a couple of the more leathery-skinned men. Within a few minutes, this tension had escalated and despite the efforts of his female companion, one of the guys flung himself over the large green plastic table in the direction of the other chap causing drinks to fly in all directions and smash into pieces of the floor. It was perhaps a good time to move on so I swiftly drank what remained of my beer and pushed Reggie discretely back towards the entrance of the station being careful not to inflict any shards of glass upon his tyres. It was gratifying to know that the British are not the only ones to go out in the evening, get drunk and fight each other. This was all the more impressive as it was a Monday evening, not even a Friday or Saturday night.

There was a handily-located police station just next to the entrance of the train station and I took up position just outside its door, ready to move inside if any of the fighting men came in my direction. However, from what I could see, things had calmed down across the street. Come on Tomasso, save me from an evening in central Sora I thought to myself. At which point a thin man with a beard and a bike appeared to my side.

'Andrew?' He enquired

'Yes. You must be Tomasso. Pleased to meet you. Thanks for meeting me.' I replied with relief. It appeared that no code word was required.

I made no mention of him being late but Tomasso did point out that I had been. It didn't seem the appropriate time or place to argue about the niceties as to who was to blame so I apologised even though I thought he was stretching the point a little. He said he had been outside the station at 6 o'clock but as I hadn't been there, he had gone off to look for me in town.

Tomasso spoke excellent English and we chatted as we cycled. I didn't quite understand the connection between Tomasso and Massimo, my contact in Benevento but it appeared to have something to do with cycling. He was older than me, perhaps in his mid 40s, but extremely fit and he was able to outpace me on the journey which forced him to pause several times to allow me to catch up. His bike lacked the four panniers that Reggie was carrying however and I had just completed a very long day indeed. I glanced down at my cycling computer as we approached the farm and noticed that I had been in the saddle for over 8 hours. It had been the longest day yet in terms of time and the third longest in terms of distance cycled; 145km.

I had done camping, done hotels, done staying in people's houses but now I was about to do something a little different; a farm stay. It was located a few kilometres to the north-east of Sora on one of the hills overlooking the town and consisted of a large three-storey house, a few out buildings and a significant amount of land. The place was run by a man called Antonello who was relatively young and who had lived there all his life. His father had farmed the land before him but it was Antonello who had seen that there was a more prosperous future for the farm if it were to be run as an organic farm stay establishment. Antonio's connection with Massimo was just as mysterious as Massimo's connection to Tomasso; they had clearly met but no explanation was forthcoming as to how or why, even when I asked.

My powers of deduction were failing me after the long day of cycling and I never managed to work out how many people were actually staying at the farm that night but I could see that they came in two categories. Some were paying guests who were there to soak up life on a farm and who were encouraged to experience the simple but plentiful life of rural Italy through home cooking, walking, horse-riding and other such wholesome country activities. The second group were those who worked on the farm and who, in return, received free food and accommodation. On my night at the farm there were two such volunteers. Both were English; Ian, a soon-to-be architecture student and Mia, an English teacher from London and it was with these two that I spent much of the evening chatting about our relative experiences that summer and our plans for the remaining few weeks before we returned back to the UK. The three of us ended the evening by making sure that the washing up had been done and things organised ready for breakfast to be served to the paying punters the following morning. We polished off the bottle of unlabelled red wine that we had been given with our meal and headed off to bed, Ian and Mia in their rooms in the house and me to a large tent in the garden just in front of the main house. It was quite a novelty having anything resembling head room and I even had the pleasure of sleeping on a camping mat that could be described as comfortable. Before nodding off to sleep I looked at the map and plotted a route for my cycle to Benevento the following day.

Cycling Day 26:

Tuesday 17th August 2010: Sora to Benevento

7 hours 44 minutes in the saddle, 172 kilometres

Tomasso had estimated that my journey to Benevento would be about 150km. On the previous days when I had cycled that kind of distance – to Luxembourg and to Pisa – it had come as a bit of a surprise. This was the first day when I knew I was in for a long day of pedalling so I had even more reasons to get out of the tent, packed and back on the road at an early hour.

I said my farewells to the volunteers and visitors who I had spent time with over dinner at the farm stay, thanked Tomasso and Antonello for their help and hospitality and cycled down the hill to Sora where I paused for a coffee before the inevitable long slog to Benevento had to start. I made excellent progress in the first couple of hours along the road to Cassino; it was long but straight and not too busy. I was able to keep up a consistent moderate speed and covered the first 50km of the day in just over two hours.

Cassino was the last major town in the Lazio region and most people have heard of it because of the events that took place in and around the area during the Second World War. By far the most impressive sight as I approached was the Benedictine Abbey that sat on top of Monte Cassino, the hill just to the west of the town. What can be seen today didn't exist after the Allied bombings of 1944 when the entire town and the monastery itself were flattened. The Abbey, founded in 529AD and the spiritual home of the Benedictines was unfortunate to be located along the German Gustav Line, Hitler's attempt at holding back the Allied advance as it crept north through Italy. For a while, it did its job quite well. The Allies thought that German soldiers were taking up positions in the monastery but this wasn't the case; the Pope, Pius XII had negotiated a 300m exclusion zone around the building. Ground attacks failed so the American Air Force was called in and they dropped over 400 tonnes of high explosives and incendiary devices on the building. The only people in the Abbey at the time were 800 refugees and twelve monks. The monks survived in an underground chapel, but many of the refugees perished. Further bombings of the town wiped it from the map. In total 20,000 soldiers of many nationalities, including of course Germans, were killed.

The monastery has since been rebuilt just as it was prior to the war but the town of Cassino was built as a new town. My guide book described it as having 'very little appeal' which although probably true, seemed a bit harsh bearing in mind the sacrifices that the inhabitants had made. I sat for a while in Piazza Antonio Labriola gazing up at the monastery on top of Monte Cassino. It was simply impossible to imagine what being in the same spot would have been like some sixty six years prior to my visit. Let's face it, I wouldn't have lived to tell the tale. Quite a sobering thought and a very sobering moment. The freedom I had to travel from my home in the UK to the south of Italy was not really thanks to the bureaucrats in Brussels doing away with visa formalities and border crossings. Rather, it was all to do with those many thousands of soldiers and their fellow fighters who had trod the same path as me only a couple of generations ago and the ultimate sacrifice that they were willing to make. We perhaps have life a little too easy at the start of the 21st century.

Soon after Cassino, I cycled into my fifth Italian region, Campania. The plan was to continue along the R6/S6/SS6 – they all seemed to refer to the same road – and then the SS372 which would take me almost all the way to Benevento.

The long straight roads were good for thinking and I spent much time en route to Benevento pondering the various challenges of cycling in Italy. Firstly there were the roads. Shortly after crossing the border from Lazio to Campania, I experienced a fabulous stretch of high quality road, so good in fact that I got off Reggie to take a picture. I had noticed this sudden change in road quality before when passing from region to region. When I emerged from the tunnel into a heavy rain shower on the day I cycled from Siena to Bolsena, I was also emerging into the region of Lazio. As you may remember the road was of exceptionally poor quality. The roads from the Swiss border to Milan were also very poor. In Tuscany they were excellent and from the evidence I had to that point, they were pretty good in Campania as well. I could only conclude that the quality of the roads I was using – the secondary town to town ones which were the responsibility of the regional administration – reflected the varying priorities of each region when it came to maintaining and developing its road infrastructure. My theory would be proven if when I cycled from Campania into Puglia, the roads deteriorated. That said, I clearly didn't want this to be the case.

A second area of thought was the drivers. Many people had warned me about cycling in Italy describing the road users as 'dangerous lunatics' or some synonym thereof. Was this standing up to scrutiny in reality? Probably not. The majority of drivers were just like anywhere else, pulling out to give you space and being patient at traffic lights. There were however a minority of idiots who took idiocy to a new level. A friend once told me that although the drivers in Italy were fast, they were also safe. This was utter rubbish. Speed kills and the sad evidence of this was in the all-too-frequent bunches of flowers tied to trees or signposts and small memorials that could be found next to most roads marking the place where someone had been killed. There was an even smaller minority of drivers who seemed to be unaware that a cyclist was in front of them, making no change to their driving position in the road and continuing on their merry way regardless. I was passed by one such lorry driver on leaving Cassino. His truck came within 50cm of Reggie. I could only hope that he wasn't on his mobile phone at the time. This is a new taboo in many countries but it doesn't seem to have caught on in Italy. Comically but fortunately not tragically, when cycling down the mountain from the Passo della Cisa as I made my way to Pisa, I was behind (thank goodness) a lorry carrying a full load of logs. As we twisted left and right along the switchback road, I could clearly see that the guy at the wheel had a mobile phone in one hand and the wheel in the other. In an old, manual truck, goodness knows how he was managing to change gear.

Pot holes in the road, excessive speed, driving too close for comfort and using a mobile phone while at the wheel. These can all be killers. The one thing that annoyed me the most while cycling in Italy however, was no killer. And it wasn't just the minority who took part in the practice, it was a large majority. We all know that the Italians like to talk (apart from the couple I witnessed in the restaurant in Bolsena) so it must be extremely frustrating for your average car driver in Italy not to have the ability to speak to the other people on the road in the way they would a passenger in the car. So how do they compensate? By using the horn of course. I was used to drivers in the UK using their car horns to say one thing which could be summed up as 'watch out, I'm taking evasive action and you need to do the same'. In Italy it could mean any of the following:

- Watch out! I have no intention of stopping or even using my brake so it's up to you whether you get out of my way.

- Hey! I'm a cyclist too and I think what you are doing is brilliant; good luck mate!

- You stupid idiot! I could have killed you and despite it clearly being my fault, my ego won't let me at least drive away without giving everyone the impression that it was your fault.

- I have brought your washing back from the cleaners but can't be bothered to get out of the car to ring your bell so I am going to sit here blaring my horn until you come down to fetch it.

– Nice tits.

Etc... It was almost impossible to decipher the meaning at any particular moment and I just wished they would all be a little less horny.

Valrano Scala was yet another town built around a long straight road; it seemed to be the way to do such things south of Rome. Having lunch on the terrace of my chosen café was a little like sitting on the hard shoulder of the M1 as all the lorries and cars roared past at speed but I persevered and ate my way through a large slice of chip (yes, chip) pizza. When I went back into the bar to buy something sweet – an equally large slice of apple tart – the guy who owned the place asked where I was heading. I explained that Benevento was my destination for the day and then Brindisi by the end of the week. There was a significant intake of breath at the mention of Benevento, an even more significant one at the mention of Brindisi at which point he called over one of his regulars who was feeding money into the fruit machine on the other side of the bar. A high-speed conversation ensued – I couldn't pick up much of what was being said – after which the barman made his offer. His customer could take me in the back of his delivery van to Benevento that afternoon but it wouldn't be possible to get me all the way to Brindisi. I was a little confused to say the least. What had I said to imply that I was looking for assistance?

'Non voglio andare in macchina. Vado in bicicletta!' I tried to explain. They looked a little confused as to why I would want to continue by bike although the customer's confusion appeared to be mixed with relief at the thought of not having to divert to Benevento.

The whole encounter was a bit of a puzzle. Was there something about the road to Benevento that I needed to know about? Judging that in this case at least, ignorance was bliss, I didn't explore their motivation for offering the lift but thanked them and sped off under my own steam in the direction of the SS372.

The SS272 was also known as the Strada Statale Telesina and was the main spur road from the A1 motorway just a couple of kilometres west of Valrano Scala to Benevento. It was quite similar to the road that I had avoided on the previous day as I made my way to Sora although it was only a single carriageway for much of its length and didn't have a central reservation separating the two flows of traffic. I looked for a sign prohibiting bicycles but couldn't see anything so ventured down the slip road and onto the Telesina itself. In one significant way it was very different from the road to Sora; it was quiet. What's more, there was a sufficient amount of tarmac to the right of the carriageway upon which to cycle. It was almost as if they had planned for it to be a cycle lane but never got around to painting the white bicycle sign on the road. Not quite sure if I was allowed to be there or not, I concluded that it wasn't the greatest crime in the world and if I was asked to leave the road by the local Carabinieri, so be it.

After a few kilometres, it wasn't the prospect of being told off by the boys in dark blue (and red stripes) so much as the sheer boredom of the route that got to me. For much of its length, trees had been planted on both sides of the road and the view was limited to say the least. When the trees did disappear for a few moments, my gaze was drawn a little too much toward the scenery in an attempt to compensate for the monotony of the exclusively green view elsewhere. This caused me to drift out of my self-proclaimed cycle path and into the kill zone frequented by the cars and lorries. It really wasn't working for me so I concluded that the only option was to leave the Telesina at the next exit and pick my way across the countryside.

When it was an imposed 'option' the previous day, I had become very frustrated. Here, however, the road network was on my side as to cut across the countryside was actually a shorter route than to continue on the Telesina which although very straight, initially headed slightly north before kinking and heading south-east. That was the theory. For about 15km I cycled through deserted villages and hamlets strewn randomly across the countryside of Campania. It was fantastic, everything you could have wished for from a cycle in southern Italy. The sun was beating down upon my back, there was only the faintest of breezes (which was wonderfully cooling), the scenery was gorgeous and I had not a care in the world. I didn't even have to worry about where I was going to sleep that evening as that was being taken care of by Massimo. What a fantastic way to make my way all the way to Benevento!

If it seems too good to be true, it probably is. And here it certainly was. I thought I was making good progress and estimated (without actually doing the maths) I had another twenty, perhaps thirty kilometres to cycle. At a roundabout in the centre of a small town called Dragoni, I noticed a sign with a string of destinations and kilometres; Baia e Latina 10, Telese 21, Benevento 68... What?! Even more shocking was that the arrow was pointing back towards the Telesina which had now returned south after its northward kink. My route across the countryside must be at least another 10km on top of the 68 on the sign. Perhaps more. It didn't escape my thoughts that this sign could be as inaccurate as the ones back in Tuscany but could I take that chance? Anyway, it could be more than 68km, not necessarily less. I looked at my watch and noted that it was already 3.30pm. Averaging just under 20km/hr it would be another three to four hours of cycling before I arrived at my destination, even longer if I had to take a break which was very likely. I reasoned that I had no choice but return to the main road and try to make as much progress within a shorter time as possible. Massimo hadn't given me exact instructions as to where to meet and when – he was presumably following my online track and would contact me as I approached Benevento – but I really didn't want to be cycling come 8 or even 9 o'clock in the evening by which time it would be dark anyway.

So back it was to the long, relentless Telesina. The frequency of the signs indicating that this town was to the right, that town to the left seemed to become more and more spaced out as I trudged further and further along the road. After only an hour of cycling I pulled into a small ESSO service station, bought a Diet Coke and a Magnum ice-cream, ignored the contradictory nature of my purchases and slumped on the path next to the forecourt trying desperately to regain a little bit of stamina to continue my journey. I still had over 40km to cycle.

I needed a boost of motivation and I found it when I checked the messages that had been posted to the website. 'I wish I was having as good a time as you!' from Chris, a cyclist from Britain who was also cycling along the Eurovelo 5 but a couple of weeks behind me. 'This is great!! I sincerely hope that I have the same experiences...while in Italy' from a Canadian cyclist who had been following me from the start and was planning his own trip for later in the year. 'You look as if you are doing well – I am most impressed!' from my boss back in the UK. And 'Mountains look magnificent!' from my cousin David.

Morale duly boosted, I climbed back on Reggie and set off once again.

I was still able to cycle in the band to the right of the carriageway but as I approached Benevento the volume of traffic increased substantially. What had started out as a jumped up minor road was now a dual carriageway with pretensions of becoming a motorway. Massimo had now texted me asking me to text him back when I arrived at a village called Ponte but by the time I had located the place on my map, I had cycled past the relevant exit. I later discovered that Massimo, following my Internet track on the website and seeing that it was probably not the best of ideas for me to continue on the major road towards Benevento was actually waiting for me in the village ready to escort me along a disused train line that had been converted into a cycle track. It was probably the first such path south of Rome and I had missed it completely only to continue on an increasingly dangerous highway going in the same direction. Had I known at the time, I would have kicked myself although that wouldn't have been the best of ideas as it could well have pushed me under a passing lorry of which there were now many.

I noticed on my map that the Telesina officially became a motorway as it approached Benevento so at that point I would have no choice but to use alternative roads. I felt as though I was in a kayak heading down the river to the Niagara Falls;

would I be able to escape the road before it became an autostrada?

To my relief and to the relief no doubt of the doctors and nurses of Benevento Hospital who would have had to try and piece me back together, I did manage to escape the Telesina before it was too late, following the centro signs all the way to the central Railway station in Benevento where I found a place to sit and texted Massimo to announce my arrival. A I waited for him to arrive, I scrolled through the statistics on Reggie's on board cycling computer;

Cycling time: 7 hrs 44 mins 5 secs

Distance: 171.55 kms

Average speed: 22.1 kms/hr

Bloody hell! I had cycled the equivalent of a trip from Reading, my home town in the Thames Valley to Birmingham. What a day. But it wasn't quite over yet.

I didn't mind waiting for Massimo in the least. When he did arrive I was a little surprised as he was in his late 30s - younger than I had expected. We chatted for a while and he explained his plan for the rest if the day. We would cycle off to the building where his cycling club was based and where I could shower. We would then cycle back into town to eat at Massimo's girlfriend's flat after which we were going to a concert. I wasn't sure about the last bit of the plan, but the rest sounded good. I was just happy to have made it to Benevento before night fall and in one piece. I had cycled well over 300km in the two days leading up to my arrival and it had clearly been a mistake. The offer of the farm stay accommodation in Sora had tempted me to cut the journey from Rome into two whereas a more rational decision would have been to divide it up into three days of cycling. But at least I had a full day off in Benevento to look forward to with my final online contact Massimo who, from first impressions, would be a good host for the next couple of days.

The cycling adrenaline must have still been pumping around my body as I didn't feel particularly tired once I had been given the chance to sit down, have a drink and eat something. The concert was a free one held in a village about half an hour's drive from Benevento. Taranta Power were a Mediterranean mix of musicians from different parts of this corner of Europe including an African rapper and it was all good foot-tapping stuff. Massimo had his flat in a small town called Apollosa a few kilometres away from Benevento and it was to there that we returned in the early hours of the following morning before I was finally allowed to crash into bed. Thankfully, that was the only collision I experienced all day.

Rest Day 6:

Wednesday 18th August 2010: Benevento

I'm not sure if I ever really understood Massimo.

As with Alain, Simone and Marcello, I had first come into contact with Massimo online. I had instigated chat forums on several bike touring sites notably the ones run by the CTC (Cyclists Touring Club), and Bike Radar in the hope of someone out there finding me and telling me just what I had to do to get from Reading to Brindisi along the Eurovelo 5. No one ever did which in the end made the experience so much more of an adventure. I did however attract a fair amount of chatter from others who were also interested in doing something similar and who had the same kind of questions. The forums were initially a swap shop of head scratching queries posed by the blind and responded to by the partially-sighted but over time they gradually developed into a useful resource of quality information.

One contributor was Massimo. He stood out just a little from the others because he could see in the Eurovelo 5 a potential business whereas the rest of us just considered it as an excuse for an extended holiday. He was very enthusiastic about the whole venture – that's what successful business people are like I suppose – and he considered my passage through Benevento as a real opportunity to promote long-distance cycling in the region of Campania.

I was very different from Massimo in my approach. The preparations were low key, the departure had been low key and it was only really once I hit the European mainland that a small but not insignificant amount of interest started to build amongst my online band of followers. This was to reach a modest peak of about 750 hits on the website on the final day of my journey. Not massive by Internet standards by any stretch of the imagination (and I was suspicious as to how many of those 750 visits were made by my mother wanting to know if I had arrived safely yet). Massimo, however, thought big from the outset.

He was a member of a local sports club and ran the website for the Benevento cycling association. My initial, tentative plan had identified Friday 20th August as the day upon which I would arrive in his home town. For Massimo this was perfect and he started to talk online about a 'European celebration' of cycling taking place on the Saturday and Sunday at which I would be the guest of honour. This was all very nice but I wasn't quite sure whether I wanted to be the guest of honour anywhere, let alone in a large town in southern Italy where I knew nobody and nobody knew me. What's more, the provisional schedule I had drawn up was just that; provisional. If I happened to arrive, let's say on the previous Tuesday evening, would Massimo expect me to hang around until the weekend? As soon as it looked likely that it would indeed be the Tuesday, I did make sure that he was aware of this but as his plans were always a little vague to say the least, I wasn't quite sure what lay in store for me when I did arrive. It was something that I had spent quite a bit of time thinking about as I cycled south. What exactly was Massimo planning? I hoped for something discrete but feared a cheering crowd waving the flag of the European Union, a massed choir singing Ode To Joy and a booking to be interviewed on the sofa of Buongiorno Campania!

At least that hadn't happened. Not yet anyway. Indeed the first evening with Massimo and his girlfriend Elena had been very pleasant indeed. Massimo had taken me in hand, ensured that I was fed and had somewhere to shower, entertained me at a cracking outdoor concert and then given me somewhere to sleep. I couldn't really complain. Far from it! So why did I still feel a little uneasy about everything?

Massimo lived in a village called Apollosa about 8km from the centre of Benevento. Before eating at Elena's flat on the previous evening, he had insisted that we go on a quick tour of the town by bike which culminated at the bus depot where he worked as the PR officer for the local bus company. It wouldn't be possible to leave Reggie at his girlfriend's flat or indeed at his flat in Apollosa so my dear travelling companion had to spend the night in Massimo's office in a deserted bus garage on the outskirts of town. I had never been separated from Reggie by such a great distance and for such a long period before. Holding back the tears, I bid Reggie adieu and we went off to the concert.

Massimo's flat was next to his parents' flat. His parents lived in Massimo's house which was somewhere else. So... while Massimo was spending the night in his parents' flat next door, I was in his flat. Does that make sense? Massimo's flat – the one in which I was sleeping – was an über bachelor pad with barely any furniture, plenty of man clutter/junk, a bathroom which indicated he showered elsewhere most of the time and a kitchen than only ever catered for the very occasional breakfast. Massimo's final instruction to me after the concert on the Tuesday night was to be at the bus stop next to the flat at midday where I should catch the bus. He would have a word with the driver when he arrived at work to make sure that I wouldn't have to buy a ticket and I would be told where to get off when the bus arrived in Benevento.

I dragged myself out of the flat at about 10am and started to wander up the hill into the village. I noticed that the bus stop was exactly where Massimo had indicated. I bought some breakfast in the local shop and sat in the sun in the middle of a small square with the village church behind me and the town hall to my right. I watched the life of a small southern Italian village go by; people were chatting outside the bar, old blokes had installed themselves for the day outside the municipio and of course some idiot went past and blew his horn for no reason whatsoever.

At around a quarter to twelve, I retraced my steps down the hill towards the bus stop and waited. I wondered what I would say to the driver to explain that I was the Englishman that Massimo had spoken to him about. I could do the 'buying a ticket' role-play in Italian but not the one that involved a complicated discussion about 'arrangements' having been made meaning I wouldn't have to pay anything. If the worst came to the worst, I would just pay up and get off at an appropriate place in the centre of Benevento. But the bus never appeared, or at least not the one that I expected.

Remember that Massimo worked for the bus company. The bus depot was full of what you would expect; big buses. Orange ones. None of these buses turned up in Apollosa. At one point a small minibus did pause for a few moments further up the road from the bus stop. Two women got off and it drove away immediately. It didn't however escape me that the name Mazzone was written on the side of the vehicle. Mazzone was Massimo's family name.

Eventually I texted Massimo explaining that the bus had never arrived. Perhaps a bus being late by 30 minutes in southern Italy was not actually 'late'. He texted me back suggesting that I either hitch my way back to Benevento or I just hang around in the village and he would pick me up later.

I chose the latter option and by 1pm I found myself sitting in a caffetteria on the other side of the village called La Rotonda eating a processed ham and cheese sandwich with a sell by date of the 24th September! If the likes of Sainsbury and Tesco knew it were possible to make sandwiches with a sell by date at least a month into the future they'd have them on the shelves before you could say 'what's that strange taste of plastic?' You better keep it to yourself.

Before indigestion could set it, Massimo arrived in his car and I jumped into the back. In the front passenger seat was Aitza, a Spanish cyclist. Massimo had mentioned that she would be arriving today and I assumed she was all part of his plans for the 'Eurovelo Celebration' that he had not yet mentioned. She was an accountant back in Spain and had just come from spending a week in Naples where she had been attending an Italian language school. After a couple of days being looked after by Massimo, she was planning on heading to the east coast to work in a hostel. Choosing to work in a hostel during your holidays puts accountancy into context quite well I think. She was young, petite, pretty and bronzed. I wondered what Elena had to say about her arrival in town. Massimo quickly explained the confusion with the bus; the local company didn't serve outlying villages like Apollosa and this is where his father's bus company had stepped in, hence the name on the side of the minibus. Massimo worked for both companies...

The three of us drove to Elena's flat and just as she had done on the previous evening, she prepared a delicious pasta dish; simple but perfect for lunch for a hot Italian day. I then snoozed on the sofa (it was my day off!) occasionally mustering the energy to spot Massimo on the Internet trying to find cheap flights for me from southern Italy to the UK. After having looked up the ticket prices when I was in Rome, I had told him earlier that at this late stage a cheap flight just wasn't available and that I would have to pay through the nose but he was having none of it! After eventually dragging myself back to life it was of little surprise to me when he announced that the cheapest flights were indeed from either Bari or Brindisi but they were far from cheap. I bought one for the following Tuesday. It was a sad sign that the end of my trip was nigh...

I was still waiting for the hinted at great events to take place to mark my arrival. I was of course quite happy for them not to do so and never mentioned them myself but Massimo liked to be in control and I was getting the distinct impression that everything and everyone around him was run on a need to know basis. I didn't need to know what he had planned for my remaining 24 hours in Benevento and he didn't seem to have any intention of telling me in any way you could describe as detailed. What I did know was that the rest of the day would be spent exploring the town itself and there was some mention of a cycle ride with members of his club that evening. What I didn't know was that Massimo was going to leave Aitza and myself to our own devices that afternoon. We were informed that we should return to Elena's flat at 8pm and I was pointed in the direction of the town centre. Aitza didn't join me as Massimo had to escort her to a sports shop to buy some shorts. This never got mentioned over lunch with Elena.

Benevento was a smallish place which was just beginning to liven up after its afternoon siesta. It had a nice triumphal arch from Roman times and a pleasant pedestrianised shopping area. I looked for a tourist office so as to be pointed in the direction of the town's other charms but couldn't find one. As a result, I couldn't find them either. It was a very long afternoon.

I felt quite trapped for the first time in weeks. My life was being controlled by a man who wasn't great when it came to collective decision making, I couldn't just leave as Reggie was (hopefully) still tethered to a water pipe back at the bus depot and I had no access to most of my things which were some 8km away in Apollosa. It wasn't turning out to be one of the highlights of my journey along the Eurovelo 5. I had been deposited in a nice but far from exciting town in southern Italy where there seemed to be bugger all to do and there was still another four hours to fill before we were expected to report back to Elena's flat. I searched in vain for anything resembling an Internet café but couldn't find one. At least it would have been nice to spend the time catching up on the messages that people had been sending and even replying to a few of them. Mind you, even if I had found a place to get online, would the strict access laws allow me to do so? I eventually managed to do so by standing outside the largest apartment block I could find and scanning for an unsecured Wi-Fi network. Much to my surprise I found quite a few and proceeded to spend the next hour or so hanging on a street corner pushing buttons on my phone. The fact that no passing curb-crawlers ever made me an offer says much for my bedraggled state after a month on the road.

After what seemed like an eternity, I rendez-voused with Aitza back outside Elena's flat and we waited. And waited. And waited just a little bit more. Darkness began to fall and eventually Massimo arrived in his car. In his first breath he announced that it wouldn't be possible for Reggie to remain at the bus depot overnight as he was not going to be able to go into work the following morning. Why? Well, we weren't privy of course to that level of high security information. We also needed to pick up a bike for Aitza to use the following day (what was happening then?) back at the sports club where I had showered the previous evening. This was a complicated logistical operation as only Massimo and Elena knew where the various places were around town, it was getting very dark and there was some debate as to whether Reggie and Elena's borrowed bike would fit in any of the various cars we had at our disposal. Aitza and I, after having spent an afternoon of doing very little indeed were now plunged into a frenzy of activity simply because Massimo was still intent on keeping control of us all. Not only that but I started to detect a certain amount of tension brewing between him and Elena. Please don't have a marital, I thought.

The next few hours are a blur in my memory. It involved many vehicle movements, lots of quizzical looks between Aitza and myself and even more sterner looks directed at Massimo by Elena. The evening ended by poor Elena, who was quite tall, cycling in the pitch black of night on a bike made for a short person without any lights because it wouldn't fit into any of the cars. It was with some relief to say the very least that we were able to close the door of the Mazzone travel agents (yes, that was part of the family empire too), Reggie and his new temporary friend securely locked inside. We didn't eat; we didn't have time to do so with all the comings and goings.

Aitza stayed at Elena's flat that night and Massimo and I returned to the flats in Apollosa. I dreaded what plans my host had for the morning but of course, whatever they were, they remained a mystery to me.

Cycling Day 27:

Thursday 19th August 2010: Benevento to The Laghi Di Monticchio

6 hours 56 minutes in the saddle, 116 kilometres

I was about to find what I had been searching for since leaving the UK. But before I did, I had to spend my last few hours under Massimo's control.

It had been decided (well, Massimo had decided and Aitza and I had our suggestions swept aside by the great man) that the three of us would cycle east along a circular cycle route that would tick my box of progressing along the Eurovelo 5 but also fulfil the requirements of Massimo and Aitza who needed to return to Benevento later in the day. In fairness, it was a good plan and I tried to put the events of the previous day to one side as we started to climb the hill that would lead us down into the valley towards Grottaminarda the town where we agreed that we would go our separate ways.

Being only a medium-sized town set in the midst of the Campania, it was only a matter of minutes before we were cycling on a deserted country road along a stunningly beautiful valley. The terrain was now hilly rather than mountainous but the vistas from our position high on the side of the valley were just as spectacular as those to be found in more topographically-challenged areas. The silence – there was no major road in the valley bottom to provide a background hum – was only punctuated by the noise of southern Europe; birds, insects, the light breeze against the low trees and bushes and the purring of our bicycles. The land itself was light brown and marked with the tell-tale lines of a harvest having recently taken place. One crop that had been growing in abundance was tobacco and as we cycled higher into the valley we passed strange barns with no walls but with cubes stacked one on top of each other and containing row after row of dark green tobacco leaves which had been hung up to dry. We British rarely see anything in our fields

274

that doesn't end up being eaten or drunk but in Campania the growing of tobacco is just as important as a herd of dairy cows might be back in the English shires. Things may however be about to change. The last European subsidies paid directly to tobacco farmers were in 2010 and it will be interesting to see how the industry fares when it is no longer supported by the European taxpayer. For we northern Europeans, it's an indignant thought that any money was every paid to any tobacco farmer in the first place but here in the south of Europe, livelihoods depend upon the killer crop and it's easy to see why they probably have a completely different attitude towards its cultivation.

Ever the man to spring a surprise, Massimo suddenly announced that we would be paying a visit to one of his friends who lived on a small holding in the valley bottom. So, just as we were beginning to make good progress vertically as well as horizontally, we descended the short but annoying distance to Apice to be introduced to Paolo and Luisa. They were charm personified and showered us with the fruits of their land, literally; figs, apricots, plums and cherries all washed down with home-made lemonade and strong coffee. We were taken on a short guided tour of the orchard of trees, continuing to pick as we walked. Paolo's attention was, just as Massimo's had been on the previous day, drawn towards Aitza's Hispanic charms and I played the bit part of the photographer as the visit ended with her being held aloft in celebratory fashion. It was very unclear what was being celebrated however. Wasn't I the one who had just cycled nearly 3,000 kilometres? That said, even the sturdy Paolo would have struggled to lift me aloft in a way he was able to do with petite Aitza. Before we had chance to start rolling our own cigars (Luisa must surely have had a hidden corner growing tobacco where she could slope off for a crafty fag every once in a while), we left the small farm and retraced our tracks back up to the road to continue the journey towards Grottaminarda.

For most of the morning I had held up the rear of our small group alongside Aitza who, with a smaller bike wasn't able to keep going at the same speed as Massimo. He very often cycled on ahead and would periodically wait for us. He didn't do so out loud, but I could see his mind tutting every time we approached him and when we arrived, he would immediately cycle on before giving us the chance of benefitting from the short rest that had been imposed upon him. Eventually the climb flattened out and I could see ahead of us the long slope of the road as it fell into the next valley. Recognising that this would be a good point to cool off in the breeze of a long, freewheeling cycle, I overtook Aitza and Massimo and, making the most of the fact that Reggie, laden not only with me but also four heavy panniers could pick up a decent speed on an incline, sped off down the hill and into the distance. After a few minutes I arrived at the bottom and at a junction. My map told me that Grottaminarda was just a few hundred metres away if I turned right and as it had been agreed that we should use the place as the point where we would split and go in our separate ways, I cycled the short distance into the centre of the small town itself to sit and await their arrival.

They never did join me. I waited for around half an hour before concluding that Massimo was probably beginning to read the signs of my frustration with his autocratic style. For over four weeks I had been making my own decisions, deciding where to go, what time to start and stop, how often to eat, when to pause and ogle the view, where to stay and who to talk to. Although Alain, Simone and Marcello had all guided me, at no point until I arrived in Benevento had I felt under the control of another person. Unfortunately, it simply wasn't in Massimo's character to guide; he was a leader and needed to set the agenda. I was happy for that to happen on my first night in Benevento but it had been verging on the rude to leave Aitza and me in the town centre on the previous day without access to our luggage and in my case, my means of transport, poor old Reggie. I can only surmise that Massimo and Aitza turned left at the junction and made their way back to Benevento. For Aitza's sake, I do hope that Massimo let her off the leash for her remaining couple of days in his company. And that Elena stopped being suspicious as to why he had invited her to Benevento in the first place.

Perhaps it was accentuated by my release back into the free world, but that afternoon as I continued to cross Campania and eventually poke my toes into the neighbouring region of Basilicata at the Laghi di Monticchio I felt as though the adventure part of my journey had finally kicked in big time. The land was rugged and barren, the towns and villages windswept and desolate, the heat was chronic and I was a long way from home. As the crow flies it was still under 2,000km back to Berkshire but as Reggie cycled it was now exactly 3,000km. The digital odometer clicked over from 2,999.9km to a three and lots of zeros on a non-descript road (the SS399 for the record) just outside the village of Piani San Pietro. The ride to that point had been equally memorable as I picked my way along a long valley bottom finally climbing towards a high plain where I was surrounded by hundreds of busy wind turbines near the town of Bisaccia.

Many people harbour a deep loathing for these modern day generators of power, especially in England where their number is still lamentable. In the whole of the southern region of England which stretches from Brighton in the east to Portland in the west and from the Isle of Wight in the south to Oxford in the north, there remains just one commercially-sized turbine. Yes, one. It's next to the M4 in my home town of Reading. The country as a whole produces only 5,500 megawatts of power through wind power compared to Germany's 27,000 and Spain's 20,000. Admittedly the figure for Italy only just eclipses that of the UK at 5,800 megawatts of power but hang on! People travel to Italy because it has beautiful weather; calm, still days drenched in sun. We can't really say the same for the UK, can we? Britain is widely acknowledged as being the windiest place in Europe so we should be up there with Germans and

Spaniards leading the way just as we were during the industrial revolution when we harnessed the power of the rivers by building water mills and connected them to the factories that made us a prosperous nation.

Apart from the fact that they are by far the best way to produce electricity, they are also things of great beauty. For decades we have been stretching power cables from ugly pylon to ugly pylon across some of the most beautiful countryside on Earth in order that you and I can switch on our TVs and boil our kettles whenever we choose. There is a great irony in us allowing that to have happened and then protesting at the installation of an elegant wind turbine across the very same stretch of land. It's also a very neat way of allowing the rural communities that for such a long time have been at the wrong end of the wedge of technological revolution to make a positive, high-tech contribution to the 21st century economy. In this little corner of Campania, the turbines came in all shapes and sizes. It was almost like a beauty contest with each thin construction strutting its stuff against the stunning backdrop of the deep blue sky. Stunningly modern and beautiful.

Not that I had found a place with everything. It would have been nice for example, to have found some food in the sizeable town of Aquilonia which was handily placed along the descent from the high position of the turbines. It was a modern town but the planners had clearly forgotten to squeeze in room for a shop or even a small bar. You can hear the discussion as the builders finally handed over the keys to the town council;

'School – tick, church – tick, town hall – tick, doctors – tick, library – tick, flower shop – tick... I think that's it Giuseppe, let's go down the bar for a drink to celebrate... Damn!'

'Not to worry Ricardo, I have to get home to the wife; it's her birthday and I need to pop to the shop for some chocolates... Damn!'

Even one small Mars bar at that point would have been pounced upon like a lion onto a wildebeest but I wasn't going to find one in Aquilonia. Sustenance was desperately needed as at the end of the rugged descent towards the border with Basilicata, there was a nice sting in the tail of my day in the saddle; a gruelling 10km ride up a 400m climb along switchback roads first through Monticchio Bagni and then to the Laghi di Monticchio themselves.

My phone app had told me there would be a place to camp somewhere at the lakes but I'd heard that one before and this was a pretty remote area. As I neared the top of the volcanic hill in which the lakes have now formed I did, much to my relief pass a hotel which I noted as a possible plan B but hoped that I would be camping. The area reminded me a little of the Vosges mountains where I had spent the night prior to my arrival in Strasbourg; remote, beautiful and green. The perfect place to camp but there was a key difference between here and the Vosges; it wasn't throwing it down, which meant that this was even more perfect. A thick ring of trees separated the lakes from the road so when I arrived at the top, I still wasn't able to see them. The road itself circumnavigated the round body of water and when I arrived at the northern end of the lake, I took an anti-clockwise route. After about a kilometre of slowly curving around the lake - which I still wasn't able to see - I came to a turning on my left – the direction of one of the lakes – and a sign; 'Parco Naturale Europa' it announced alongside a red triangle of a tent. On the other side of the entrance a second sign confirmed that I had indeed found a camp-site; 'camping' it said, in English.

Relieved to have found somewhere to stay the night, there were a couple of worrying aspects. I seemed to be the only person around and the large metal gate that spanned the entrance was closed. This was the middle of August; where were all the other campers? On closer investigation there was a second, smaller gate to one side of the main gate and this was open. I pushed Reggie through and towards a hut that was marked as the reception. Not that there was anyone around to do the welcoming and anyway, that too was shut. I could, however, see the lake for the first time at the far end of the park beyond another hut where there were some people sat around wooden picnic benches eating. The hut, from what I could see, was serving food and drink, a sight which almost made me throw Reggie to the ground, run over and devour the first thing I could grab hold of. At that point, the man serving noticed me, came out from behind the counter and over to the reception.

'Buongiorno' he said.

'Buongiorno' I replied and yet again failed to convince anyone in Italy I was anything but British as he proceeded to speak to me in English without even questioning the fact.

'But where are all the other campers?' I enquired after being told that I could stay the night.

'There are a few. They are around the other side of the wash-block, near the lake.'

'Does anyone work here during the night?'

'No. I will be leaving in about an hour and after that there will be someone in the morning from about 9 o'clock.'

I couldn't get out of my mind those American horror films where a group of friends go camping at a deserted lake and then in turn, each one gets brutally murdered during the night. But what could I do otherwise? Rationalising that I probably wasn't going to get hacked to death by a disgruntled Vietnam war veteran wearing a creepy mask in southern Italy, I went through the formalities of checking in and made my way towards the lake.

It was unbelievably beautiful. Circular, with the opposite shore not even a kilometre away it was ringed by low, deeply wooded hills. The water was barely moving and reflected almost perfectly the contours on the near horizon. A rowing boat was resting nonchalantly, half in the water, half on land and a slightly larger boat resting peacefully to one side waiting to ferry people across to the other side the following morning. To my left was a large open area where I could see three or four tents and a caravan. They were spaced out widely and it would be a tricky job trying to work out exactly where to pitch my own little home. Before I did, I took a few moments to take a photo of the serene scene before me. It lacked the drama of many of the views that I had cast my eyes upon over the previous few weeks but this was by far the most gorgeous, most perfect, most awe-inspiring thing I had seen since setting off. The colours, the light, the sky, the land and the water had all come together to create the perfect, intimate view.

I wanted to share the photo via the website but I couldn't; there was, of course, no mobile signal here in this remote corner of countryside. That, I thought, was the icing on the cake. I had finally found a point of escape. All along my journey, I had not known what I was looking for but this was it. Remote, relaxing, quiet and beautiful. Just perfect.

If someone had tooted their horn at that point I would probably have gone into murderous Vietnam war veteran mode myself, but fortunately they didn't. I pitched the tent, bought some beers and some food from the snack bar before it shut and sat by the lake delighting in what I had found and delighting in my trip which was now entering its final few days.

Cycling Day 28:

Friday 20th August 2010: The Laghi Di Monticchio to Matera

6 hours 47 minutes in the saddle, 128 kilometres

I didn't need any excuses to wake up in the middle of the night; over the several weeks of on-off camping, I had mastered the art of interrupting any spell of slumber lasting more than half an hour without any outside intervention whatsoever. So the assistance I was afforded by the packs of wolves howling in the distance and from the smaller pack of night-time fishermen was unnecessary but nevertheless annoying. The wolves were only doing just what nature intended them to do (although I remain oblivious as to why). The fishermen on the other hand were doing what their leisure-time activity manual told them to do and from which it was entirely possible to opt out. There were three of them, all in their 30s, from Germany and all of whom had a heavily made-up girlfriend on hand to cook the poor fish once they had been plucked from the lake. The fish that is rather than the girlfriends. I had seen them setting up their long rods during the evening and it was a complex arrangement of poles, sensors and electronic devices. What happened, I wondered, to sitting next to the river with a length of string attached to a short piece of wood? No rod activity took place during the evening, at least not with the ones dangling over the water. In the early hours however, I started to hear loud electronic beeps followed by a frenzy of human movement, muffled but high-speed conversations, zips being zipped and then people running and panting. Sid James would have been in his element. Having seen the men set up earlier however, my imagination didn't have to go into overdrive for logic to lead me to a different conclusion to that of Sid's. It was all a bit excessive and quite frankly, cheating. If you want to night fish then fill yourself up with black coffee and sit by the water; don't let sensors and beeps do the job for you. I did hope they had been unsuccessful but as they were still sleeping soundly when I left Parco

Naturale Europa just after 7.30, I never had the chance to exchange smug glances with them.

Had I turned left and made my way around the larger of the two lakes in a clockwise direction on the previous evening, I may have come to a slightly different conclusion as to how tranquil a place I had discovered. On leaving the campsite and completing most of what remained of the circular road around the lake I discovered a strip of bars, cafés and restaurants to rival even the liveliest of southern Italian towns. At breakfast time however, all the establishments were still shuttered but clearly there was a less sedate side to the Laghi di Monticchio if you came at the right time of day.

I turned south and started my journey away from the lakes in the direction of Rionero in Vulture, a town on the opposite side of the Monte Vulture. The references to 'vulture' made me wonder if a large, ugly bird would sweep down from the sky and carry me off. Soon however I was more concerned with the animals I could see on the road in front of me rather than what was or most likely wasn't in the sky above me. The wolves I had heard in the far distance during the night had made their way much closer to the lakes, presumably to scavenge discarded food from the tourists who were about to descend upon the area. I tried to play it cool as Reggie and I glided past the point where they were lingering and fortunately their noses were more interested in what they had found on the floor rather than the juicy piece of living meat that was cycling up the hill just a few metres away.

After an initial short climb, it was a much longer descent into Rionero where the Friday market was in full swing. My aim was to make it as far as Matera by the end of the day. Matera is a World Heritage site with houses built into the rock of the valley where it stands but I found it difficult to make a decision as to which route to take. I had been climbing a lot in recent days and yearned for a nice flat bit of cycling but I couldn't pick out a route that was both sufficiently direct and avoided the hills between Rionero and Matera. Food usually did the trick when it came to decision-making so I took up position outside a modern café overlooking the buying and selling of the market and filled up on pastries and an espresso coffee. It worked; I decided to head off in the direction of Venosa but before doing so I joined the throng of the market to buy a peach that washed my breakfast down well as it melted into liquid upon contact with my mouth. You can't beat a continental peach, certainly compared to the cannonballs we have to break our teeth on in the UK.

My choice of flatter, longer route made for slow progress which was confirmed when I took a few moments out to compare the as-the-crow-flies distance that I could estimate using the map with the number of kilometres recorded on Reggie's on-board computer. On arrival in Venosa, the former was standing at 20km, the latter at 35km. The point to point distance from the Laghi di Monticchio to Matera was about 90km so I groaned as I sat down in the main square upon realising that although it was already nearly lunchtime, I wasn't even a quarter of the way along my route!

As I tucked into a high-calorie boost courtesy of an ice-cream, Reggie rested to my side leaning against the wall of the café. Since his technical problems in Switzerland and northern Italy during the third week of the journey, he had been working well but ever wary that even at this late stage the hand of fate could deal a fatal blow to my plan to complete my journey as far as Brindisi, I took a rare decision to spend a few minutes giving him the once over. If you read bike repair manuals and choose to follow them to the letter you would end up spending more time checking for faults (and presumably preventing them before they got serious) than you would actually cycling. You are certainly encouraged to do basic checks before every single ride and then there are lists of things that need to be done every week, every month and then, if there is anything left to do, every year. So far on the trip however, my alternative method of looking after Reggie seemed to be working just as well. This could be summed up as follows; ignore him until he started screaming. It wasn't so much for Reggie's peace of mind that I took this radical approach, more for mine and let's face it is a typical 'man' attitude when it comes to anything medical. OK, I had suffered in terms of time and anguish when his spokes had broken and I had to make arrangements for them to be repaired, but for the rest of the trip I remained serenely ignorant of any developing issues and this only helped keep me in a calm holiday mood. That said, there was one new element that had entered the equation of my trip along the Eurovelo 5 which was that I now had a ticket for a flight back to the UK for the following Tuesday morning. It was Friday and I didn't want to arrive in Puglia, meet my friends Basil and Liz and then immediately jump on a plane. A couple of days of rest, relaxation, good food and good wine were in the back of my mind. Any mechanical hiccups at this stage could potentially flush this tentative plan down the toilet so I checked Reggie in a way that neither of us were accustomed to. I felt like the most junior of junior doctors taking part in his first ever intimate examination. Tyres were OK, chain was still greased and the brakes were fine. Dare I examine the wheels? The front one spun perfectly but the back one did have a distinct wobble. Was this a hangover from the work carried out by the mechanics in Airolo and Parma or was it a sign of something, probably another spoke, going wrong. I plucked each spoke individually and all seemed fine but I would have to keep a careful eye upon the wobbliness as I made my way towards the coast over the next couple of days. If I had been a doctor, it would have been a case of asking the patient to come back in a couple of weeks if the condition got worse but quite frankly, as Reggie's first stop back in Britain was the shop where we had first met for a full and sustained session of mechanical attention and therapy, that was fine by me. Reggie didn't seem to argue either.

The further I travelled south and east, the more distant were the towns and villages from each other and they became little oasis of replenishment. The square in Venosa which I had turned into a temporary bicycle medical centre even had a couple of palm trees making the oasis analogy even more apt. My guidebook informed me that Venosa was the largest colony of the Roman world '...in its time', whenever that was and that it was the birthplace of Quintus Horatius Flaccus who must still be grumbling in his tomb that we have shortened such a majestic name to simply Horace. He was a Roman poet by the way but don't worry, I wouldn't have been able to tell you that either had I not had my book at hand.

With still three-quarters (as-the-crow flies!) of the day ahead of me, I made tracks out of Quintus Horatius Flaccus' home town and continued cycling south-east. Following a gentle descent from Venosa I joined the main road to Spinazzola. It was a good quality road that allowed me to bank quickly some desperately-needed kilometres.

Spinazzola would have been my first town in Puglia had I chosen to turn left before continuing to Gravina in Puglia but from a distance it didn't shout 'stop here and write something whimsical about me on your blog'. So I didn't. I did however make a stop at Spinazzola's most unfriendly service station to buy two bottles of water. The woman behind the counter didn't even ring my 3€ into the till, a till whose money drawer seemed to be permanently open. This despite there being two policemen standing at the bar having a drink. What happened to the Italian regulation requiring everyone to keep hold of their receipt within 100m of where the purchase had been made? Fully laden with illicitly-purchased water I set off across the desert of Puglia. That was no exaggeration. Hot, arid and barren. All it needed were a few snakes and David Attenborough in a linen suit with a film crew in tow to prove me right. Many of the farmers had decided to burn off the stubble from their land and at one point the flames were just next to the road. If I had paused, I'm not sure who would have melted first; me or Reggie. The tent, strapped above the back wheel would have dissolved into the ground quicker than the Wicked Witch of the West.

36km later with a slight sunburn on the exposed parts of the right-hand side of my body I approached Gravina in Puglia.

Certain names conjured up images of certain kinds of places and with a name like Gravina in Puglia, this town was certainly in that category. Lime-washed houses and marble-clad squares hosting ancient cathedrals and stunning arcades? It was just a shame that in Gravina's case it was a bit of a dump. Think Mad Max (we'll come back to Mel Gibson in a few moments by the way) with more litter. I did need sustenance however and sat outside an ice-cream bar consuming a delicious melon, lemon and peach cone wondering if it counted as three of my five-a-day. It struck me that there was a killing to be made in Italy for anyone who decided to open up the first 24 hour shop. My choice of places to eat at 3pm was either the ice-cream parlour or, err... well, that was it. There is a niche in the Italian market that someone, someday will exploit. Probably Tesco.

There is a patron saint of cyclists. She is called the Madonna del Ghisallo and had I known this on the day that I was passing through Como a few weeks earlier, I would have paid her small church in a place called Magréglio a visit. It is, apparently, quite a tourist attraction for passing cyclists (who know about it) and is filled with cycling banners and even bikes in memorial to those who have perished on the roads. This being the 21st century, the Madonna del Ghisallo has a Facebook page all of her own, but then again, so does Reggie.

Why is all this relevant? Well, the Madonna del Ghisallo was smiling down upon Reggie and myself that morning as we left Gravina. Not only was the road to Matera predominantly flat, it was slightly downhill for more or less the entire journey. My decision to have taken what looked like the flatter but longer route was finally paying off and I was able to tick off the kilometres more quickly than you could say 'thank God for a Catholic obsession with iconography'.

Late in the afternoon as I approached what I thought was Matera I started to ask myself two questions; What is that horrible place over there on my left? and Why is it not on my map?. All I could see were modern apartment blocks raising their ugly heads out of the desert. No sign of any houses built into the rock, but as I neared the blot on the landscape the signs confirmed what I didn't want to know; it was indeed Matera. Not at all what I had expected. I continued up the long hill that lead me to the centre of the development contenting myself in the knowledge that the centro signs had still not run out so I was able to remain hopeful of an improvement in my surroundings. After battling through the suburbs, they eventually did and I discovered the delightful historic centre of Matera a few minutes later.

There was something quaintly biblical about the main square in the old part of town. There was nothing grand about it, just old two and three story buildings with trees sporadically placed around its long thin shape. There was a small fountain in the middle next to which was a simple arch leading to a panoramic terrace. I didn't really have the time to linger and take in much of the view but what I could see was a striking; a valley full of small houses tightly-packed one on top of the other. Clearly I would have to come back after having found some accommodation but it was immediately evident to understand why Mel Gibson had come here to make his film The Passion of The Christ. This was a little piece of the Holy Land in southern Europe and quite a significant jewel in Italy's crown.

The tourist office took one look at me in my increasingly shabby Lycra, sweating from the afternoon's exertions and pointed me in the direction of the bed and breakfast accommodation. I informed them that I preferred a hotel, and not a crap one at that! Well, OK, I didn't, but that's what I wanted them to read in my facial expression. I was ready to launch into 'do you know that I have just cycled all the way from London and this is my last night on the road...' rant but held back. They suggested a hotel which was actually back in Mel Gibson's part of town so I pushed Reggie along the windy alleys, down two levels of houses and found the hotel. It was very 'boutique' and I begun to regret my clearly very effective facial expression back at the tourist office. Although my taste may have been 'boutique', my budget certainly wasn't so when they informed me they were completo it wasn't a crushing blow.

But that did still leave me with the problem of finding somewhere else. I wandered around for a while but couldn't find anything that didn't have a completo sign in the window. After all these days of successfully finding accommodation across Europe, had I finally met my match? I reached for my guidebook which came up with a few suggestions but the ones I tried were also full, even the Italia '...where Mel Gibson and his cast stayed and the best option if you don't fancy sleeping in a cave'. I was sure the boutique place wouldn't refer to their rooms as 'caves'.

Feeling a little dejected, I continued to stroll around the town centre. It would be such a pity to end up staying back in those horrid suburbs I had seen earlier. Suddenly on the right, only a few metres up a street just opposite to where the tourist office was located in the main square, appeared the '4-star' Hotel San Domenica. What the hell? I thought. This is my last night on the road and I'll blow the budget in style. They even had a red carpet up the short flight of steps leading to the main entrance so leaving Reggie tethered to a tree on the street, I stepped inside. Expecting a three-figure number for the price I almost squealed with delight when the guy behind the desk informed me a room would only be 80€. Not only had I been blessed that day by the patron saint of cycling, the patron saint of finding somewhere to sleep (she must exist!) had yet again and for the final time seen fit to kiss my perspiring brow.

When I reappeared from the hotel an hour or so later, having managed to transform myself from weathered cyclist to stylish traveller for almost the last time, the passeggiata was in full swing. I joined the Italians, strolling around, pausing briefly at a small canteen on the Via del Corso to eat a large slice of pizza and then at a small bar in the square for a beer. I could barely wipe the smile off my face; I was nearly there!

Cycling Day 29:

Saturday 21st August 2010: Matera to Cisternino

4 hours 39 minutes in the saddle, 90 kilometres

I had started out with eleven pristine 1:200,000 maps bundled neatly together with a thick rubber band. I envisaged that I would finish the trip with eleven rather ragged-looking maps bundled not-so-neatly together in similar fashion. But it didn't quite work out that way. Once I had cycled off the end of a particular map I was more than happy to screw it up and throw it into the nearest bin. There was something far more satisfying in doing it that way rather than putting the map back at the bottom of the stack. I had also taken to cutting off any unnecessary parts of the map that I was using the result being that all that I was left with in the hotel room in Matera on my penultimate morning of the trip was a thin strip of paper showing the route due east from Matera to Brindisi.

The distance between the two was only about 130km, the terrain would be flat and the roads direct. I had already cycled more than that distance on at least half a dozen occasions in the previous 28 days of cycling so I could have been dipping my toes into the Adriatic by some time later that day. However, my friends Basil and Liz lived in a small town called Cisternino about 50km west of Brindisi so it made more sense to cut the final leg of my journey into two, pausing overnight in Cisternino and then making my triumphal entrance into Brindisi on Sunday morning.

But before doing any of that, I needed to spend a little more time exploring Mel Gibson's film set so, after checking out of the hotel and paying only 60€ for my room (I had a single and the 80€ tariff had been for a double – result!) I returned to the Belvedere Luigi Guerricchio viewpoint to study the Sassi of Matera in a little more detail.

The word sassi translates as stones but this was no pile of discarded rubble. The area is a World Heritage Site and

UNESCO describe the Sassi as '...an outstanding example of a rock-cut settlement, adapted perfectly to its geomorphological setting and its ecosystem and exhibiting continuity over more than two millennia. They represent an outstanding example of a traditional human settlement and land use showing the evolution of a culture that has maintained over time a harmonious relationship with its natural environment'. You can see why UNESCO have never branched out into the guide book market. Basically, the Sassi are a bunch of houses built into the rock of a gorge, one on top of another over many, many centuries. The resulting chaotic mish-mash of buildings and lanes is fascinating to a passing tourist but can't be anything but a vision of hell to the local postman who must scratch his head every time he arrives in town. The view was truly amazing and there was so much to look at; it was the architectural equivalent of a Where's Wally? cartoon (without, as far as I could see, Wally) with an air of repetition but where, on closely inspection, not a house, roof, wall, window or terrace was exactly the same. The original troglodyte dwellings were dug out of the soft tufa rock, a kind of limestone that was also used to build the houses and churches that now cover each side of the valley. The soft light brown colour of this rock made the entire place shine like a new penny under the gaze of the morning sun. I had immediately thought I had stepped into the Holy Land on arrival in the old part of Matera on the previous evening and this impression was only being embedded by what I could see now.

It was why Mel and his crew had come here to film The Passion of The Christ but also why many other film makers had passed this way rather than to more unstable Palestine or Israel to film their own biblically-themed oeuvres. That said, one film that was made in Matera which, despite its name, didn't have a direct link to the time of Jesus was Francesco Rosi's interpretation of Carlo Levi's 1945 novel Cristo si è Fermato a Eboli or Christ Stopped at Eboli. Levi's book is autobiographical and recounts his experiences of being a doctor in an impoverished town in southern Italy in the mid 1930s to where he had been exiled for his anti-fascist views. The notion of Christ stopping at Eboli, a town near Salerno in the west of Italy, was used to emphasise how in the very south of the Italy, life had changed little since medieval times with people leading abandoned, primitive lives. This is certainly how people lived in the Sassi of Matera until the government started to forcibly re-house families (partly as a result of the impact of Carlo Levi's book) in more modern apartment blocks away from the squalor of the valley in the 1950s. These were no doubt the ones that I had seen on my arrival in town from the west on the previous day. But some people did stay put in the sassi and it wasn't until the 1990s when someone at the town council woke up one day and realised that they could have a tourist gold mine sitting in the very heart of their town that the boutique hotels started to move in.

I was sceptical as to whether I would be able to get any closer to the buildings of the sassi without having to wheel Reggie down countless flights of twisting steps. With his dodgy back wheel in mind I wanted to avoid such a tortuous and bumpy mini adventure. In addition, I was unsure as to how I would be able to return to the top of the valley once I had made it to the bottom; if this meant re-negotiating the same steep steps, I would have to be content with the view from the panoramic terrace. That said, I could see cars in one of the lanes below me so I decided to give it a try. If I met any steps I would simply have to turn back.

After several minutes of twisting and turning lanes which were mercifully stair-free, I was able to get Reggie and myself to the other side of the valley and then to the bottom of the settlement from where it was possible to inspect the buildings from much closer quarters. The lanes had actually been well-cobbled and everywhere I looked were shiny BMWs and Mercedes cars. My initial scepticism had been misplaced to say the least; who else would be frequenting the chic hotels, bars and restaurants to be found in the sassi other than the middle classes with their big, air-conditioned vehicles? A well-paved access road was probably the first thing that had been built once the decision to assist the area in dragging itself out of abject poverty had been made. It was interesting to note however, that the transition from working-class slum to top holiday destination was still very much a work-in-progress with many buildings, especially on the periphery of the area still derelict with boards up stating that they were for sale. So, if you fancy a little holiday retreat in the south of Italy with cracking views, a fantastic cellar in which to keep your wine cool and an interesting back story to boot, you know where to go. Just don't expect your birthday cards to be delivered on time by a cheerful postie.

By the time I was ready to hit the road, it was still only 10 o'clock and few tourists or indeed locals had yet to venture out onto the streets. It was a Saturday and all that passeggiata night-time strolling can certainly take it out of you so I left the residents of Matera, both temporary and permanent, to their beds and caves, made my way out of town, returned to the main road and headed east.

Actually, my route was initially north-east as coming to Matera had been a little detour off the general route towards Cisternino and Brindisi but it wasn't too long before I crossed the provincial border taking me from Matera to Bari and in doing so back into Puglia for proper. I had, if you remember, rolled Reggie's tyres into Puglia on the previous day when I had stopped at Spinazzola's unfriendly service station and paused at Gravina-in-Puglia's only open purveyor of nutrition, an ice-cream parlour. But here I was doing it properly, heading into my final region of the trip for good. The terrain was just as flat, the heat just as intense and the towns just as distant from each other as they had been on the previous day. At Santeramo in Colle, my direction changed and for the remainder of that day's cycling I would be heading along one long, continuous road due east towards Cisternino, a journey only punctuated with the occasional medium-sized town at which I would pause for quick pit-stop.

The first of these was Gioia del Colle some 30km from Matera where I stopped for lunch. The people of southern Italy had now been roused. The temptation of not having to go to work but having a car sitting in your driveway with a fully-functioning horn was too much for many and they had jumped in their Fiats, Lancias and Alfa Romeos and congregated along the main road of the town where they were keen to keep testing them repeatedly at any given opportunity. In fairness, many of the annoying blasts that morning were emanating from a wedding procession and it's not just the Italians who think it appropriate to celebrate the nuptials of a happy couple by disturbing the peace of every other person in the vicinity of the wedding in such a headache-inducing way. Practically every other nation on earth has adopted the same thoughtless ritual. Apart from the British. At last, an aspect of our misery-ridden lives at which we excel! It can only, however, be a matter of time before we succumb...

After having failed to come up with more than just this one reason to spend the rest of your life living in the UK, I continued heading east and my next stop was the town of Alberobello. If you translate the name of the famous Italian operatic composer Giuseppe Verdi into English you get the rather prosaic 'Joe Green' and you wonder how, with a name like that, he ever made it further than playing the recorder at primary school. If, however, you translate the name Alberobello into English you get 'beautiful tree' which although as equally simple as 'Joe Green', only adds to its beauty. And Alberobello is another stunning destination in southern Italy. That said, it's not really as famed for its trees as it is for its trullo buildings. These are small, square, white-washed houses with conical roofs made from piled-up stones. They are distinctly Puglian and you can find them dotted all across the countryside in this corner of the world. The thing that makes Alberobello stand out from the tourist-attracting crowd is that there are so many of them all in one place.

It was actually my second visit to Alberobello; I had explored the town on my visit to see Basil and Liz some three-years before my cycling efforts of 2010. At the time, Basil had explained that one theory as to why the dry-stone buildings were built as they were was so that they could be easily dismantled if a tax inspector was thought to be passing. No house equalled no tax. It seems a little excessive to say the least to go to the bother of tearing down your house to avoid such a fiscal imposition from the authorities but perhaps, if the story is true, it says much about the levels of tax at the time. Whatever the motivation for them being built as they were, the result is that now, just as similar working-class dwellings in Matera have become beacons for modern-day tourists, so have the trulli of Puglia.

Unfortunately, just as the relative urban tranquillity of Gioia del Colle had been somewhat disturbed by the wedding procession driving repeatedly up and down the town's main street, the even greater tranquillity of Alberobello was even more disturbed by the alarm of a car that had been parked at the very bottom of one of the lanes funnelling visitors up and through the trulli buildings. There are few things that can make you yearn for someone to come along and peep their horn for no good reason, but a car alarm repeatedly sounding its dull, monotone and loud cry is one of them. For the half an hour or so that I stayed, the entire atmosphere was ruined by some idiot who had never seen fit to have the sensitivity settings on the alarm adjusted appropriately. He or she was no doubt happily quaffing fine food and wine on the other side of town oblivious to the fact that for everyone on my side of town the visit to Alberobello would forever be associated with the racket of that car. The only saving grace was to think that perhaps the owner of the car wasn't sitting on the terrace of a restaurant on the other side of town but sitting on a similar terrace on this side of town, suffering the same attack on their ears as we were. Had earplugs been available, I might have been tempted to stay and observe the hopefully violent retribution meted out on the owner's return by the poor unfortunate family who had chosen to sit down for a meal at the restaurant next to the car prior to the alarm starting.

I needed no incentive to escape Alberobello although I did have one; the thought of meeting up with Basil and Liz at the next but one town. I did hope they were in. It would have been very embarrassing for all concerned if they had decided to go away for the weekend. Logic said that they would be there; they had, after all, been following my journey all the way since the day I shook Basil's hand back in our home town of Reading and told him, a little nervously, that I would see him again in Puglia. In many ways it seemed such a long time ago when I thought about the places that I had visited, the people I had met and the adventures that I had taken part in en route. But it was only five weeks.

As I approached the town of Cisternino, my emotions were a little mixed. I was happy to be nearing the end of the journey and having had Puglia in mind as the destination for the previous two years of planning, I had no enthusiasm (or indeed time) to continue cycling to Greece, Turkey or beyond. But my heart and mind were giving me mixed messages about what would happen over the course of the next day or so. The shaking of hands, embraces, telling of stories, dare I say adulation for what I had done would come in Cisternino when I met my friends and perhaps their friends and acquaintances in the town. But this was not the end of the Eurovelo 5. That would be at the harbour wall in Brindisi the following morning where, unless someone was keeping a very big surprise from me, there would be just me, Reggie and the vast expanse of the Mediterranean Sea to mark the real end of my journey. The events that were about to take place in Cisternino would seem to be a bit like opening your presents on the day before your birthday.

Parking my emotions to one side, I approached Cisternino. I had not visited the town on my previous visit to Basil and Liz as when I did, they were living in the restored and expanded trullo that they owned near the town of Ostuni some 10km down the road from Cisternino. This ever-more-luxurious trullo was now rented out to paying guests during the summer months and Basil and Liz had moved into a small flat in the centre of Cisternino. It was here that I would be spending most of my time in Puglia. On the outskirts of town there was a large yellow sign informing me that I was about to enter the town. I paused to take a picture and texted it to Basil so that he could estimate where I was and so that hopefully, he would text back some instructions as to where I should meet him.

I continued up and hill and sure enough there was a loud beep indicating that a message had arrived. I was to cycle into the centre of town until the crossroads as which point I should turn right onto the Via 24 Maggio. After a couple of hundred metres I would see the terrace of a bar upon which Basil, Liz and a large beer would be sitting. I hoped.

I found the Via 24 Maggio without problem. I found a bar with a terrace. But I didn't find Basil, Liz or the beer. I cycled around aimlessly for a few moments checking and double-checking that what I could see matched up with the instructions given to me by Basil. It made no sense that he would have sent me a text message only a few moments before I arrived which was wrong. There were a couple of elderly gentlemen sitting on a wall in the park next to the bar but all they could do was confirm that yes, I was where I thought I was.

It would be ironic indeed if, after having successfully navigated a route across an entire continent, I was unable to find the people who had been one of the main reasons why I had chosen to come all the way to southern Italy in the first place. It was all becoming a little anti-climatic. Here I was at one of the two finishing lines – the other one was the real one in Brindisi of course – but no-one was here to greet me. I had never expected so much as a white tape to be held out in front of me, but a familiar face and welcoming smile would have been nice.

I decided to venture a bit further along the road. It dipped a little under a long wall and to my left I began to see the white-washed buildings of the old part of town. If Basil and Liz were not to be found, I would at least be able to wander around some pretty streets. With my eyes distracted by the beauty of the architecture, I almost missed the faint but familiar voice that shouted 'hello' just a few metres away. I turned to see Basil, distinctly more tanned that he had been a few weeks earlier in Berkshire but whose equally distinctive Geordie twang confirmed, if confirmation was needed, that it was indeed him. 'Welcome to Puglia!' he cried.

At the bar with the terrace where Liz had already arrived and ordered drinks, the celebration that wasn't really a celebration ensued. It was a different bar than the one that I had initially found although it matched the description in the text message just as well. We spent the next couple of hours happily consuming far too many beers, certainly for a hot afternoon in the south of Italy but who cared? Although not quite finished, I did have something to celebrate and I certainly wasn't going to wait to do it with just Reggie by my side in Brindisi the following day. Well done to me!

Apart from the joy of seeing friendly, familiar faces after such a long period of seeing only friendly but mainly unfamiliar faces, it was good to relax and begin to unwind. It was great to let others make the decisions once again but unlike the frenzy of the first night with Massimo in Benevento, that evening in Cisternino was taken at a very leisurely pace, nothing hurried, nothing forced. Think slow and then slow it down just a little bit more. We ate in a local restaurant, drank more beer in the squares of the old town and once again I joined the passeggiata but this time I was able to do so in true Italian style, with good friends. The evening drew to close on the roof-top terrace above Basil and Liz's flat in the very heart of the old town where we could look east toward the sea and from where I was able to contemplate the final morning of cycling towards Brindisi itself.

Cycling Day 30

Sunday 22nd August 2010: Cisternino to Brindisi

2 hours 39 minutes in the saddle, 62 kilometres

It was a very slim line-looking Reggie who was carried down the exterior staircase leading from the front door to Basil and Liz's flat in Cisternino. It made no sense to continue cycling with the panniers fully-laden or indeed at all. Everything I needed for the relatively short cycle to the coast at Brindisi could be secured either on the map board on Reggie's handlebars or on the rack above his back wheel. Not only was this shedding of weight a no-brainer for logistical reasons – I would be picked up by Basil in his car later in the day and would not be cycling any further than our meeting point in Brindisi – it also made eminent sense in light of the condition of Reggie's back wheel which, although still turning without problem, was continuing to wobble. I prayed that it wouldn't let me down at this very late stage of the trip. Panniers or no panniers, it would be no fun pushing a bike even part of the way to the sea but it was something I would be prepared to do if it became necessary; nothing would stop me now from being able to say that I had indeed travelled, on (or off) a bike from Berkshire to Brindisi.

Fortunately the ride was uneventful. If anything, a little too uneventful as once I had made it as far as Ostuni, the roads were dead straight only kinking slightly in the towns of Carovigno and San Vito dei Normanni to keep me heading in the right direction towards Brindisi. Along these long, straight roads, the land was as flat and as featureless as it had been for most of the cycling during the previous two days. At one point as Reggie and I were about half way along the road from San Vito dei Normanni to Brindisi, there was minor excitement as I could see that the road ahead appeared to curve off to the left. On my map this was depicted as a small lump along the long yellow that that was the SS16 but from what I could see, this extravagant break from the monotony of the rest of the road was just an overly-fancy way of crossing the railway track below it. Perhaps the road builders had been just as bored as the future road users would be and fancied making their working lives a tad more exciting. Who knows?

Gradually, the urban sprawl of Brindisi started to take over from the countryside of Puglia. To my left I could see the occasional plane taking off or landing at Brindisi airport in the north of the city. I would be heading there later in the day to rendez-vous with Basil, but I first needed to make my way into the centre of city and towards the harbour. This was an iconic part of the journey that I had cycled many, many times before in my head but despite all those imaginary practice runs, it was just as unknown as most of the previous 3,300km had been and I struggled to find my way through the complex grid of roads, pedestrian precincts, bridges and very occasional cycle paths. It became a little frustrating to say the least as I turned repeatedly left and right in my quest to locate the point, any point, where land stopped and water started.

When I finally did so, it was a little disappointing. I wanted a view of nothing but the sea but what I could see was a bit of sea and a lot of land on all sides. My 1:200,000 map wasn't helping me much with trying to figure out why I wasn't able to stand in front of the vast expanse of the Mediterranean Sea and had to make do with what I perceived as just a glorified harbour. I needed a more detailed map and found one on a board next to where a number of fishermen had set up their rods trying to catch Sunday lunch. The map showed how the extensive harbour of Brindisi came right into the city centre and where I was standing was actually the harbour within the harbour which curved around most of the centre of Brindisi like two thin claws. I was standing at the point opposite where the claws were attached to the arm which itself was extended by a long thin harbour wall stretching far out into the sea. I had seen this harbour wall when poring over maps prior to the trip, fantasising as to how my journey would end. Wouldn't it be great if I were able to make it all the way to the end of this man-made peninsula at which point I would have nowhere else to go unless it involved deserting Reggie, pulling on a pair of Speedos, diving in and swimming to Albania.

But how would I get there? The end of the harbour wall that is, rather than Albania. I noticed that a short way away on the quayside was a very small ferry. I pushed Reggie towards the queue of people waiting to board and inspected the sign. It indicated that the destination of the ferry was the other side of the harbour a few hundred metres away so I joined the queue and after a few minutes we were allowed to board. This was no cross-channel vessel and it didn't even have the grandeur of the boat we had taken to cross Lake Lucerne. It was really just a living room-sized shed sitting on top of a hull.

After quite a few minutes of waiting for more customers who never arrived, we set off, but in what appeared to be the wrong direction. Rather than panicking that I might be seeing Albania after all (the 1€ price for the journey hinted that we weren't going too far), I correctly reasoned that it was probably a circular route and that we were just going to pick up more customers elsewhere. We did just that before sailing to the opposite side of the harbour where I remounted Reggie and cycled along the substantial harbour walls towards an oddly-shaped monument dedicated to the navy. I wasn't quite sure whether or not I would be successful in making it as far as the end of the long harbour wall but was conscious of capturing the end of my trip with a thought-provoking photograph which is why I spent a few minutes positioning Reggie near a gate that blocked entry to part of the monument that jutted out into the harbour. Was this the end of the road? Blocked by an iron gate? It could have been.

I cycled a little further, trying to remember the geography of Brindisi harbour from the map I had seen on the other side of the water. I appeared to be very close to the airport as I could hear a loud noise emanating from what I assumed was a jet engine. The area was also very militarised with signs attached to high barbed-wire topped fences warning of the consequences of getting too close. At one point it was necessary to pass through a tunnel under what appeared to be part of the airport but it was too short to be the runway itself. On the other side, the area was more residential so I continued until once again I met water. In front of me I could see the very long tail of the harbour wall stretching out into the sea. Was this the end of the road? There was a crumbling lighthouse just next to the more modern harbour wall and it appeared to be blocking access to the road that ran out to sea. The wall itself was heavily graffitied with the opinions of Brindisi football supporters towards their local rivals; Lecce Merda being written just next to the lighthouse amongst more traditional declarations of love.

I noticed figures on the harbour wall in the far distance so it appeared that there was some way of continuing my journey. I investigated the area behind the lighthouse and there were no barriers or warning signs so I didn't stop there and continued cycling.

This was one serious harbour wall and after 2km of cycling, I still hadn't reached the second lighthouse that I could see at the far end. I had passed and left behind the other people who were on the wall many minutes previously. There was not another soul around as I cycled the final few metres to a point where I knew that my journey would finally be at an end. As I glanced to my right, I could see the view of Brindisi that I did recognise from the photographs I had first seen when researching my journey.

I slowed slightly to take in the moment but also because the ground beneath Reggie's well-worn (but remarkably un-punctured) tyres was deteriorating the further we travelled along the wall. This made everything attached to Reggie vibrate just a little bit more but they were good vibrations. It was perhaps his way of celebrating the climax of what had been an incredible journey from the south of England to the south of Italy over more than 3,000km and five weeks. I thought I would be emotional about what I had achieved but my feelings were more of pride and satisfaction at having not just planned such a journey but actually having carried it out. The dream had become a reality.

As the end of the wall approached, I squeezed Reggie's brakes for the very last time and we came to a halt. Our journey had ended at a deserted, graffitied, litter-strewn lighthouse in the middle of the sea. It was beautiful.

Brindisi to home

Making my way back along the long harbour wall, past the airport boundary fence, through the short tunnel and to the terminal where I had arranged to meet Basil, I relived the thirty days of cycling leading up to my arrival in Brindisi. I also relived the two-years of preparation prior to the trip. It was inevitable that somewhere amongst the euphoria of having achieved what I had done, there was an element of sadness that now I had to put it all to one side and get on with other things in my life. I had lived and breathed the Eurovelo 5 for many months and now I needed to find some other obsession to occupy my time. If that were to be another cycling trip it would have to be one step further up the ladder of adventure; I had started by cycling south through the north of England for a ten days and then graduated to a trans-European expedition. But what could come next? I wasn't sure but I did know that having done what I had just finished, there was no reason why I couldn't at least try to aim higher.

I wasn't very chatty as we drove back to Ostuni that afternoon. I had dismantled poor Reggie at Brindisi airport so that he would fit in the back of Basil's small car and when we arrived at the villa where we would be spending one night before my final night back at the flat in Cisternino, I took him out of the car and left him in an ignominious pile around the back of the building. I felt guilty at having treated him in such a way but he was, after all, just a collection of metal, rubber and plastic. Albeit one with soul.

We were able to stay at the villa for one night because of a break in the holiday lettings and there can be few places on the European continent where you will find greater peace that that patch of ground in southern Italy. We sat on the terrace with some of Basil and Liz's ex-pat friends who were complimentary as they were quizzical about the trip from the UK. I remained polite but just yearned to get on the plane and be delivered to my own front door where I would be able to relax in the way that I needed by doing absolutely nothing for a couple of days before I had to go back to work at the start of September.

We returned to stay in Cisternino on the Monday where much of our time was spent finding a suitable box in which to transport Reggie back on the plane with me. Liz had a brainwave of asking at a local bike shop for one of the boxes in which brand new bikes are delivered so once Reggie's Bianchi box had been given to us, we then just had the problem of transporting the box with Reggie inside back to Brindisi airport in Basil's small car.

As with most problems of this nature, it is best solved after good food and wine which we ate and drank in abundance that evening. It was my 37th away from home and it ended with the three of us once again joining the lively passeggiata in the streets of Cisternino before climbing to the roof-top terrace to drink yet more local red wine. I would have been happy to sleep on the roof if only to save the energy of having to make my way downstairs and back into the flat.

First thing Tuesday, I bid farewell to Liz who would be staying in Puglia to manage the villa until later in the year while Basil, who would be returning to the UK just a few days after me, drove me back to Brindisi airport. It was not an inconsequential job ensuring that Reggie was secure inside his Bianchi box but eventually we succeeded.

At 11.05 am the flight for Stanstead departed and soon both Reggie and I were at cruising height above Europe. I had fought for a window seat as I wanted to spend the two-hour flight staring back down upon the land mass that I had just traversed. There weren't many things I could see which were familiar although when the Alps appeared I had to hold myself back from turning to the other passengers and telling them that I wasn't on a return ticket and that I had done the outward journey the hard way.

At the very start of the planning process for the ride I wanted someone to tell me when to turn left, when to turn right and when to go straight forward. People still write to me asking the question that I had been asking myself for much of the two-years of planning; where can I find a route map of the Eurovelo 5?

In the end, I'm glad that one didn't exist and I'm even happier that I never wrote one. As with many things in life, it's often better just to work it out for yourself. I did and I don't regret it for a moment.

About the author

Andrew P. Sykes was born and grew up in the small town of Elland in the foothills of the Pennines in West Yorkshire. He studied for a degree in mathematics at the University of York and immediately after graduation went to work in London for a firm of city accountants. The world of auditing was not however for him and in 1993 he left the U.K to go and work in France, initially in the tourist industry and then for four years teaching English in the Loire Valley city of Tours. He returned to the U.K. in 1999 to train as a secondary school teacher of French at the University of Reading. He still lives in the town and can currently be found working as the Head of Modern Languages at a secondary school in South Oxfordshire. You may well spot him each morning and each evening during term time cycling to work through the picturesque countryside that lies between the Thames Valley towns of Reading and Henley-on-Thames. Please don't knock him off!

Lightning Source UK Ltd.
Milton Keynes UK
UKOW031851310512

193729UK00009B/42/P